Fodor's
Europe
Ports of Call

Portions of this book appear in *Fodor's Europe*

Fodor's Travel Publications, Inc.
New York • Toronto • London • Sydney • Auckland
www.fodors.com

Europe Ports of Call

EDITOR: Lauren A. Myers

Editorial Contributors: Wendy Determan, M. T. Schwartzman, Heidi Sarna

Editorial Production: Linda K. Schmidt

Maps: David Lindroth, *cartographer*; Robert Blake, *map editor*

Design: Fabrizio La Rocca, *creative director*; Guido Caroti, *art director*; Jolie Novak, *photo editor*

Production/Manufacturing: Mike Costa

Cover Photograph: *top photo,* Princess Cruises/Island Princess/Santorini, Greece; *bottom photo,* Michele & Tom Grimm/Tony Stone Images

Cover Design: Allison Saltzman

Copyright

ISBN 0–679–00348–7

ISSN 1525–5840

Special Sales

Fodor's Travel Publications are available at special discounts for bulk purchases for sales promotions or premiums. Special editions, including personalized covers, excerpts of existing guides, and corporate imprints, can be created in large quantities for special needs. For more information, contact your local bookseller or write to Special Markets, Fodor's Travel Publications, 201 East 50th Street, New York, NY 10022. Inquiries from Canada should be directed to your local Canadian bookseller or sent to Random House of Canada, Ltd., Marketing Department, 2775 Matheson Boulevard East, Mississauga, Ontario L4W 4P7. Inquiries from the United Kingdom should be sent to Fodor's Travel Publications, 20 Vauxhall Bridge Road, London SW1V 2SA, England.

PRINTED IN THE UNITED STATES OF AMERICA

10 9 8 7 6 5 4 3 2 1

CONTENTS

Index   **208**

Maps

Important Tip

Although all prices, opening times, and other details in this book are based on information supplied to us at press time, changes occur all the time in the travel world, and Fodor's cannot accept responsibility for facts that become outdated or for inadvertent errors or omissions. So **always confirm information when it matters,** especially if you're making a detour to visit a specific place.

Don't Forget to Write

Keeping a travel guide fresh and up-to-date is a big job. So we love your feedback—positive and negative—and follow up on all suggestions. Contact the Europe Ports of Call editor at editors@fodors.com or c/o Fodor's, 201 East 50th Street, New York, New York 10022. And have a wonderful trip!

Karen Cure
Editorial Director

1 Cruise Primer

BEFORE YOU GO

Tickets, Vouchers, and Other Travel Documents

After you make the final payment to your travel agent, the cruise line will issue your cruise tickets and vouchers for airport–ship transfers. Depending on the airline, and whether you have purchased an air-sea package, you may receive your plane tickets or charter-flight vouchers at the same time; you may also receive vouchers for any shore excursions, although most cruise lines issue these aboard ship. Should your travel documents not arrive when promised, contact your travel agent or cruise line. If you book late, tickets may be delivered directly to the ship.

Passports and Visas

All U.S. citizens will need a passport to travel to Europe. Visas may also be required for visits to or through Turkey, Romania, Poland, Estonia, and Latvia, among other countries. Your cruise documents will specify whether visas are needed, and, generally, the line or your travel agent can obtain the visa for you for a fee. (There may be a charge of up to $25 for this service, added to the visa charge.)

What to Pack

Certain packing rules apply to all cruises: Always take a sweater in case of cool evening ocean breezes or overactive air-conditioning. A rain slicker usually comes in handy. Men should pack a dark suit, a tuxedo, or a white dinner jacket. Women should pack one long gown or cocktail dress for every two or three formal evenings on board.

For exploring port towns, take at least one pair of comfortable walking shoes—walking is the best and sometimes only way to explore in port. Your wardrobe for land excursions will be determined by your cruise itinerary. In the Mediterranean, casual summer wear will usually do. For visits to churches, cathedrals, and mosques, avoid shorts and revealing outfits; in Italy, women should cover their shoulders and arms (a shawl is fine). In Greece many monasteries bar women wearing pants, and long skirts are often provided at the entrance as a cover-up for women wearing pants and men dressed in shorts. In Turkey women must have a head covering, and a long-sleeved shirt and a long skirt or slacks are required. Pack clothing that can be layered and is suitable for hot days and cooler evenings.

Plan on one outfit for every two days of cruising, especially if your wardrobe contains many interchangeable pieces. Fortunately, ships often have laundry facilities. Don't overload your luggage with extra toiletries and sundry items; they are available in port and in the ship's gift shop (though usually at a premium price). Soaps, shampoos, and body lotion are often placed in your cabin.

Outlets in cabin bathrooms are usually compatible with U.S.-purchased appliances. This may not be the case on older ships or those with European registries; call ahead if this is a concern for you. Most cabin bathrooms are equipped with low-voltage outlets for electric shavers, and many newer ships have built-in hairdryers.

Take an extra pair of eyeglasses or contact lenses in your carry-on luggage. If you have a health problem that requires a prescription drug, pack enough to last the duration of the trip or have your doctor write a prescription using the drug's generic name, because brand names vary from country to country. Always carry prescription drugs in their original packaging to avoid problems with customs officials. Don't pack them in luggage that you plan to check, in case your bags go astray. Pack a list of the offices that supply refunds for lost or stolen traveler's checks.

Although no two cruises are quite the same, evening dress tends to fall into three categories:

FORMAL
Formal cruises celebrate the ceremony of cruising. Jackets and ties for men are the rule for dinner, and tuxedos are not uncommon.

SEMIFORMAL
Semiformal cruises are a bit more relaxed than their formal counterparts. Men wear a jacket and tie most nights.

CASUAL

Casual cruises are the most popular. Shipboard dress and lifestyle are informal. Men dress in sport shirts and slacks for dinner most nights, in jackets and ties only two or three evenings of a typical seven-day sailing.

ARRIVING AND DEPARTING

If you have purchased an air-sea package, you will be met by a cruise-company representative when your plane lands at the port city and then shuttled directly to the ship in buses or minivans. Some cruise lines arrange to transport your luggage between airport and ship—you don't have to hassle with baggage claim at the start of your cruise or with baggage check-in at the end. If you decide not to buy the air-sea package but still plan to fly, ask your travel agent if you can use the ship's transfer bus anyway. Otherwise, you will have to take a taxi to the ship. If you live close to the port of embarkation, bus transportation may be available.

Embarkation

Check-In

On arrival at the dock, you must check in before boarding your ship. (A handful of smaller cruise ships handle check-in at the airport.) An officer will collect or stamp your ticket, inspect or even retain your passport or other official identification, ask you to fill out a tourist card, check that you have the correct visas, and collect any unpaid port or departure tax. Seating assignments for the dining room are often handed out at this time, too. You may also register your credit card to open a shipboard account, although that may be done later at the purser's office.

After this you may be required to go through a security check and to pass your hand baggage through an X-ray inspection. These are the same machines in use at airports, so ask to have your photographic film inspected by hand.

Although it takes only five or ten minutes per family to check in, lines are often long, so aim for off-peak hours. The worst time tends to be immediately after the ship begins boarding; the later it is, the less crowded. For example, if boarding is from 2 PM to 4:30, try to arrive after 3:30.

Boarding the Ship

Before you walk up the gangway, the ship's photographer will probably take your picture; there's no charge unless you buy the picture (usually $6). On board, stewards may serve welcome drinks in souvenir glasses—for which you're usually charged between $3 and $5 in cash.

You will either be escorted to your cabin by a steward or, on a smaller ship, given your key by a ship's officer and directed to your cabin. Some elevators are unavailable to passengers during boarding, since they are used to transport luggage. You may arrive to find your luggage outside your stateroom or just inside the door; if it hasn't arrived a half hour before sailing, contact the purser. If you are among the unlucky few whose luggage doesn't make it to the ship in time, the purser will have it flown to the next port.

Visitors' Passes

Some cruise ships permit passengers to invite guests on board prior to sailing, although most cruise lines prohibit all but paying passengers from boarding for reasons of security and insurance liability. Cruise companies that allow visitors usually require that you obtain passes several weeks in advance; call the lines for policies and procedures.

Most ships do not allow visitors while the ship is docked in a port of call. If you meet a friend on shore, you won't be able to invite him or her back to your stateroom.

Disembarkation

The last night of your cruise is full of business. On most ships you must place everything except your hand luggage outside your door, ready to be picked up by midnight. Color-coded tags, distributed to your cabin in a debarkation packet, should be placed on your luggage before the crew collects it. Your color will determine when you leave the ship and help you retrieve your luggage on the pier.

Your shipboard bill is left in your room during the last day; to pay the bill (if you haven't already put it on your credit card) or to settle any questions, you must stand in line at the purser's office. Tips to the cabin steward and dining staff are distributed on the last night.

The next morning, in-room breakfast service is usually not available because stewards are too busy. Most passengers clear out of their cabins as soon as possible, gather their hand luggage, and stake out a chair in one of the public lounges to await the ship's clearance through customs. Be patient—it takes a long time to unload and sort thousands of pieces of luggage. Passengers are disembarked in groups according to the color-coded luggage tags; those with the earliest flights get off first. If you have a tight connection, notify the purser before the last day, and he or she may be able to arrange faster preclearing and debarkation.

Customs and Duties

U.S. Customs

Upon re-entering the U.S., each individual or family must fill out a customs declaration, regardless of whether anything was purchased abroad. If you have less than $1,400 worth of goods, you will not need to itemize purchases. Be prepared to pay whatever duties are owed directly to the customs inspector, with cash or check.

Allowances. You may bring home $400 worth of foreign goods duty-free if you've been out of the country for at least 48 hours and haven't already used the $400 exemption, or any part of it, in the past 30 days. Note that these are the *general* rules, applicable to most countries. Antiques and works of art more than 100 years old are duty-free, as are original works of art done entirely by hand, including paintings, drawings, and sculptures.

Alcohol and Tobacco. Travelers 21 or older may bring back 1 liter of alcohol duty-free, provided the beverage laws of the state through which they reenter the United States allow it. In addition, 100 non-Cuban cigars and 200 cigarettes are allowed, regardless of your age.

Canadian Customs

Allowances. If you've been out of Canada for at least seven days, you may bring in C$500 worth of goods duty-free.

If you've been away less than seven days but more than 48 hours, the duty-free exemption drops to C$200. You cannot pool exemptions with family members. Goods claimed under the C$500 exemption may follow you by mail; those claimed under the lesser exemption must accompany you. Check ahead of time with Revenue Canada or the Department of Agriculture for policies regarding meat products, seeds, plants, and fruits.

Alcohol and Tobacco. Alcohol and tobacco products may be included in the seven-day and 48-hour exemption. If you meet the age requirements of the province or territory through which you reenter Canada, you may bring in, duty-free, 1.14 liters (40 imperial ounces) of wine or liquor *or* two dozen 12-ounce cans or bottles of beer or ale. If you are 16 or older, you may bring in, duty-free, 200 cigarettes and 50 cigars. Alcohol and tobacco must accompany you on your return.

U.K. Customs

If you are a U.K. resident and your journey was wholly within the European Union (EU), you won't have to pass through customs when you return to the United Kingdom. If you're returning from outside the EU, prohibited items include meat products, seeds, plants, and fruits.

Allowances. You may bring home 60 milliliters of perfume; 250 milliliters of toilet water; and £136 worth of other goods, including gifts and souvenirs.

Alcohol and Tobacco. If you plan to bring back large quantities of alcohol or tobacco, check EU limits beforehand. From countries outside the EU, you may bring home, duty-free, 200 cigarettes or 50 cigars; one liter of spirits or two liters of fortified or sparkling wine or liqueurs; and two liters of still table wine.

ON BOARD

Checking Out Your Cabin

The first thing to do upon arriving at your cabin or suite is to make sure that everything is in order. If there are two twin beds instead of the double bed you wanted, or other problems, ask to be moved *before* the ship departs. Unless the ship is full, you can usually persuade the chief house-keeper or hotel manager to allow you to change cabins. It is customary to tip the stewards who help you move.

Since your cabin is your home for a few days or weeks, everything should be to your satisfaction. Take a good look around: Is the cabin clean and orderly? Do the toilet, shower, and faucets work? Check the telephone and television. Again, major problems should be addressed immediately. Minor concerns, such as a shortage of pillows, can wait until the frenzy of embarkation subsides.

Your dining-time and seating-assignment card may be in your cabin; now is the time to check it and immediately request any changes. The maître d' usually sets up shop in one of the public rooms specifically for this purpose.

Shipboard Accounts

Virtually all cruise ships operate as cashless societies. Passengers charge onboard purchases and settle their accounts at the end of the cruise with a credit card, traveler's checks, or cash. You can sign for wine at dinner, drinks at the bar, shore excursions, gifts in the shop—virtually any expense you may incur aboard ship. On some lines, an imprint from a major credit card is necessary to open an account. Otherwise, a cash deposit may be required and a positive balance maintained to keep the shipboard account open. Either way, you will want to open a line of credit soon after settling in if an account was not opened for you at embarkation. This can easily be arranged by visiting the purser's office, in the central atrium or main lobby.

Tipping

For better or worse, tipping is an integral part of the cruise experience. Most companies pay their cruise staff nominal wages and expect tips to make up the difference. Most cruise lines have recommended tipping guidelines, and on many ships "voluntary" tipping for beverage service has been replaced with a mandatory 15% service charge, which is added to every bar bill. On the other hand, the most expensive luxury lines include tipping in the cruise fare and may prohibit crew members from accepting any additional gratuities. On most small adventure ships, a collection box is placed in the dining room or lounge on the last full day of the cruise, and passengers contribute anonymously.

Dining

Ocean liners serve food nearly around the clock. There may be up to four breakfast options: early-morning coffee and pastries on deck, breakfast in bed through room service, buffet-style in the cafeteria, and sit-down in the dining room. There may also be several lunch choices, mid-afternoon hors d'oeuvres, and midnight buffets. You can eat whatever is on the menu, in any quantity, at as many of these meals as you wish. Room service is traditionally, but not always, free (*see* Shipboard Services, *below*).

Restaurants

The chief meals of the day are served in the main dining room, which on most ships can accommodate only half the passengers at once. Meals are therefore usually served in two sittings—early (or main) and late (or second) seatings. Early seating for dinner is generally between 6 and 6:30, late seating between 8 and 8:30.

Most cruise ships have a cafeteria-style restaurant, usually near the swimming pool, where you can eat lunch and breakfast (dinner is usually served only in the dining room). Many ships provide self-serve coffee or tea in their cafeteria around the clock, as well as buffets at midnight.

Increasingly, ships also have alternative restaurants for ethnic cuisines, such as Italian, Chinese, or Japanese food. These are found mostly on newer vessels, although some older liners have been refitted for alternative dining. Other ships have pizzerias, ice-cream parlors, and caviar or cappuccino bars; there may be an extra charge at these facilities.

More and more lines are banning smoking in their main dining rooms. Smoking policies vary; contact your cruise line to find out what the situation will be on your cruise.

Seatings

When it comes to your dining-table assignment, you should have options on four important points: early or late seating; smoking or no-smoking section (if smoking is allowed in the dining room); a table for two, four, six, or eight; and special dietary needs. When you receive your cruise documents, you will usually receive a card asking for your dining preferences. Fill this out and return it to the cruise line, but remember that you will not get your seating assignment until you board the ship. Check it out immediately, and if your request was not met, see the maître d'—usually there is a time and place set up for changes in dining assignments.

On some ships, seating times are strictly observed. Ten to 15 minutes after the scheduled mealtime, the dining-room doors are closed. On other ships, passengers may enter the dining room at their leisure, but they must be out by the end of the seating. When a ship has just one seating, passengers may enter at any time while the kitchen is open.

Seating assignments on some ships apply only for dinner. Several have open seating for breakfast or lunch, which means you may sit anywhere at any time. Smaller or more luxurious ships offer open seating for all meals.

CHANGING TABLES

Dining is a focal point of the cruise experience, and your companions at meals may become your best friends on the cruise. However, if you don't enjoy the company at your table, the maître d' can usually move you to another one if the dining room isn't completely full—a tip helps. He will probably be reluctant to comply with your request after the first full day at sea, however, because the waiters, busboys, and wine steward who have been serving you up to that point won't receive their tips at the end of the cruise. Be persistent if you are truly unhappy.

Cuisine

Most ships serve food geared to the American palate, but there are also theme dinners featuring the cuisine of a particular country. Some European ships, especially smaller vessels, may offer a particular cuisine throughout the cruise—Scandinavian, German, Italian, or Greek, perhaps—depending on the ship's or the crew's nationality. The quality of the cooking is generally good, but even a skilled chef is hard put to serve 500 or more extraordinary dinners per hour. The presentation is often spectacular, especially at gala midnight buffets.

There is a direct relationship between the cost of a cruise and the quality of its cuisine. The food is very sophisticated on some (mostly expensive) lines, among them Crystal Cruises, Cunard Line, Seabourn Cruise Line, and Silversea Cruises. In the more moderate price range, Celebrity Cruises has gained renown for the culinary stylings of French chef Michel Roux, who acts as a consultant to the line.

Special Diets

With notification well in advance, many ships can provide a kosher, low-salt, low-cholesterol, sugar-free, vegetarian, or other special menu. However, there's always a chance that the wrong dish will somehow be handed to you. Especially when it comes to soups and desserts, it's a good idea to ask about the ingredients.

Large ships usually offer an alternative "light" or "spa" menu based upon American Heart Association guidelines, using less fat, leaner cuts of meat, low-cholesterol or low-sodium preparations, smaller portions, salads, fresh-fruit desserts, and healthy garnishes. Some smaller ships may not be able to accommodate special dietary needs. Vegetarians generally have no trouble finding appropriate selections.

Wine

Wine at meals costs extra on most ships; the prices are usually comparable to those in shoreside restaurants and are charged to your shipboard account. A handful of luxury vessels include both wine and liquor.

The Captain's Table

It is both a privilege and a marvelous experience to be invited to dine one evening at the captain's table. Although some seats are given to celebrities, repeat passengers, and passengers in the most expensive suites, other invitations are given at random to ordinary passengers. You can request an invitation from the chief steward or the hotel manager, although there is no guarantee you will be accommodated. The captain's guests always wear a suit and tie or a dress, even if the dress code for that evening is casual. On many ships, passengers may also be invited to dine at the other officers' special tables, or officers may visit a different passenger table each evening.

Bars

A ship's bars, whether adjacent to the pool or attached to one of the lounges, tend to be its social centers. Except on a handful of luxury-class ships where everything is included in the ticket price, bars operate on a pay-as-it's-poured basis. Rather than demand cash after every round, however, most ships allow you to charge drinks to an account.

In international waters there are, technically, no laws against teenage drinking, but almost all ships require passengers to be over 18 or 21 to purchase alcoholic drinks. Many cruise ships have chapters of Alcoholics Anonymous (a.k.a. "Friends of Bill W.") or will organize meetings on request. Look for meeting times and places in the daily program slipped under your cabin door each night.

Entertainment

Lounges and Nightclubs

On ocean liners, the main entertainment lounge or showroom schedules nightly musical revues, magic acts, comedy performances, and variety shows. During the rest of the day the room is used for group activities, such as shore-excursion talks or bingo games. Generally, the larger the ship, the bigger and more impressive the productions. Newer ships have elaborate showrooms that often span two decks. Some are designed like an amphitheater while others have two levels—a main floor and a balcony. Seating is sometimes in clusters of armchairs set around cocktail tables. Other ships have more traditional theater-style seating.

Many larger ships have a second showroom. Entertainment and ballroom dancing may go on here late into the night. Elsewhere you may find a disco, nightclub, or cabaret, usually built around a bar and dance floor. Music is provided by a piano player, a disc jockey, or by performing ensembles such as country-and-western duos or jazz combos.

On smaller ships the entertainment options are more limited, sometimes consisting of no more than a piano around which passengers gather. There may be a main lounge where scaled-down revues are staged.

Library

Most cruise ships have a library with up to 1,500 volumes, from the latest best-sellers to reference works. Many shipboard libraries also stock videotapes.

Movie Theaters

All but the smallest vessels have a room for screening movies. On older ships and some newer ones, this is often a genuine cinema-style movie theater. On other ships, it may be just a multipurpose room. The films are frequently one or two months past their first release date but not yet available on videotape or cable TV. Films rated "R" are edited to minimize sex and violence. On a weeklong voyage, a dozen different films may be screened, each one repeated at various times during the day. Theaters are also used for lectures, religious services, and private meetings.

With a few exceptions, ocean liners equip their cabins with closed-circuit TVs; these show movies (continuously on some newer ships), shipboard lectures, and regular programs (thanks to satellite reception). Ships with VCRs in the cabins usually provide a selection of movies on cassette at no charge (a deposit is sometimes required).

Casinos

Once a ship is 12 mi off American shores, it is in international waters and gambling is permitted. (Some "cruises to nowhere," in fact, are little more than sailing casinos.) All ocean liners, as well as many cruise yachts and motor-sailing ships, have casinos. On larger vessels, they usually have poker, baccarat, blackjack, roulette, craps, and slot machines. House stakes are much more modest than those in Las Vegas or Atlantic City. On most ships the maximum bet is $200; some ships allow $500. Payouts on the slot machines (some of which take as little as a nickel) are generally much lower, too. Credit is never extended, but many casinos have handy credit-card machines that dispense cash for a hefty fee.

Children are officially barred from the casinos, but it's common to see them playing the slots rather than the adjacent video machines. Most ships offer free individual instruction and even gambling classes in the off-hours. Casinos are usually open from early morning to late night, although you may find only unattended slot machines before evening. In adherence to local laws, casinos are always closed while a ship is in port.

Game Rooms

Most ships have a game or card room with card tables and board games. These rooms are for serious players and are often the site of friendly round-robin competitions and tournaments. Most ships furnish everything for free (cards, chips, games, and so forth), but a few charge $1 or more for each deck of cards. Be aware that professional cardsharps and hustlers have been fleecing ship passengers almost as long as there have been ships. There are small video arcades on most medium and large ships. Family-oriented ships often have a computer learning center as well.

Bingo and Other Games

The daily high-stakes bingo games are even more popular than the casinos. You can play for as little as a dollar a card. Most ships have a snowball bingo game with a jackpot that grows throughout the cruise into hundreds or even thousands of dollars. Another popular cruise pastime is the so-called "horse races": fictional horses are auctioned off to "owners." Individual passengers can buy a horse or form "syndicates." Bids usually begin at around $25 and can top $1,000 per horse. Races are then "run" according to dice throws or computer-generated random numbers. Audience members bet on their favorites.

Sports and Fitness

Swimming Pools

All but the smallest ships have at least one pool, some of them elaborate affairs with water slides or retractable roofs; hot tubs and whirlpools are quite common. Pools may be filled with fresh water or salt water; some ships have one of each. While in port or during rough weather, the pools are usually emptied or covered with canvas. Many are too narrow or too short to allow swimmers more than a few strokes in any direction; none have diving boards, and not all are heated. Often there are no lifeguards. Wading pools are sometimes provided for small children.

Sun Deck

The top deck is usually called the Sun Deck or Sports Deck. On some ships this is where you'll find the pool or whirlpool; on others it is dedicated to volleyball, table tennis, shuffleboard, and other such sports. A number of ships have paddle-tennis courts, and a few have golf driving ranges. Often, after the sun goes down, the Sun Deck is used for dancing, barbecues, or other social activities.

Exercise and Fitness Rooms

Most newer ships and some older ones have well-equipped fitness centers, many with massage, sauna, and whirlpools. An upper-deck fitness center often has an airy and sunny view of the sea; an inside, lower-deck health club is often dark and small unless it is equipped with an indoor pool or beauty salon. Many ships have full-service exercise rooms with bodybuilding and cardiovascular equipment, aerobics classes, and personal fitness instruction. Some ships even have cruise-length physical-fitness programs, which may include lectures on weight loss or nutrition. These often are tied in with a spa menu in the dining room. Beauty salons adjacent to the health club may offer spa treatments such as facials and mud wraps. The more extensive programs are often sold on a daily or weekly basis.

Promenade Deck

Many vessels designate certain decks for fitness walks and may post the number of laps per mile. Fitness instructors may lead daily walks around the Promenade Deck. A number of ships discourage jogging and running on the decks or ask that no one take fitness walks before 8 AM or after 10 PM, so as not to disturb passengers in cabins. With the advent of the megaship, walking and jogging have in many cases moved up top to tracks on the Sun or Sports deck.

Shipboard Services

Room Service

A small number of ships have no room service at all, except when the ship's doctor orders it for an ailing passenger. Many offer only breakfast (Continental on some, full on others), while others provide no more than a limited menu at certain hours of the day. Most, however, have selections that you can order at any time. Some luxury ships have unlimited round-the-clock room service. There usually is no charge other than for beer, wine, or spirits.

Minibars
An increasing number of ships equip their more expensive cabins with small refrigerators or minibars stocked with snacks, soda, and liquors, which may or may not be free.

Laundry and Dry Cleaning
All but the smallest ships and shortest cruises offer laundry services—full-service, self-service, or both. Use of machines is generally free, although some ships charge for detergent, use of the machines, or both. Valet laundry service includes cabin pickup and delivery and usually takes 24 hours. Most ships also offer dry-cleaning services.

Hair Stylists
Even the smallest ships have a hair stylist on staff. Larger ships have complete beauty salons, and some have barbershops. Book your appointment well in advance, especially before such popular events as the farewell dinner.

Film Processing
Many ships have color-film processing equipment to develop film overnight. It's expensive but convenient.

Photographer
The staff photographer, a near-universal fixture on cruise ships, records every memorable, photogenic moment. The thousands of photos snapped over the course of a cruise are displayed publicly in special cases every morning and are offered for sale, usually for $6 for a $5'' \times 7''$ color print or $12 for an $8'' \times 10''$. If you want a special photo or a portrait, the photographer is usually happy to oblige. Many passengers choose to have a formal portrait taken before the captain's farewell dinner—the dressiest evening of the cruise. The ship's photographer usually anticipates this demand by setting up a studio near the dining-room entrance.

Religious Services
Most ships provide nondenominational religious services on Sundays and religious holidays, and a number offer

Catholic masses daily and Jewish services on Friday evenings. The kind of service held depends upon the clergy the cruise line invites on board. Usually religious services are held in the library, the theater, or one of the private lounges, although a few ships have actual chapels.

Communications

SHIPBOARD

Most cabins have loudspeakers and telephones. Generally, the loudspeakers cannot be switched off because they are needed to broadcast important notices. Telephones are used to call fellow passengers, order room service, summon a doctor, request a wake-up call, or speak with any of the ship's officers or departments.

SHIP TO SHORE

As a rule, cruise ships sell local stamps at the front desk, and you can send postcards from an onboard mailbox as well, eliminating the need to find a post office. Satellite facilities make it possible to call anywhere in the world from most ships. Most are also equipped with telex and fax machines, and some provide credit card–operated phones. It may take as long as a half hour to make a connection, but unless a storm is raging outside, conversation is clear and easy. On older ships, voice calls must be put through on shortwave wireless or via the one phone in the radio room. Newer ships are generally equipped with direct-dial phones in every cabin for calls to shore. Be warned: the cost of sending any message, regardless of the method, can be quite expensive—up to $15 a minute. (On some ships, though, it's much cheaper, costing as little as $3.95 a minute.) If possible, wait until you go ashore to call home.

Safety at Sea

Fire Safety

The greatest danger facing cruise-ship passengers is fire. All of the lines reviewed in this book must meet certain international standards for fire safety. The latest rules require that ships have sprinkler systems, smoke detectors, and other safety features. However, these rules are designed to protect against loss of life. They do not guarantee that a fire will not happen; in fact, fire is relatively common on cruise ships. The point here is not to alarm, but to emphasize the importance of taking fire safety seriously.

Fire safety begins with you, the passenger. Once settled into your cabin, find the location of your life vests and review the emergency instructions inside the cabin door or near the life vests. Make sure your vests are in good condition and learn to secure them properly. Make certain the ship's purser knows if you have some physical infirmity that may hamper a speedy exit from your cabin. In case of a real emergency, the purser can quickly dispatch a crew member to assist you. If you are traveling with children, be sure that child-size life jackets are placed in your cabin.

Within 24 hours of embarkation, you will be asked to attend a mandatory lifeboat drill. Do so and listen carefully. If you are unsure how to use your vest, now is the time to ask. Only in the most extreme circumstances will you need to abandon ship—but it has happened. The time you spend learning the procedure may serve you well in a mishap.

Health Care

Quality medical care at sea is another important safety issue. All big ships are equipped with medical infirmaries to handle minor emergencies. However, these should not be confused with hospitals. There are no international standards governing medical facilities or personnel aboard cruise ships, although the American Medical Association has recommended that such standards be adopted. If you have a preexisting medical condition, discuss your upcoming cruise with your doctor. Pack an extra supply of any medicines you might need. Once aboard, see the ship's doctor and alert him or her to your condition, and discuss treatments or emergency procedures before any problem arises. Passengers with potentially life-threatening conditions should seriously consider signing up with a medical evacuation service, and all passengers should review their health insurance to make sure they are covered while on a cruise.

If you become seriously ill or injured and happen to be near a modern major city, you may be taken to a medical facility shoreside. But if you're farther afield, you may have to be airlifted off the ship by helicopter and flown either to the nearest American territory or to an airport where you can be taken by charter jet to the United States. Many standard health insurance policies, as well as Medicare, do not cover these or other medical expenses incurred outside the United States. You can, however, buy supplemental health insurance to cover you while you're traveling.

The most common minor medical problems confronting cruise passengers are seasickness and gastrointestinal distress. Modern cruise ships, unlike their transatlantic predecessors, are relatively motion-free vessels with computer-controlled stabilizers, and they usually sail in relatively calm waters. If, however, you do feel queasy, you can always get seasickness pills aboard ship. (Many ships give them out for free at the front desk.)

Outbreaks of food poisoning happen from time to time aboard cruise ships. Episodes are random; they can occur on ships old and new, big and small, budget and luxury. The Centers for Disease Control and Prevention (CDC) monitors cruise-ship hygiene and sanitation procedures, conducting voluntary inspections twice a year of all ships that sail regularly from U.S. ports (this program does not include ships that never visit the United States). For a free listing of the latest ship scores, write the CDC's National Center for Environmental Health (Vessel Sanitation Program, 1015 North America Way, Room 107, Miami, FL 33132). You can also get a copy from the CDC's fax-back service at 888/232–3299. Request publication 510051. Another alternative is to visit the Centers' Web site at www.cdc.gov.

A high score on the CDC report doesn't mean you won't get sick. Outbreaks have taken place on ships that consistently score very highly; conversely, some ships score very poorly yet passengers never get sick.

Crime on Ships
Crime aboard cruise ships has become headline news, thanks in large part to a few well publicized cases. Most people never have any type of problem, but you should exercise the same precautions aboard ship that you would at home. Keep your valuables out of sight—on big ships virtually every cabin has a small safe in the closet. Don't carry too much cash ashore, use your credit card whenever possible, and keep your money in a secure place, such as a front

pocket that's harder to pick. Single women traveling with friends should stick together, especially when returning to their cabins late at night. And be careful about whom you befriend, whether it's a fellow passenger or a member of the crew. Don't be paranoid, but do be prudent.

GOING ASHORE

Traveling by cruise ship presents an opportunity to visit many places in a short time. The flip side is that your stay in each port of call will be limited. For this reason, cruise lines offer shore excursions, which maximize passengers' time by organizing tours for them. There are a number of advantages to shore excursions: In some destinations, transportation may be unreliable, and a ship-packaged tour is the best way to see distant sights. Also, you don't have to worry about missing the ship. The disadvantage of a shore excursion is the cost—you pay more for the convenience of having the ship do the legwork for you. Of course, you can always book a tour independently, hire a taxi, or use foot power to explore on your own. Ask your shore-excursions office for recommended companies in each port.

Currency

Currencies vary by country, and U.S. dollars are accepted at some ports. It is advisable to change only a small amount on your ship or ashore for purchasing trinkets or snacks. When making major purchases and eating at better restaurants, use credit cards, which offer the best exchange rate.

Arriving in Port

When your ship arrives in a port, it will tie up alongside a dock or anchor out in a harbor. If the ship is docked, passengers walk down the gangway to go ashore. Docking makes it easy to move between the shore and the ship.

Tendering

If your ship anchors in the harbor, however, you will have to take a small boat—called a launch or tender—to get ashore. Tendering is a nuisance. When your ship first arrives in port, everyone wants to go ashore. Often, in order to avoid a stampede at the tenders, you must gather in a public room, get a boarding pass, and wait until your number is called. This continues until everybody has disembarked. Even then, it may take 15–20 minutes to get ashore if your ship is anchored far offshore. Because tenders can be difficult to board, passengers with mobility problems may not be able to visit certain ports. The larger the ship, the more likely it will use tenders. It is usually possible to learn before booking a cruise whether the ship will dock or anchor at its ports of call. (For more information about where ships dock, tender, or both at each port, *see* Chapter 2.)

Before anyone is allowed to walk down the gangway or board a tender, the ship must be cleared for landing. Immigration and customs officials board the vessel to examine passports and sort through red tape. It may be more than an hour before you're allowed ashore. You will be issued a boarding pass, which you'll need to get back on board.

Returning to the Ship

Cruise lines are strict about sailing times, which are posted at the gangway and elsewhere and announced in the daily schedule of activities. Be certain to be back on board at least a half hour before the announced sailing time or you may be stranded. If you are on a shore excursion that was sold by the cruise line, however, the captain will wait for your group before casting off. That is one reason many passengers prefer ship-packaged tours.

If you're not on one of the ship's tours and the ship sails without you, immediately contact the cruise line's port representative, whose phone number is often listed on the daily schedule of activities. You may be able to hitch a ride on a pilot boat, though that is unlikely. Passengers who miss the boat must pay their own way to the next port.

2 Ports of Call

EUROPE AND THE MEDITERRANEAN

For sheer diversity, there is no cruise destination quite like Europe. From the majesty of Norway's fjords to the ruins of ancient Greece, the Old World has more than one could possibly hope to see in a single cruise vacation. Depending on your ship choice, your cruise companions may be as varied as the places you visit; you may find yourself mostly with North Americans or a mix of North Americans and Europeans. If your cruise is during peak season—May through August—you will be joining the crowds, as the weather is usually best during this time. If you're visiting in the early spring or late fall, you'll avoid the fray and get lower prices. Temperatures can be very comfortable, and it is possible to swim in the Mediterranean through early October.

Amsterdam, the Netherlands

If you've come to Holland expecting to find its residents shod in wooden shoes, you're years too late; if you're looking for windmills at every turn, you're looking in the wrong place. The bucolic images that brought tourism here in the decades after World War II have little to do with the Netherlands today. Modern Holland is a marriage of economic power and cultural wealth, a mix not new to the Dutch: in the 17th century, for example, money raised through colonial outposts was used to buy or commission portraits and paintings by young artists such as Rembrandt, Hals, Vermeer, and van Ruisdael.

Amsterdam is the cultural focal point of the nation. It is characterized by small, densely packed buildings, many dating from the 17th century or earlier. The heart of the city consists of canals, with narrow streets radiating out like spokes of a wheel.

Currency

The unit of currency in Holland is the guilder, written as NLG (for Netherlands guilder), Fl., or simply F. Each guilder is divided into 100 cents. Don't confuse the 1- and

2.5-guilder coins and the 5-guilder and 5-cent coins. At press time, the exchange rate for the guilder was Fl. 2.1 to the U.S. dollar, Fl. 1.4 to the Canadian dollar, Fl. 3.3 to the pound sterling.

Telephones

The country code for the Netherlands is 31. All towns and cities have area codes that are used only when you are calling from outside the area. When dialing from outside the country, drop the initial zero in the local area code. All public phone booths require phone cards, which may be purchased from post offices, railway stations, and newsagents for Fl. 10 or Fl. 25. Pay phones in bars and restaurants take 25¢ or Fl. 1 coins. Dial 0800/0410 for an English-speaking operator. Direct-dial international calls can be made from any phone booth. To reach an **AT&T** long-distance operator, dial 0800/022–9111; for **MCI,** dial 0800/022–9122; for **Sprint,** dial 0800/022–9119.

Shore Excursions

The following is a good choice in Amsterdam. It may not be offered by all cruise lines. Time and price are approximate.

City Tour Cruise. By motor coach and canal boat, you'll see Amsterdam's major sights, including the Dam Square, Royal Palace, New Church, and Rijksmuseum. The route also passes some of Amsterdam's architectural highlights, such as the Mint Tower and Weeping Tower. *3½ hrs. Cost: $36.*

Coming Ashore

Ships dock at the cruise terminal; it's about a 10-minute drive to the main square. Central Station, the hub of the city, is the most convenient point to begin sightseeing. Across the street, in the same building as the Old Dutch Coffee House, is a tourist information center that offers helpful advice.

Getting Around

Amsterdam is a small, congested city of narrow streets, which makes it ideal for exploring on foot. The most enjoyable way to get to know Amsterdam is by taking a boat trip along the canals. There are frequent departures from points opposite Central Station. Taxis are expensive: a 5-km (3-mi) ride costs around Fl. 15. Rental bikes are readily available

for around Fl. 12.50 per day with a Fl. 50–Fl. 200 deposit.
Several rental companies are close to Central Station.

Exploring Amsterdam

*Numbers in the margin correspond to points of interest on
the Amsterdam map.*

① The **Centraal Station** (Central Station), designed by P.J.H.
Cuijpers, was built in 1884–89 and is a good example of
Dutch architecture at its most flamboyant. It provides an
excellent viewpoint for both the Beurs van Berlage and the
Scheepvaartshuis, two of the city's best examples of early-
20th-century architecture. The street directly in front of the
station square is Prins Hendrikkade.

② The most important of Amsterdam's museums is the **Rijksmuseum** (State Museum), easily recognized by its towers.
It was founded in 1808, but the current, rather lavish,
building dates from 1885. The museum's fame rests on its
unrivaled collection of 16th- and 17th-century Dutch masters. Of Rembrandt's masterpieces, make a point of seeing
The Nightwatch, concealed during World War II in caves
in Maastricht. The painting was misnamed because of its
dull layers of varnish; in reality it depicts the Civil Guard
in daylight. Also worth searching out are Frans Hals's family portraits, Jan Steen's drunken scenes, van Ruisdael's romantic but menacing landscapes, and Vermeer's glimpses
of everyday life bathed in his usual pale light. *Stadhouderskade 42, tel. 020/6732121. Admission: Fl. 12.50. Open
daily 10–5.*

③ The not-to-be-missed **Van Gogh Museum** contains the
world's largest collection of the artist's works—200 paintings and nearly 500 drawings—as well as works by some
50 of his contemporaries. The new wing, a spaceship-like
stone and titanium oval structure connected to the main
building by an underground walkway, provides space to exhibit Van Gogh's prints and accommodate temporary exhibitions. *Paulus Potterstraat 7, tel. 020/5705200.
Admission: Fl. 12.50. Open daily 10–5.*

④ The **Stedelijk Museum** (Museum of Modern Art) has a stim-
ulating collection of modern art and ever-changing displays
of contemporary art. Before viewing the works of Cézanne,

28

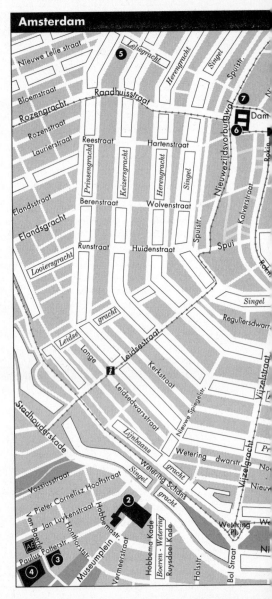

Amsterdam

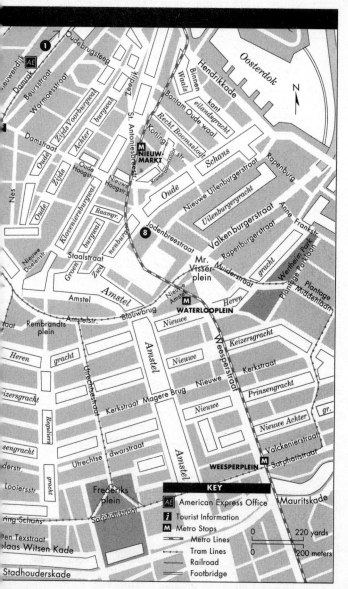

Oosterdok

N

Oudebrugsteeg

Nieuwendijk

Damrak

Beursstraat

Warmoesstraat

Hendrikkade

Binnen kant

Waals

Bantam eilandsgracht

Oude waal

Zijds Voorburgwal

Achter burgwal

St. Antoniesbreestr.

Recht Boomssloot

Koningsstr.

Damstraat

Oude

Zijds

Oude Hoogstr.

Nieuwe Hoogstr.

Kromme

M NIEUW-MARKT

Schans

Rapenburg

Oude

Nieuwe Uilenburgerstraat

Nes

Nieuwe Doelenstr.

Klovenirsburgwal

Raamgr.

Zand burgwal

nenburg

8

Jodenbreestraat

Uilenburgergracht

Valkenburgerstraat

Rapenburgerstraat

Anne Franksstr.

gracht

Wertheim Park

Plantage Parklaan

Staalstraat

Groen

Mr. Visser-plein

Muiderstraat

Heren

Plantage Middenlaan

Amstel

Amstel

Nieuwe Amstel

M WATERLOOPLEIN

faat

Rembrandts plein

Amstelstr.

Blauwbrug

Nieuwe

Keizersgracht

Heren

gracht

Amstel

Nieuwe

Weesperstraat

Kerkstraat

iersgracht

Utrechtsestraat

Kerkstraat Magere Brug

Nieuwe

Prinsengracht

Regulier

Nieuwe

Nieuwe Achter

gr.

sengracht

Utrechtse dwarsstraat

Amstel

Valckenierstraat

derstr.

gracht

WEESPERPLEIN M Sarphatistraat

Looiersstr.

Frederiks plein

KEY

ring Schans

Sarphatistraat

Mauritskade

en Texstraat

plaas Witsen Kade

Stadhouderskade

AE	American Express Office
i	Tourist Information
M	Metro Stops
	Metro Lines
	Tram Lines
	Railroad
	Footbridge

0   220 yards

0   200 meters

Chagall, Kandinsky, and Mondrian, check the list of temporary exhibitions in Room 1. Exhibits trace an artists' development rather than just showing a few masterpieces. *Paulus Potterstraat 13, tel. 020/5732911. Admission: Fl. 9. Open Apr.–Sept., daily 10–5; Oct.–Mar., daily 11–5.*

5 Arguably the most famous house in Amsterdam is the **Anne Frankhuis** (Anne Frank House), immortalized by the poignant diary kept by the young Jewish girl from 1942 to 1944, when she and her family hid here from the German occupying forces. An exhibition including documents about the Holocaust and civil liberty can also be seen in the house. *Prinsengracht 263, tel. 020/5567100. Admission: Fl. 10. Open June–Aug., Mon.–Sat. 9–7, Sun. 10–7; Sept.–May, Mon.–Sat. 9–5, Sun. 10–5.*

The infamous *rosse buurt* (red-light district) is bordered by Amsterdam's two oldest canals (Oudezijds Voorburgwal and Oudezijds Achterburgwal). In the windows at canal level, women in lingerie slouch, stare, or do their nails. Although the area can be shocking, with its sex shops and porn shows, it is generally safe. If you decide to explore the area, beware purse-snatchers and pickpockets. Midnight walks down dark side streets are not advised.

6 Dominating Dam Square is **Het Koninklijk Paleis te Amsterdam** (The Royal Palace at Amsterdam), a vast, well-proportioned structure that was completed in 1655. It is built on 13,659 pilings sunk into the marshy soil. The great pediment sculptures are an allegorical representation of Amsterdam surrounded by Neptune and mythological sea creatures. *Dam, tel. 020/6248698. Admission: Fl. 7. Open Tues.–Thurs. 1–4; daily 12:30–5 in summer. Occasionally closed for state events.*

7 The **Nieuwe Kerk** (New Church), a huge Gothic structure, stands next to the royal palace on a corner of the Dam. The original 16th-century structure was gutted by fire in the 17th century and rebuilt in a Renaissance style. As the national church, the Nieuwe Kerk is the site of all coronations; in democratic Dutch spirit, it is also used as a meeting place, has a lively café, and hosts special exhibitions and concerts. *Dam, tel. 020/6268168. Admission free, except for exhibitions. Daily 11–5; exhibitions daily 10–6.*

From 1639 to 1658, Rembrandt lived at Jodenbreestraat
❽ 4, now the **Museum Het Rembrandthuis** (Rembrandt House
Museum). For more than 20 years, the ground floor was
used by the artist as living quarters; the sunny upper floor
was his studio. It contains a superb collection of his etch-
ings. The new, modern wing next door includes more exhibition space, an auditorium, and a shop. From St. Antonies
Sluis Bridge, just by the house, there is a canal view that
has barely changed since Rembrandt's time. *Jodenbreestraat
4–6, tel. 020/6249486. Admission: Fl. 7.50. Open Mon.–
Sat. 10–5, Sun. 1–5.*

Shopping

Amsterdam is a cornucopia of interesting markets and
quirky specialty shops selling antiques, art, and diamonds.
The chief shopping districts, which have largely been turned
into pedestrian-only areas, are the **Leidsestraat, Kalver-
straat, Utrechtsestraat,** and **Nieuwendijk.** The **Rokin,** hec-
tic with traffic, houses a cluster of diamond houses,
boutiques, and renowned antiques shops selling 18th- and
19th-century furniture, antique jewelry, Art Deco lamps,
and statuettes. The **Spiegelkwartier** is another good place
for antiques, with a mix of collectors' haunts and old cu-
riosity shops. Haute couture and other fine goods are at
home on **P.C. Hooftstraat, Van Baerlestraat,** and **Beethoven-
straat.** For trendy small boutiques and unusual crafts shops,
locals browse through the **Jordaan.** For A-to-Z shopping
in a huge variety of stores, visit the **Magna Plaza** shopping
center, built inside the glorious old post office behind the
Royal Palace at the Dam.

Athens/Piraeus, Greece

Athens is essentially a village that outgrew itself, spread-
ing out from the original settlement at the foot of the
Acropolis. Back in 1834, when it became the capital of modern Greece, the city had a population of fewer than 10,000.
Now it houses more than a third of the Greek population—
around 4.3 million. A modern concrete city has engulfed
the old village and sprawls for 388 square km (244 square
mi), covering almost all the surrounding plain from the sea
to the encircling mountains.

The city is crowded, dusty, and overwhelmingly hot during the summer. It also has an appalling air-pollution problem. Still, Athens is an experience not to be missed. Its tangible vibrancy makes it one of the most exciting cities in Europe, and the sprawling cement has failed to overwhelm the astonishing reminders of ancient Athens.

Currency

The Greek monetary unit is the drachma (dr.). At press time, there were approximately 305 dr. to the U.S. dollar, 202 dr. to the Canadian dollar, and 485 dr. to the pound sterling.

Telephones

The country code for Greece is 30. When dialing Greece from outside the country, drop the first zero from the regional area code. Telephone kiosks are easy to find, although many can only be used for local calls. The easiest way to make a local or an international call is with a phone card, available at kiosks, convenience stores, or Hellenic Telecommunications Organization (OTE) offices. Go to an OTE office for convenience and privacy if you plan to make several international calls; there are several branches in Athens. For an **AT&T** long-distance operator, dial 00/800–1311; **MCI,** 00/800–1211; **Sprint,** 00/800–1411. For operator-assisted calls in English, dial 161 or 162.

Shore Excursions

The following are good choices in Athens. They may not be offered by all cruise lines. Times and prices are approximate.

Athens and the Acropolis. A must for the first-time visitor. Drive by motor coach to Athens, passing the Olympic Stadium, the former Royal Palace, and the Tomb of the Unknown Warrior on the way to the Acropolis, where a guide will lead an extensive walking tour. *4 hrs. Cost: $40.*

Agora and Plaka. Athens's ancient shopping district and its beautiful 19th-century quarter are the centerpieces of this half-day tour into historic Greece. *4 hrs. Cost: $44.*

Coming Ashore

Cruise ships dock at Piraeus, 10 km (6 mi) from Athens's center. From Piraeus, you can take the nearby metro right into Omonia Square. The trip takes 20 minutes and costs

120 dr. Alternatively, you can take a taxi, which may well take longer due to traffic and will cost around 1,100 dr. Cruise lines nearly always offer bus transfers for a fee.

The central area of modern Athens is small, stretching from the Acropolis to Mt. Lycabettus, with its little white church on top. The layout is simple: Three parallel streets—Stadiou, Panepistimiou, and Akademias—link two main squares—Syntagma and Omonia. In summer, closing times often depend on the site's available personnel, but throughout the year, arrive at least 45 minutes before the official closing time to ensure that you can buy a ticket.

Many of the sights you'll want to see, and most of the hotels, cafés, and restaurants, are within the central area of Athens, and it's easy to walk everywhere. Taxis are plentiful and heavily used. Although you'll eventually find an empty one, it's often faster to call out your destination to one carrying passengers; if the taxi is going in that direction, the driver will pick you up. Most drivers speak basic English and are familiar with the city center. The meter starts at 200 dr., and there is a basic charge of 66 dr. per km (½ mi), which increases to 130 dr. between midnight and 5 AM. The minimum fare is 500 dr. There is an additional 150 dr. charge for trips to, but not from, the port. Some drivers overcharge foreigners; make sure they turn on the meter and use the high tariff ("Tarifa 2") only after midnight.

Exploring Athens

Numbers in the margin correspond to points of interest on the Athens map.

❶ A steep, zigzag path leads to the **Akropolis** (Acropolis). The Athenians built this complex during the 5th century BC to honor the goddess Athena, patron of the city. It is now undergoing conservation as part of an ambitious 20-year rescue plan launched with international support in 1983 by Greek architects.

The first ruins you'll see are the Propylaea, the monumental gateway that led worshipers from the temporal world into the spiritual world of the sanctuary; now only the columns of Pentelic marble and a fragment of stone ceiling remain. Above, to the right, stands the graceful Naos

34

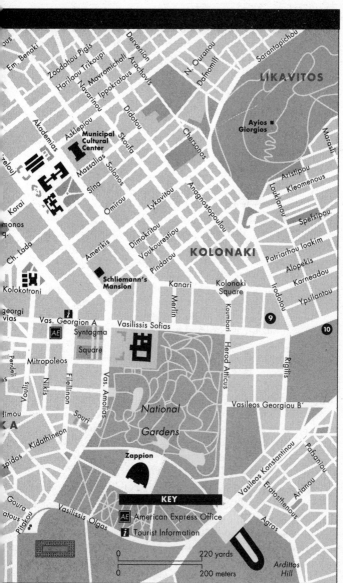

LIKAVITOS

Ayios ■
Giorgios

Em. Benaki
Zoodohou Pigis
Harilaou Trikoupi
Mavromichali
Navarinou
Ippokratous
Dervenion
Arachovis
N. Ouranou
Dahomiti
Sarantapichou
Marasli

Akademias
Asklepiou
Didotou
Skoufa
Chesronos

Municipal
Cultural
Center

Massalias
Sina
Solonos
Omirou
Lykavitou
Anagnostopoulou

'ielou
Korai
monos
q.
Ch. Lada

Aristipou
Loukianou
Kleomenous
Spefsipou

Dimokritou
Voukourestiou
Pindarou

KOLONAKI

Patriarhou Ioakim
Alopekis
Karneadou
Ypsilantou

Kolokotroni

Schliemann's
Mansion

Kanari

Kolonaki
Square

Irodotou

georgi
vias

Vas. Georgion A
Syntagma
Square

Vasilissis Sofias

Koumbari
Herod Atticus
Rigillis

Amerikis

Marlin

9

10

Mitropoleos
Filellinon
Souri
Nikis
Vas. Amolias

pendali
Voulis
timou
KA

Kidathineon
spidos

Vasileos Georgiou B'

*National
Gardens*

Zappion

Vasileos Konstantinou
Eratosthenous
Arianou
Patsanou

Goura
atous
Pitakou
Vasilissis Olgas
Agras

KEY

AE American Express Office

ℹ️ Tourist Information

0   220 yards

0   200 meters

Ardittos
Hill

Athenas Nikis or Apterou Nikis (Wingless Victory). The temple was mistakenly called the latter because common tradition often confused Athena with the winged goddess Nike. The elegant and architecturally complex Erechtheion temple, most sacred of the shrines of the Acropolis and later turned into a harem by the Turks, has emerged from repair work with dull, heavy copies of the caryatids (draped maidens) supporting the roof. The Acropolis Museum houses five of the six originals, their faces much damaged by acid rain; the sixth is in the British Museum in London.

❷ The **Parthenonas** (Parthenon) dominates the Acropolis and indeed the Athens skyline. It was completed in 438 BC and is the most architecturally sophisticated temple of that period. Even with hordes of tourists wandering around the ruins, it still inspires wonder. The architectural decorations were originally painted in vivid red and blue, and the roof was of marble tiles, but time and neglect have given the marble pillars their golden-white shine, and the beauty of the building is all the more stark and striking. The British Museum houses the largest remaining part of the original 532-ft frieze (the Elgin Marbles). The building has 17 fluted columns along each side and eight at the ends, and these lean slightly inward and bulge to cleverly counterbalance the natural optical distortion. The Parthenon was made into a brothel by the Romans, a church by the Christians, and a mosque by the Turks. The Turks also stored gunpowder in the Propylaea, and when this was hit by a Venetian bombardment in 1687, a fire raged for two days and 28 columns of the Parthenon were blown out, leaving the temple in its present condition. *Top of Dionyssiou Areopagitou, tel. 01/321–4172. Admission: 2,000 dr., joint ticket to Acropolis and museum. Open May–Oct., weekdays 8–7, weekends 8–2:30; Nov.–Apr., daily 8–2:30.*

❸ The **Museo Akropoleos** (Acropolis Museum), tucked into one corner of the Acropolis, contains some superb sculptures from the Acropolis, including the Caryatids and a large collection of colored *korai* (statues of women dedicated by worshipers to the goddess Athena, patron of the ancient city). *Southeastern corner of Acropolis, tel. 01/323–6665. Admission: 2,000 dr., joint ticket to the Acropolis. Open*

Mon. 11–6:30 (11–2:30 in winter), Tues.–Sun. 8–6:30 (8–2:30 in winter).

On Areopagus, the rocky outcrop facing the Acropolis, St. Paul delivered his Sermon to the Unknown God. Legend also claims that Orestes was tried here for the murder of
❹ his mother. To the right stands the **Archaia Agora** (Ancient Agora) which means "marketplace," the civic center and focal point of community life in ancient Athens, where Socrates met with his students while merchants haggled over the price of olive oil.

The sprawling confusion of stones, slabs, and foundations at the Agora is dominated by the best-preserved temple in
❺ Greece, the **Hephaisteion** (often wrongly referred to as the Theseion), built during the 5th century BC.

The impressive **Stoa Attalou** (Stoa of Attalos II), reconstructed in the mid-1950s by the American School of Classical Stud-
❻ ies in Athens, houses the **Museo tis Agoras** (Museum of Agora Excavations), which offers a glimpse of everyday life in ancient Athens. *Three entrances: from Monastiraki, on Adrianou; from Thission, on Apostolos Pavlou; from Acropolis, on descent along Ag. Apostoli. Tel. 01/321–0185. Admission: 1,200 dr. Open Tues.–Sun. 8–2:30.*

❼ The **Plaka** is almost all that's left of 19th-century Athens, a lovely quarter with winding lanes, neoclassical houses, and sights such as the Museo Ellinikis Laikis Technis (Greek Folk Art Museum; Kidathineon 17); the Aerides (Tower of the Winds), a 1st-century BC water clock near the Roman Agora; and the Mnimeio Lysikratous (Monument of Lysikrates; Herefondos and Lysikratous Sts.). Above the Plaka, at the base of the Acropolis, is Anafiotika, the closest thing you'll find to a village in Athens. To escape the city bustle, take some time to wander among its whitewashed, bougainvillea-framed houses and its tiny churches. *Stretching east from the Agora.*

❽ Make time to see the **Ethniko Archaiologiko Museo** (National Archaeological Museum). Among the collection of antiquities are the sensational archaeological finds of Heinrich Schliemann in 1874 at Mycenae; 16th-century BC frescoes from the Akrotiri ruins on Santorini; and the 6½-ft-tall bronze sculpture *Poseidon,* an original work of circa 470 BC, which was found in the sea off Cape Artemision in 1928. *28 Oktovriou (Patission) 44, 10-min walk north of Pl. Omonia, tel. 01/821–7717. Admission: 2,000 dr. Open May–Oct., Mon. 12:30–7, Tues.–Fri. 8–7, weekends 8–2:30; Nov.–Apr., Mon. 10:30–5, Tues.–Sun. 8–2:30.*

❾ The **Goulandri Museo Kikladikis ke Ellinikis Archaias Technis** (Goulandris Museum of Cycladic and Greek Ancient Art) collection spans 5,000 years, with nearly 100 exhibits of the Cycladic civilization (3000–2000 BC), including many of the marble figurines that so fascinated artists such as Picasso and Modigliani. *Neofitou Douka 4 or Irodotou 1, tel. 01/722–8321. Admission: 400 dr. Open Mon. and Wed.–Fri. 10–4, Sat. 10–3.*

Housed in an 1848 mansion built by an eccentric French **❿** aristocrat is the **Vizantino Museo** (Byzantine Museum). Since the museum is undergoing renovation, not all its pieces are on display, but it has a unique collection of icons, re-creations of Greek churches through the centuries, and very beautiful 14th-century Byzantine embroidery of the body of Christ, in gold, silver, yellow, and green. Sculptural fragments give an excellent introduction to Byzantine architecture. *Vasilissis Sofias 22, tel. 01/721–1027. Admission: 500 dr. Open Tues.–Sun. 8:30–3 (8–2:30 in winter).*

Shopping

Better tourist shops sell copies of traditional Greek jewelry, silver filigree, Skyrian pottery, onyx ashtrays and dishes, woven bags, attractive rugs (including *flokatis*—shaggy wool rugs, often brightly colored), worry beads called *koboloi* in amber or silver, and blue-and-white amulets to ward off the *mati* (evil eye). Prices for gold and silver are much lower in Greece than in many Western countries, and jewelry is of high quality. Some museums sell replicas of small items in their collections. The best handicrafts are sold in the **Organismos Ethnikos Pronoias** (National Welfare Organization; Vas. Sofias 135, Ambelokipi; Ipatias 6 and Apollonos, Plaka) and the **Kentro Ellinikis Paradosis** (Center of Hellenic Tradition; Mitropoleos 59 or Pandrossou 36, Monastiraki). Other shops sell dried fruit, packaged pistachios, and canned olives. Natural sponges and Greek coffee also make good gifts.

Barcelona, Spain

Barcelona, capital of Catalunya (Catalonia), thrives on its business acumen and industrial muscle. The hardworking citizens of this thriving metropolis are proud to have and use their own language—street names, museum exhibits, newspapers, radio programs, and movies are all in Catalan. An important milestone here was the city's long-awaited opportunity to host the Olympic Games, in summer 1992; the Olympics were of singular importance in Barcelona's modernization. Their legacy includes a vastly improved ring road and several other highways; four new beaches; and an entire new neighborhood in what used to be the run-down industrial district of Poble Nou. Few cities can rival the medieval atmosphere of the Gothic Quarter's narrow alleys, the elegance and distinction of the Moderniste (Art Nouveau) Eixample, or the many fruits of Gaudí's whimsical imagination.

Currency

The unit of currency in Spain is the peseta (pta.). There are bills of 1,000, 2,000, 5,000, and 10,000 ptas. Coins are 1, 5, 25, 50, 100, 200, and 500 ptas. At press time, the exchange rate was about 156 ptas. to the U.S. dollar, 103 ptas. to the Canadian dollar, and 248 ptas. to the pound sterling.

Telephones

The country code for Spain is 34. Note that to call anywhere within the country—even locally—from any kind of phone, you need to dial the area code first; all provincial codes begin with a 9. Pay phones generally take the new, smaller 5- and 25-pta. coins; the minimum charge for short local calls is 25 ptas. Newer pay phones take only phone cards, which can be purchased at any tobacco shop in denominations of 1,000 or 2,000 ptas. International calls can be made from any pay phone marked TELÉFONO INTERNACIONAL. Use 50-pta. (or 100-pta. if the phone takes them) coins initially, then coins of any denomination to prolong your call. For lengthy international calls, go to the *telefónica*, a telephone office, where an operator assigns you a private booth and collects payment at the end of the call; this is the least expensive and by far the easiest way of phoning abroad. Dial 07 for international calls, wait for the tone to change, then dial the country code, area code, and the number. For the operator and directory information for any part of Spain, dial 1003 (some operators speak English). To reach an **AT&T** operator, dial 900/99–00–11; **MCI,** 900/99–00–14; **Sprint,** 900/99–00–13.

Shore Excursions

The following is a good choice in Barcelona. It may not be offered by all cruise lines. Time and price are approximate.

Barcelona Highlights. This comprehensive excursion winds its way from the pier to the Gothic Quarter. Along the way you'll see the unfinished Sagrada Familia cathedral and visit Montjuïc, one of the city's highest points, before reaching Plaza Catalunya for a walking tour of the Gothic Quarter. *3½ hrs. Cost: $30.*

Coming Ashore

Ships visiting Barcelona dock near the Gothic Quarter and the Columbus Monument, but it's too far to walk. Take the cruise-line bus.

Modern Barcelona above the Plaça de Catalunya is mostly built on a grid system, though there's no helpful numbering system as in the United States. The Gothic Quarter from the Plaça de Catalunya to the port is a warren of narrow streets, however, and you'll need a good map to get around. Most sightseeing can be done on foot—you won't have any other choice in the Gothic Quarter—but you may need to use the metro, taxis, or buses to link sightseeing areas. The subway is the fastest way of getting around. Maps of the system are available at main metro stations and branches of the Caixa savings bank. For both subways and city buses, you pay a flat fare of 150 ptas. or purchase a *tarjeta multiviatge,* good for 10 rides (780 ptas.). Taxis are black and yellow and when available for hire show a LIBRE sign in the daytime and a green light at night. The meter starts at 315 ptas., and there are small supplements for rides to the port. There are cab stands all over town; cabs may also be flagged down on the street.

Exploring Barcelona

Numbers in the margin correspond to points of interest on the Barcelona map.

① Head to the bottom of Rambla and take an elevator to the top of the **Monument a Colom** (Columbus Monument) for a breathtaking view over the city. Columbus faces out to sea, pointing east toward Naples. (Nearby you can board the cable car that crosses the harbor to Barceloneta or goes up to Montjuïc.) *Admission: 450 ptas. Open Tues.–Sat. 10–2 and 3:30–6:30, Sun. 10–7.*

② The **Museu Marítim** (Maritime Museum) is housed in the 13th-century Drassanes Reiales (Royal Shipyards). The museum is packed with ships, figureheads, nautical paraphernalia, and several early navigation charts, including a map by Amerigo Vespucci and the oldest chart in Europe, the 1439 chart of Gabriel de Valseca. *Plaça Portal de la Pau 1, tel. 93/318–3245. Admission: 850 ptas.; ½ price Wed., free 1st Sun. of month. Open Tues.–Sat. 10–2 and 4–7, Sun. 10–2.*

③ Gaudí's **Palau Güell** mansion was built between 1886 and 1890 for his patron, Count Eusebi de Güell, and is the only one of Gaudí's houses that is open to the public. *Nou de la Rambla, 3, tel. 93/317–3974. Admission: 500 ptas.; ½ price Wed., free 1st Sun. of month. Open weekdays 10–1:30 and 4–6:30.*

④ An impressive square built in the 1840s in the heart of the Gothic Quarter, the **Plaça Sant Jaume** features two imposing buildings facing each other. The 15th-century Ajuntament, or City Hall, has an impressive black and gold mural (1928) by Josep María Sert and the famous Saló de Cent, from which the first European parliament, the Council of One Hundred, ruled the city from 1372 to 1714. You can wander into the courtyard, but to visit the interior, you will have to arrange entrance with the protocol office. The Palau de la Generalitat, seat of the Catalan Regional Government, is a 15th-century palace open to the public on special days or by appointment. *Jct. of C. de Ferràn and C. Jaume I.*

⑤ At the Plaça de la Seu, step inside the magnificent Gothic **Catedral de la Seu** (cathedral) built between 1298 and 1450, though the spire and Gothic facade were not added until 1892. Highlights are the beautifully carved choir stalls, Santa Eulàlia's tomb in the crypt, the battle-scarred crucifix from Don Juan's galley in the Lepanto Chapel, and

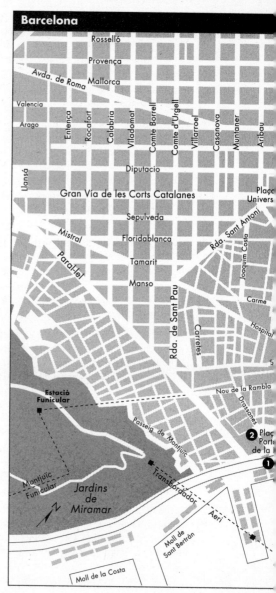

Barcelona

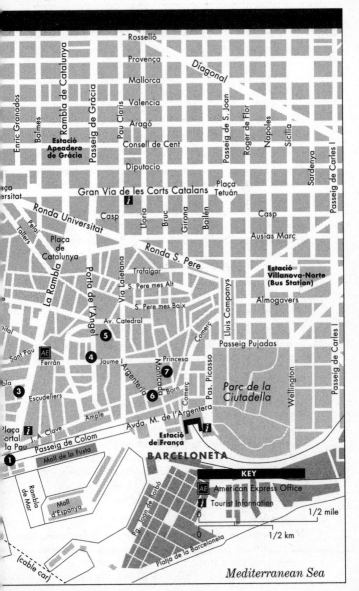

Rosselló

Provença

Mallorca

Diagonal

Valencia

Aragó

Consell de Cent

Diputacio

Enric Granados

Balmes

Rambla de Catalunya

Passeig de Gràcia

Pau Claris

Estació
Apeadero
de Gràcia

Passeig de S. Joan

Roger de Flor

Napoles

Sicilia

Sardenya

Passeig de Carles I

Gran Via de les Corts Catalans

Plaça
Tetuán

Plaça
ersitat

Ronda Universitat

Casp

Lloria

Bruc

Girona

Bailén

Casp

Ausias Marc

Pelai

Tallers

Plaça
de
Catalunya

Ronda S. Pere

Estació
Villanova-Norte
(Bus Station)

La Rambla

Porta de l'Angel

Via Laietana

Trafalgar

S. Pere mes Alt

S. Pere mes Baix

Av. Catedral

Lluís Companys

Almogavers

Sant Pau

AE

Ferràn

5

4

Jaume I

Argenteria

Princesa

Montcada

7

Comerç

Pas. Picasso

Passeig Pujadas

Wellington

Passeig de Carles I

3

Escudellers

Ample

6

Born

Comerç

Parc de la
Ciutadella

Plaça
ortal
la Pau

i

J. A. Clavé

Passeig de Colom

Avda. M. de l'Argentera

Estació
de França

i

bla

1

Moll de la Fusta

BARCELONETA

Rambla
de Mar

Moll
d'Espanya

Pg. Joan de Borbó

KEY

AE American Express Office

i Tourist Information

0   1/2 mile

0   1/2 km

Platja de la Barceloneta

(cable car)

Mediterranean Sea

the cloisters. *Plaça de la Seu, tel. 93/315–1554. Admission free. Open daily 7:45–1:30 and 4–7:45.*

❻ Santa Maria del Mar (Saint Mary of the Sea) is Barcelona's best example of a Mediterranean Gothic church and is widely considered the city's loveliest. It was built between 1329 and 1383 in fulfillment of a vow made a century earlier by James I to build a church for the Virgin of the Sailors. Its simple beauty is enhanced by a colorful rose window and slender soaring columns. *Plaça Santa Maria. Open weekends 9–12:30 and 5–8.*

❼ One of Barcelona's most popular attractions, the **Museu Picasso** (Picasso Museum) is actually two 15th-century palaces that provide a striking setting for the collections donated in 1963 and 1970, first by Picasso's secretary, then by the artist himself. The collection ranges from early childhood sketches to exhibition posters done in Paris shortly before his death. Of particular interest are his Blue Period paintings and his variations on Velázquez's *Las Meninas. Carrer Montcada 1519, tel. 93/319–6310. Admission: 750 ptas; Wed. ½ price, free 1st Sun. of month. Open Tues.– Sat. 10–8, Sun. 10–3.*

Above the Plaça de Catalunya you come into modern Barcelona and an elegant area known as the **Eixample,** which was laid out in the late 19th century as part of the city's expansion scheme. Much of the building here was done at the height of the Moderniste movement, a Spanish and mainly Catalan offshoot of Art Nouveau whose leading exponents were the architects Gaudí, Luís Domènech i Montaner, and Josep Puig i Cadafalch. The principal thoroughfares of the Eixample are the Rambla de Catalunya and the Passeig de Gràcia, on which stand some of the city's most elegant shops and cafés. For the Ruta Modernista tour of the city's main Art Nouveau sights, stop at the Casa Lleó Morera (⊠ Passeig de Gràcia 35, 3rd floor).

Shopping
There are no special handicrafts associated with Barcelona, but you'll have no trouble finding typical Spanish goods anywhere in town. If you're into fashion and jewelry, then you've come to the right place, as Barcelona makes all the

headlines on Spain's booming fashion front. **Xavier Roca i Coll** (Sant Pere mes Baix 24, just off Laietana) specializes in silver models of Barcelona's buildings. Barcelona and Catalonia have passed along a playful sense of design ever since Antoni Gaudí began creating shock waves over a century ago. Stores and boutiques specializing in design items (jewelry, furnishings, knickknacks) include **Bd** (Barcelona Design, at Mallorca 291–293) and **Dos i Una** (Rosselló 275).

Bullfighting

Barcelona's bullring is the **Monumental** (Gran Via and Carles I), where bullfights are held on Sundays between March and October; check the newspaper for details. For tickets with no markup, go to the official ticket office (Muntaner 24, near Gran Via, tel. 93/453–3821). There's a **Bullfighting Museum** at the Monumental ring (open Mar.–Oct., daily 10–1 and 5:30–7).

Bergen, Norway

Norway has some of the most remote and dramatic scenery in Europe. Along the west coast, deep fjords knife into steep mountain ranges. In older villages, wooden houses spill down toward docks where Viking ships—and later, whaling vessels—once were moored. Norway is most famous for its fjords, which were formed during an ice age a million years ago. The entrances to most fjords are shallow, about 500 ft, and inland depths reach 4,000 ft.

Bergen is the gateway to the fjord region. The town was founded in 1070 and is now Norway's second-largest city; for the year 2000, it is one of the nine European Cities of Culture and is presenting three season-based programs of art and folk festivals; ask for details at the tourist office (Bryggen 7, tel. 55321480). Bergen was a member of the medieval Hanseatic League and offered an ice-free harbor and convenient trading location on the west coast. Despite numerous fires in its past, much of medieval Bergen has survived. Seven surrounding mountains set off the weathered wooden houses, cobbled streets, and Hanseatic-era warehouses of Bryggen (the harbor area).

Currency

The unit of currency in Norway is the krone, written as Kr. on price tags but officially written as NOK (bank designation), NKr, or kr. The krone is divided into 100 øre. Bills of NKr 50, 100, 200, 500, and 1,000 are in general use. Coins are in denominations of 50 øre and 1, 5, 10, and 20 kroner. The exchange rate at press time was NKr 7.82 to the U.S. dollar, NKr 5.18 to the Canadian dollar, and NKr 12.44 to the pound sterling.

Telephones

The country code for Norway is 47. Public phones accept either coins or phone cards. Be sure to read the instructions; some phones require the coins to be deposited before dialing, some after. The minimum deposit is NKr 2 or NKr 3, depending on the phone. You can buy telephone cards at Narvesen kiosks or at the post office. International calls can be made from any pay phone. For calls to North America, dial 00–1, then the area code and number. You will need to dial 00 for an international connection. To reach an **AT&T** long-distance operator, dial 80019011.

Shore Excursions

The following are good choices in Bergen. They may not be offered by all cruise lines. Times and prices are approximate.

City Tour. Head past the central harbor area to Bryggen, where rows of gabled merchants' houses line the streets. Stop at Troldhaugen, once the estate of composer Edvard Grieg, for a tour and concert. *3 hrs. Cost: $44.*

Historic Bergen. The open-air Old Bergen Museum, the 13th-century royal ceremonial hall of King Haakon, and a replica of a 12th-century stave church are highlights of this short tour. *3 hrs. Cost: $40.*

Coming Ashore

Ships calling at Bergen dock at the harbor area at Bryggen. The city is small and easily toured on foot.

Exploring Bergen

The best way to get a feel for Bergen's medieval trading heyday is to visit the **Hanseatisk Museum.** One of the oldest and best-preserved of Bergen's wooden buildings, it is furnished in 16th-century style. *Bryggen, tel. 55314189. Admission: NKr 35. Open May–Aug., daily 10–4; Sept.–Apr., weekdays 11–3, Sat. noon–3, Sun. noon–4.*

On the western end of the Vågen is the Rosenkrantztårnet (Rosenkrantz tower), part of the **Bergenhus Festning** (Bergenhus Fortress), the 13th-century fortress guarding the harbor entrance. The tower and fortress were destroyed during World War II, but were meticulously restored during the 1960s and are now rich with furnishings and household items from the 16th century. *Bergenhus, tel. 55314380. Admission: NKr 15 for tower; NKr 15 for fortress. Open mid-May–mid-Sept., daily 10–4; mid-Sept.–mid-May, Sun. noon–3, or upon request.*

From Ævregaten, the back boundary of Bryggen, you can walk through the meandering back streets to the popular **Fløybanen** (Fløyen Funicular). It climbs 1,070 ft to the top of Fløyen, one of seven mountains guarding the city. *Øvregt. Open May–Sept., weekdays every half hour 7:30 AM–11 PM, Sat. from 8 AM, Sun. from 9 AM until midnight.*

Shopping

Galleriet, on Torgalmenningen, is one of the best downtown shopping malls. Here you will find the more exclusive small shops along with all the chains, like Hennes & Mauritz and Lindex. **Prydkunst-Hjertholm** (Olav Kyrresgt. 7) is full of excellent, locally made glassware and pottery. **Husfliden** (Vågsalmenning 3) includes a department of traditional Norwegian costumes; also, don't miss the troll cave.

Canary Islands, Spain

Closer to North Africa than to mainland Spain, the ruggedly exotic Canary Islands are becoming a year-round destination for sun seekers and nature lovers alike. The Canaries lie 112 km (70 mi) off the coast of southern Morocco in the Atlantic Ocean and enjoy mild, sunny weather throughout the year, except for the north coast of Tenerife, which has above-average rainfall for the Canaries and below-average temperatures year-round. Each of the seven volcanic islands in the archipelago is distinct. Some have lush tropical vegetation, poinsettias as tall as trees, and banana plantations, while others are arid and resemble an exotic moonscape of lava rock and sand dunes. Mt. Teide (12,198 ft), Spain's highest peak, snowcapped for much of the year, is here. The islands house national parks and dozens of other protected ecological zones in which visitors can hike through mist-shrouded forests of virgin laurel trees, climb mountains, eat food cooked by nature over volcanic craters, or scuba dive off long stretches of unspoiled coastline.

Currency

The unit of currency in Spain is the peseta (pta.). There are bills of 1,000, 2,000, 5,000, and 10,000 ptas. Coins are 1, 5, 25, 50, 100, 200, and 500 ptas. At press time, the exchange rate was about 156 ptas. to the U.S. dollar, 103 ptas. to the Canadian dollar, and 248 ptas. to the pound sterling.

Telephones

The country code for Spain is 34. Note that to call anywhere within the country—even locally—from any kind of phone, you need to dial the area code first; all provincial codes begin with a 9. Pay phones generally take the new, smaller 5- and 25-pta. coins; the minimum charge for short local calls is 25 ptas. Newer pay phones take only phone cards, which can be purchased at any tobacco shop in denominations of 1,000 or 2,000 ptas. International calls can be made from any pay phone marked TELÉFONO INTERNACIONAL. Use 50-pta. (or 100-pta. if the phone takes them) coins initially, then coins of any denomination to prolong your call. For lengthy international calls, go to the *telefónica,* a telephone office, where an operator assigns you a private booth and collects payment at the end of the call; this is the least expensive and by far the easiest way of phoning abroad. Dial 07 for international calls, wait for the tone to change, then dial the country code, area code, and the number. To reach an **AT&T** operator, dial 900/99–00–11; **MCI,** 900/99–00–14; **Sprint,** 900/99–00–13.

Shore Excursions

The following are good choices in the Canary Islands. They may not be offered by all cruise lines. Times and prices are approximate.

Mt. Teide and Countryside. A motor coach takes you through the Esperanza mountain range to Mt. Teide National Park with picturesque scenery along the way. *4½ hrs. Cost: $40.*

Botanical Gardens. This motor-coach excursion takes you to the Orotava Valley, with its banana plantations and views of Mt. Teide, before reaching the Botanical Gardens. *4½ hrs. Cost: $33.*

Timanfaya National Park and Winery Tour. By motor coach, this tour visits the park of Timanfaya (fire mountains), before heading off to El Golfo, Los Hervideros, and Janubio, which feature a variety of different forms of volcanic activity. A visit to the La Geria vineyards includes a tasting. *4 hrs. Cost: $40.*

Coming Ashore
Ships dock in Tenerife at the Santa Cruz pier in the island's provincial capital.

Most visitors rent a car or Jeep—driving is by far the best way to explore the countryside. **Hertz** and **Avis** have locations in both Tenerife and Lanzarote, though better rates can be obtained from the Spanish company **Cicar** (tel. 928/802790), located at airports.

Exploring the Canary Islands
Of all the Canary Islands, Tenerife is the most popular and has the greatest variety of scenery. Its beaches are small, though, with volcanic black sand or sand imported from the Sahara Desert. The **Museo de la Naturaleza y el Hombre** (Museum of Nature and Man) in the island's capital, Santa Cruz, contains ceramics and mummies from the stone-age Guanches. *Fuentes Morales s/n, tel. 922/209320. Admission: 450 ptas.; free Sun. Open Tues.–Sun. 10–8.*

The best thing to visit in Santa Cruz is the colorful weekday-morning market, **Mercado de Nuestra Señora de Africa** (Market of Our Lady of Africa), which sells everything from tropical fruits and flowers to canaries and parrots. *Avda. de San Sebastín. Open Mon.–Sat. 5AM–noon.*

Inland, past banana plantations, almond groves, and pine forests, is the entrance to **Parque Nacional del Teide** (Teide National Park). The visitors' center offers trail maps, guided hikes, educational videos, and bus tours. Before arriving at the foot of the mountain, you pass through a stark landscape called Las Cañadas del Teide, a violent jumble of rocks and minerals created by millions of years of volcanic activity. A cable car will take you within 534 ft of the top of Mt. Teide, where there are good views of the southern part of the island and neighboring Gran Canaria. *Cable car: Admission: 2,000 ptas. Open daily 9–5, last trip up at 4. Visitor center: Open daily 9–2.*

Also worth a visit are the north-coast towns of **Icod de los Vinos,** which boasts a 3,000-year-old, 57-ft-tall dragon tree once worshiped by the ancient Guanches and a plaza surrounded by typical wood-balconied Canarian houses; farther west, **Garachico** is the most peaceful and best-preserved village on this touristy isle.

LANZAROTE

Lanzarote is stark and dry, with landscapes of volcanic rock, good beaches, and tasteful low-rise architecture. The **Parque Nacional Timanfaya** (Timanfaya National Park), popularly known as the fire mountains, takes up much of the southern part of the island. Here you can have a camel ride, take a guided coach tour of the volcanic zone, and eat lunch at one of the world's most unusual restaurants, El Diablo, where meat is cooked over the crater of a volcano using the earth's natural heat. *4 km (2½ mi) north of Yaiza, tel. 928/840057. Admission: 1,000 ptas. Open daily 9–6; last trip at 5.*

The **Jameos del Agua** (Water Cavern) is a natural wonder, created when molten lava streamed through an underground tunnel and hissed into the sea. The site also features an auditorium with fantastic acoustics for concerts and a restaurant-bar. *Rte. GC710, 21 km (13 mi) north of Arrecife, tel. 928/835010. Admission: days 1,000 ptas., nights 1,100 ptas. Open daily 9:30–6:45; Tues., Fri., and Sat. also 7 PM–3 AM.*

Shopping

IN TENERIFE

The Canary Islands are famous for lacy, hand-embroidered tablecloths and place mats. The largest selection is available in Puerto de la Cruz at **Casa Iriarte** (San Juan 17). Contemporary crafts and traditional musical instruments can be found at the government-sponsored shop **Casa Torrehermosa** (Tomás Zerolo 27) in Orotava.

Beaches

Las Teresitas beach, 7 km (4 mi) east of Santa Cruz, was constructed using white sand imported from the Sahara Desert and is popular with local families. **Playa de las Américas** is the newest, sunniest, and brashest beach area on Tenerife. The yellow sand is ringed with high-rise hotels, restaurants, and nightspots.

Playa de la Garita is a wide bay with crystal-clear water that's great for surfing and snorkeling. The **Playa Blanca** resort area, reached by traveling down hard-packed dirt roads on Punta de Papagayo, features white-sand beaches. Bring your own picnic.

Copenhagen, Denmark

When Denmark ruled Norway and Sweden in the 15th century, Copenhagen was the capital of all three countries. Today it is still a lively northern capital, with about 1 million inhabitants. It's a city meant for walking, the first in Europe to recognize the value of pedestrian streets in fostering community spirit. As you stroll through the cobbled streets and squares, you'll find that Copenhagen combines the excitement and variety of big-city life with a small-town atmosphere. If there's such a thing as a cozy metropolis, you'll find it here.

You're never far from water, be it sea or canal. The city itself is built upon two main islands, Slotsholmen and Christianshavn, connected by drawbridges. The ancient heart of the city is intersected by two heavily peopled walking streets—part of the five such streets known collectively as Strøget—and around them curls a maze of cobbled streets packed with tiny boutiques, cafés, restaurants—all best explored on foot. In summer Copenhagen moves outside, and the best views of city life are from the sidewalk cafés in the sunny squares. The Danes are famous for their friendliness

and have a word—*hyggelig*—for the feeling of well-being
that comes from their own brand of cozy hospitality.

Currency

The monetary unit in Denmark is the krone (kr., DKr, or
DKK), which is divided into 100 øre. At press time, the krone
stood at about DKr 6.9 to the U.S. dollar, DKr 4.6 to the
Canadian dollar, and DKr 11.1 to the pound sterling.

Telephones

The country code for Denmark is 45. Pay phones take 1-,
2-, 5-, and 10-kr. coins. You must use area codes even
when dialing a local number. Calling cards, which are sold
at DSB stations, post offices, and some kiosks, cost DKr
25, DKr 50, or DKr 100, and are increasingly necessary as
coin phones become a thing of the past. For international
calls dial 00, then the country code, the area code, and the
number. To reach an **AT&T** long-distance operator, dial 800/
10010; **MCI WorldCom,** 800/10022; **Sprint,** 800/10877.

Shore Excursions

The following are good choices in Copenhagen. They may
not be offered by all cruise lines. Times and prices are approximate.

City Tour. This quick overview of the sights takes you to the
Citadel, the Little Mermaid statue, the Renaissance castle,
City Hall Square, Tivoli Gardens, Christiansborg Palace,
the Stock Exchange, the Canal District, and the courtyard
of Amalienborg Palace. *2½ hrs. Cost: $38.*

Royal Castle Tour. Castle aficionados can see two on this
tour: Christiansborg and Rosenborg, as well as other sites.
3 hrs. Cost: $50.

Coming Ashore

Ships visiting Copenhagen dock at Langelinie Pier, a short
distance from the central part of the city.

Copenhagen is a city for walkers, not drivers. Attractions
are relatively close together, and public transportation is excellent. Buses and suburban trains operate on a ticket system and divide Copenhagen and its environs into three zones.
Tickets are validated on the time system: on the basic ticket,
which costs DKr 11 for an hour, you can travel anywhere

in the zone in which you started. Computer-metered taxis are not cheap. The base charge is DKr 15, plus DKr 8–DKr 10 per km. You can either hail a cab (though this can be difficult outside the center), pick one up at a taxi stand, or call (35/35–35–35); there's a surcharge of DKr 20.

Exploring Copenhagen

Numbers in the margin correspond to points of interest on the Copenhagen map.

❶ Copenhagen's best-known attraction is **Tivoli.** In the 1840s, the Danish architect Georg Carstensen persuaded King Christian VIII that an amusement park was the perfect opiate for the masses, preaching that "when people amuse themselves, they forget politics." In the season from May to September, about 4 million people come through the gates. Tivoli is more sophisticated than a mere amusement park: it offers a pantomime theater and an open-air stage; elegant restaurants; a museum chronicling its own history; and numerous classical, jazz, and rock concerts. On weekends there are elaborate fireworks displays. In recent years Tivoli has also been opened a month before Christmas with a gift and decorations market and children's rides. Try to see Tivoli at least once by night, when the trees are illuminated along with the Chinese Pagoda and the main fountain. *Vesterbrog. 3, tel. 33/15–10–01. Open May– mid-Sept., daily 11 AM– midnight.*

The hub of Copenhagen's commercial district is Rådhus Pladsen, which is dominated by the mock-Renaissance **❷ Rådhus** (city hall), completed in 1905. A statue of Copenhagen's 12th-century founder, Bishop Absalon, sits atop the main entrance. Inside, you can see the first World Clock, an astrological timepiece invented and built by Jens Olsen and put in motion in 1955. If you're feeling energetic, take a guided tour partway up the 350-ft tower for a panoramic view. *Rådhus Pladsen, tel. 33/66–25–82. Admission: tour DKr 20, tower DKr 10. Open Mon.–Wed., Fri. 9:30–3, Thurs. 9:30–4, Sat. 9:30–1. Tours in English weekdays at 3, Sat. at 10. Tower tours: Oct.–May, Mon.–Sat. at noon; June–Sept. at 10, noon, and 2. Call to confirm hrs.*

❸ The elaborately neoclassical **Ny Carlsberg Glyptotek** (New Carlsberg Sculpture Museum) has one of Europe's great-

54

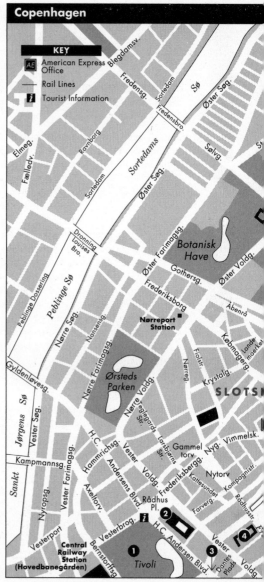

Copenhagen

KEY

🅰🅴 American Express
Office

— Rail Lines

ℹ Tourist Information

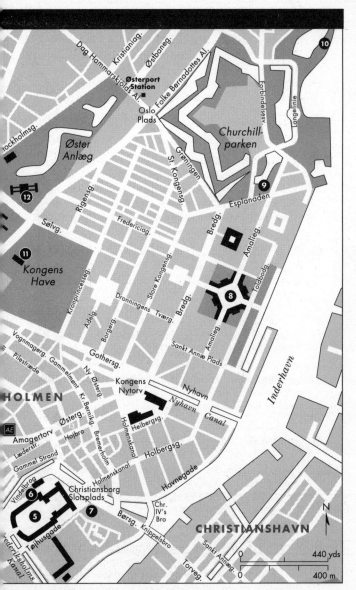

Dag Hammarskjölds Al.

Kristianiag.

Østbaneg.

Østerport
Station

Oslo
Plads

stockholmsg.

Øster
Anlæg

Forbindelsesv.

Langelinie

Churchill-
parken

Grønningen

St. Kongensg.

Esplanaden

Rigensg.

Sølvg.

Fredericiag.

Bredg.

Amalieg.

Kongens
Have

Kronprincessg.

Store Kongensg.

Dronningens Tværg.

Bredg.

Adelg.

Borgerg.

Toldbodg.

Sankt Annæ Plads

Amalieg.

Vognmagerg.

Gammelment.

Gothersg.

Pilestræde

Ny Østerg.

Kr. Berrikg.

Bremerholm

Kongens
Nytorv

Nyhavn

Nyhavn Canal

HOLMEN

Østerg.

Højbro

Holmenskanal

Heibergsg.

Inderhavn

AE

Amagertorv

Lædersstr.

Gammel Strand

Holmenskanal

Holbergsg.

Havnegade

Vindelbrog

Christiansborg
Slotsplads

Chr.
IV's
Bro

CHRISTIANSHAVN

Frederiksholms

Tøjhusgade

Børsg.

Knippelsbro

Sankt Annæg.

Kanal

Torveg.

N

0   440 yds

0   400 m

est collections of Greek and Roman antiquities and sculpture. In 1996 a modern painting wing, envisioned as a three-story treasure chest and designed by acclaimed Danish architect Henning Larsen, was completed. It houses an impressive pre-Impressionist collection including works from the Barbizon school; Impressionist paintings, including works by Monet, Sisley, and Pissarro; and a post-Impressionist section, with 50 Gauguin paintings plus 12 of his rare sculpures. *Dantes Pl. 7, tel. 33/41–81–41. Admission: DKr 30; free Wed. and Sun. Open Tues.–Sun. 10–4.*

❹ The city's **Nationalmuseet** (National Museum) houses extensive collections that chronicle Danish cultural history to modern times, and displays Egyptian, Greek, and Roman antiquities. Viking enthusiasts may want to see the Runic stones in the Danish cultural-history section. *Ny Vesterg. 10, tel. 33/13–44–11. Admission: DKr 30. Open Tues.–Sun. 10–5.*

❺ Castle Island is dominated by the massive gray **Christiansborg Slot** (Christiansborg Castle). The complex, which contains the Folketinget (Parliament House) and the Royal Reception Chambers, is on the site of the city's first fortress, built by Bishop Absalon in 1167. While the castle was being built at the turn of the century, the National Museum excavated the ruins beneath the site. *Christiansborg ruins, tel. 33/92–64–92. Admission: DKr15. Open May–Sept., daily 9:30–3:30; Oct.–Apr., Tues., Thurs., Fri., Sun. 9:30–3:30. Folketinget: tel. 33/37–55–00. Admission free. Tour times vary; call ahead. Reception Chambers: tel. 33/92–64–92. Admission: DKr 28. Hrs and tour times vary; call ahead.*

The 19th-century Danish sculptor Bertel Thorvaldsen is
❻ buried at the center of the **Thorvaldsen Museum.** He was greatly influenced by the statues and reliefs of classical antiquity. In addition to his own works, there is a collection of paintings and drawings by others that illustrate the influence of Italy on Denmark's Golden Age artists. *Porthusg. 2, tel. 33/32–15–32. Admission: DKr 20 (free Wed.) Open Tues.–Sun. 10–5.*

❼ With its steep roofs, tiny windows, and gables, the **Børsen,** the old stock exchange, is one of Copenhagen's treasures. It is believed to be the oldest building of its kind in use—although it functions only on special occasions. It was built by the 16th-century monarch King Christian IV, a scholar, warrior, and architect of much of the city. The king is said to have had a hand in twisting the tails of the four dragons that form the structure's distinctive green copper spire. *Christiansborg Slotspl. Not open to the public.*

⑧ Amalienborg (Amalia's Castle) has been the principal royal residence since 1784. During the fall and winter, when the royal family returns to its seat, the Royal Guard and band march through the city at noon to change the palace guard. Among the museum's highlights are the study of King Christian IX (1818–1906) and the drawing room of his wife, Queen Louise. The collection also includes Rococo banquet silver, highlighted by a bombastic Viking-ship centerpiece, and a small costume collection. *Amalienborg Pl.; museum, tel. 33/12–21–86. Admission: DKr 35. Open May–late Oct., daily 11–4; late Oct.–Apr., Tues.–Sun. 11–4.*

⑨ The **Frihedsmuseet** (Liberty Museum) in Churchillparken gives an evocative picture of the heroic World War II Danish resistance movement, which managed to save 7,000 Jews from the Nazis by hiding them and then smuggling them across to Sweden. *Churchillparken, tel. 33/13–77–14. Admission free. Open Sept. 16–Apr., Tues.–Sat. 11–3, Sun. 11–4; May–Sept. 15, Tues.–Sat. 10–4, Sun. 10–5.*

Near the Langelinie, which on Sunday is thronged with promenading Danes, is **Den Lille Havfrue** (Little Mermaid), **⑩** the 1913 statue commemorating Hans Christian Andersen's lovelorn creation and the subject of hundreds of travel posters. *East on Langelinie.*

⑪ Rosenborg Slot, a Renaissance castle—built by Renaissance man Christian IV—houses the Crown Jewels, as well as a collection of costumes and royal memorabilia. Don't miss Christian IV's pearl-studded saddle. *Øster Voldg. 4A, tel. 33/15–32–86. Admission: DKr 40. Castle open late Oct.–Apr., Tues., Fri., and Sun. 11–2; treasury open Tues.–Sun. 11–3. Both open May, Sept.–late Oct., daily 11–3; June–Aug., daily 10–4.*

⑫ The **Statens Museum for Kunst** (National Art Gallery) re-opened in fall 1999 with a complete refurbishment of the original 100-year-old building and a new, modern building that doubles the exhibition space. Though the collection remains the same—including works of Danish art from the Golden Age (early 19th century) to the present, as well as paintings by Rubens, Dürer, the Impressionists, and other European masters—there is also a children's museum, an amphitheater, and other resources. *Sølvg. 48–50, tel. 33/74–84–94. Admission: DKr 20–DKr 40 (depending on exhibit). Open Tues.–Sun. 10–5, Wed. until 9.*

Shopping

Strøget's pedestrian streets are synonymous with shopping. Just off Østergade is Pistolstræde, a typical old courtyard that has been lovingly restored and is filled with intriguing boutiques. **Magasin** (Kongens Nytorv 13), one of the largest department stores in Scandinavia, offers everything in terms of clothing and gifts, as well as an excellent grocery. In **Illums Bolighus** (Amagertorv 10), designer furnishings, porcelain, quality clothing, and gifts are displayed in near-gallery surroundings. **Royal Copenhagen Porcelain** (Amagertorv 6) carries both old and new china and porcelain patterns and figurines. **Georg Jensen** (Amagertorv 4) is one of the world's finest silversmiths and gleams with a wide array of silver patterns and jewelry. Don't miss the **Georg Jensen Museum** (Amagertorv 6, tel. 33/14–02–29), which showcases glass and silver beauties, ranging from tiny, twisted-glass shot glasses to an $85,000 silver fish dish.

Corfu, Greece

The northernmost of the seven major Ionian islands, Corfu has a colorful history, reflecting the commingling of Corinthians, Romans, Goths, Normans, Venetians, French, Russians, and British; it was not until 1864 that it was ceded to Greece. The climate of the island is rainy, which makes it green. Moderated by westerly winds, scored with fertile valleys, and punctuated by enormous, gnarled olive trees, the island is perhaps the most beautiful in Greece.

Currency

The Greek monetary unit is the drachma (dr.). At press time, there were approximately 305 dr. to the U.S. dollar, 202 dr. to the Canadian dollar, and 485 dr. to the pound sterling.

Telephones

The country code for Greece is 30. When dialing Greece from outside the country, drop the first zero from the regional area code. Telephone kiosks are easy to find, although many can only be used for local calls. The easiest way to make a local or an international call is with a phone card, available at kiosks, convenience stores, or Hellenic Telecommunications Organization (OTE) offices. Go to an OTE office for convenience and privacy if you plan to make several international calls. For an **AT&T** long-distance operator, dial 00/800–1311; **MCI,** 00/800–1211; **Sprint,** 00/800–1411. For operator-assisted calls in English, dial 161 or 162.

Shore Excursions

The following are good choices in Corfu. They may not be offered by all cruise lines. Times and prices are approximate.

Paleokastritsa, Achilleion, and Corfu Town. Visit the pretty resort of Paleokastritsa and the 100-year-old Achilleion Palace, and drive past the major sights of the town. *3–4 hrs. Cost: $45–$50.*

City tour with Achilleion and Kanoni. Visit the Achilleion Palace and the village of Kanoni and enjoy a walking tour of Corfu. *4 hrs. Cost: $43.*

Coming Ashore

Most cruise ships dock at Corfu Town.

Radio-dispatched taxis are available, and rates, set by the government, are reasonable. The bus network on the island is extensive, and buses tend to run fairly close to their schedules. Motorbike rentals are available, but caution is advised.

Exploring Corfu

The **New Fortress** was built by the Venetians and expanded by the French and the British. It was a Greek naval base until 1992, when it was opened to the public. You can now wander through the fascinating maze of tunnels, moats, and fortifications. A classic British citadel stands at its heart, and there are stunning views of Corfu Town, the sea, and the countryside in all directions. The best times to come here are early morning and late afternoon. *Above the Old Port on north side of Corfu Town.*

The huge parade ground on the land side of the canal is the **Esplanade,** central to life in Corfu Town. It is bordered on the west by a street lined with a row of tall houses and arcades, called Liston, which was once the exclusive preserve of Corfiot nobility. Now the arcades are lively with cafés that spill out onto the square. Cricket matches are played on the northern side of the Esplanade. *Between Old Fortress and Old Town.*

The narrow streets that run west from the Esplanade lead to the medieval parts of the city, where Venetian buildings stand cheek-by-jowl with the 19th-century ones built by the British. This is a great shopping area—you can buy nearly anything on earth.

The **Archaeological Museum** displays artifacts from ongoing excavations. Note the Gorgon from the pediment of the 6th-century BC Temple of Artemis. *South of the Esplanade along Leoforos Dimokratias, tel. 0661/30680. Admission: 800 dr. Open daily 9–4:30.*

The oldest cultural institution in modern Greece, the **Corfu Reading Society,** contains archives (dating back several centuries) of the Ionian islands. In the early 19th century, Corfu was the literary center of Greece. One of the island's loveliest buildings, it has an exterior staircase leading up to a loggia. *Kapodistriou. Open Sat.–Wed. 9–1, Thurs.–Fri. 9–1 and 5–8.*

The **Garrison Church of St. George** (1830) in the Old Fortress has a Doric portico. In summer there's folk dancing, and in August sound-and-light shows relate the fortress's history. The views from here, east to the Albanian coast and west over the town, are splendid. *In middle of Old Fortress. Admission free. Open 8–7.*

Shopping
The downside of Corfu's popularity with tourists is that merchants have become greedy, at times charging outrageous prices in order to squeeze as much money as possible out of visitors. Ask your ship's cruise or shore-excursion director for the names of reputable shops.

Beaches

The resort areas of Ermones and Glyfada, which are south of the popular resort area Paleokastritsa, offer good sunning. On the north coast, Roda and Sidari have good beaches.

Crete, Greece

The mountains, blue-gray and barren, split with deep gorges and honeycombed with caves, define both landscape and lifestyle in Crete. No other Greek island is so large and rugged. To Greeks, Crete is the Great Island, where rebellion was endemic for centuries—against Arab invaders, Venetian colonialists, Ottoman pashas, and German occupiers in World War II. Situated in the south Aegean, Crete was the center of Europe's earliest civilization, the Minoan, which flourished from about 2000 BC to 1200 BC. It was struck a mortal blow in about 1450 BC by some unknown cataclysm, perhaps political.

Currency

The Greek monetary unit is the drachma (dr.). At press time, there were approximately 278 dr. to the U.S. dollar, 183 dr. to the Canadian dollar, and 464 dr. to the pound sterling.

Telephones

The country code for Greece is 30. When dialing Greece from outside the country, drop the first zero from the regional area code. Telephone kiosks are easy to find, although many can only be used for local calls. The easiest way to make a local or an international call is with a phone card, available at kiosks, convenience stores, or Hellenic Telecommunications Organization (OTE) offices. Go to an OTE office for convenience and privacy if you plan to make several international calls. For an **AT&T** long-distance operator, dial 00/800–1311; **MCI**, 00/800–1211; **Sprint**, 00/800–1411. For operator-assisted calls in English, dial 161 or 162.

Shore Excursions

The following are good choices in Crete. They may not be offered by all cruise lines. Times and prices are approximate.

Knossos and the Museum. Minoan life is on display at the Archaeological Museum and Knossos, the largest Minoan palace. *4 hrs. Cost: $46.*

Chania and Akrotiri. This excursion explores the old town of Chania before heading to Akrotiri peninsula to see the tomb of Eleftherios Venizelos and the Ayia Triada Monastery. *Half day. Cost: $45.*

Coming Ashore

Most ships dock at Heraklion. A few tie up at Souda Bay, which is about 15 minutes from Chania. Smaller vessels may dock at Ayios Nikolaos.

You can rent cars, Jeeps, and motorbikes in all the island's towns. Bus companies offer regular service between main towns.

Exploring Crete

The most important Minoan objects are housed in the **archaeological museum** in Heraklion, Crete's largest city. The museum's treasures include frescoes and ceramics from Knossos and Agia Triada depicting Minoan life and snake goddesses, and the Phaestos disc, with Europe's first writing. *Xanthoudidou 1, Platia Eleftherias, tel. 081/226–092. Admission: 1,500 dr. Open May–Oct., Mon. 12:30–7, Tues.–Sun. 8–7; Nov.–Apr., Mon. 12:30–5, Tues.–Sun. 8–5.*

The partly reconstructed **Palace of Knossos** will give you a feeling for the Minoan world. From 2000 to 1400 BC it was the chief site of Europe's first civilization. Note the simple throne room, with its tiny gypsum throne, pipes for running water, and splendid decorations. Its complexity and rituals probably suggested the myth of the Minotaur: the monstrous man-bull, offspring of Queen Pasiphae and a white bull was confined by King Minos to the labyrinth. *Tel. 081/231–940. Admission: 1,500 dr. Open May–Oct., daily 8–7; Nov.–Apr., daily 8–5.*

The town of **Ayios Nikolaos** on the Gulf of Mirabellow was built just a century ago by Cretans and is good for an afternoon of strolling and shopping. *24 km/15 mi from Heraklion.*

Beaches

In addition to archaeological treasures, Crete can boast of beautiful mountain scenery and a large number of beach resorts along the north coast. One is **Mallia,** which contains the remains of another Minoan palace and has good sandy beaches. Two other beach resorts, **Ayios Nikolaos** and the nearby **Elounda,** are farther east. The south coast offers good beaches that are quieter.

Dublin, Ireland

Europe's most intimate capital has become a boomtown—the soul of the new Ireland is in the throes of what is easily the nation's most dramatic period of transformation since the Georgian era. Dublin is riding the back of the Celtic Tiger (as the roaring Irish economy has been nicknamed), and massive construction cranes are hovering over both shiny new hotels and old Georgian houses. Travelers are coming to Dublin in ever greater numbers, so don't be surprised if you stop to consult your map in Temple Bar—the city's most happening neighborhood—and are swept away by the ceaseless flow of bustling crowds. Literary Dublin can still be recaptured by those who want to follow the footsteps of Leopold Bloom's progress, as described in James Joyce's *Ulysses*. And Trinity College—alma mater to Oliver Goldsmith, Jonathan Swift, and Samuel Beckett, among others—still provides a haven of tranquillity.

Currency

The unit of currency in Ireland is the pound, or punt (pronounced poont), written as IR£ to avoid confusion with the pound sterling. The currency is divided into 100 pence (written *p*). Ireland is now a member of the European Monetary Fund (EMU) and since January 1, 1999, all prices have been quoted in pounds and euros. January 2002 is to see the introduction of euro coins and notes and the gradual withdrawal of the local currency. The rate of exchange at press time was 74 pence to the U.S. dollar, 50 pence to the Canadian dollar, and IR£1.18 to the British pound sterling.

Telephones

The country code for the Republic of Ireland is 353, and for Northern Ireland it's 44. When dialing from outside the country, drop the initial zero from the regional area code. There are pay phones in all post offices and most hotels and bars, as well as in street booths. Telephone cards are available at all post offices and most newsagents. Booths accepting cards are as common as coin booths. For calls to the United States and Canada, dial 001 followed by the area code; for calls to the United Kingdom, dial 0044 and then the area code (dropping the beginning zero). To reach an **AT&T** long-distance operator, dial 1–800/550–000; **MCI,** 1–800/551–001; **Sprint,** 1–800/552–001.

Shore Excursions

The following is a good choice in Dublin. It may not be offered by all cruise lines. Time and price are approximate.

City Tour. Two of Dublin's main attractions, St. Patrick's Cathedral and Trinity College, are the highlight of this excursion, which passes other city sights, such as St. Stephen's Square, Georgian Dublin, the River Liffey, and the Customs House. *3½ hrs. Cost: $48–$64.*

Coming Ashore

Ships dock at the Ocean Pier in the city's industrial port area, about a 20-minute drive to downtown.

Dublin is small as capital cities go—the downtown area is compact—and the best way to see the city and soak in the full flavor is on foot. The River Liffey divides the city north and south. Official licensed taxis, metered and designated by roof signs, do not cruise; they are located beside the central bus station, at train stations, at O'Connell Bridge, at St. Stephen's Green, at College Green, and near major hotels. They are not of a uniform type or color. Make sure the meter is on. The initial charge is £1.80 with an additional charge of about £1.60 per mile thereafter; the fare is displayed in the cab.

Exploring Dublin

Numbers in the margin correspond to points of interest on the Dublin map.

❶ O'Connell Bridge is the city's prime landmark. Look closely and you will notice a strange feature: the bridge is wider than it is long. The north side of O'Connell Bridge is dominated by an elaborate memorial to Daniel O'Connell, "the Liberator," erected as a tribute to the great 19th-century orator's achievement in securing Catholic emancipation in 1829.

Henry Street, to the left beyond the General Post Office, is a pedestrian-only shopping area that leads to colorful **Moore Street Market,** where street vendors recall their most famous ancestor, Molly Malone, by singing their wares—mainly flowers and fruit—in traditional Dublin style.

❷ The **General Post Office,** known as the GPO, occupies a special place in Irish history. It was from the portico of its handsome classical facade that Padraig Pearse read the Proclamation of the Republic on Easter Monday 1916. You can still see the scars of bullets on its pillars from the fighting that ensued. The GPO remains the focal point for political rallies and demonstrations. *O'Connell St., tel. 01/872–8888. Open Mon.–Sat. 8–8, Sun. 10:30–6:30.*

Charlemont House, whose impressive Palladian facade **❸** dominates the top of Parnell Square, now houses the **Hugh Lane Municipal Gallery of Modern Art.** Sir Hugh Lane, a nephew of Lady Gregory, was a keen collector of Impressionist paintings and 19th-century Irish and Anglo-Irish works. Among them are canvases by Jack Yeats (W. B.'s brother) and Paul Henry. *Parnell Sq., tel. 01/874–1903. Admission free. Open Tues.–Thurs. 9:30–6 (Apr.–Aug. Thurs. 9:30–8), Fri.–Sat. 9:30–5, Sun. 11–5.*

The Parnell Square area is rich in literary associations. **❹** They are illustrated in the **Dublin Writers Museum,** which opened in 1991 in two carefully restored 18th-century buildings. Rare manuscripts, diaries, posters, letters, limited and first editions, photographs and other mementos commemorate the lives and works of the nation's greatest writers, including Joyce, Shaw, Wilde, Yeats, and Beckett. The bookshop and café make this an ideal place to spend a rainy afternoon. *18–19 Parnell Sq. N, tel. 01/872–2077. Admission: IR£2.95. Open June–Aug., Mon.–Sat. 10–6, Sun. 11–5; Sept.–May, Mon.–Sat. 10–5, Sun. 11–5.*

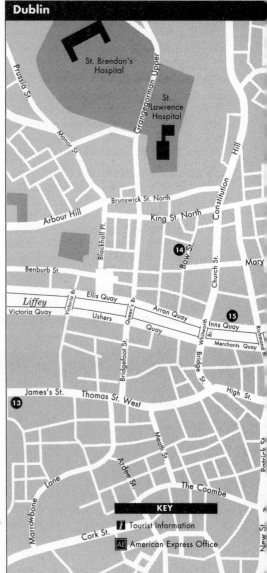

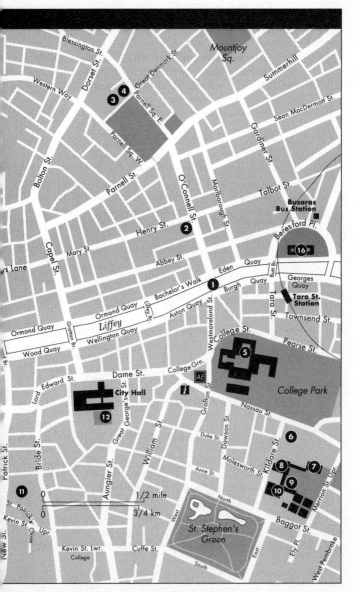

⑤ A must for every visitor is a stop at **Trinity College.** The college, officially titled Dublin University but familiarly known as Trinity, was founded by Elizabeth I in 1592 and offered a free education to Catholics—provided that they accepted the Protestant faith. As a legacy of this condition, right up until 1966, Catholics who wished to study at Trinity had to obtain a dispensation from their bishop or face excommunication. Today more than 70% of Trinity's students are Catholics, a clear indication of how far away those days seem to today's generation. The college's facade, built between 1755 and 1759, consists of a magnificent portico with Corinthian columns. The design is repeated on the interior, so the views from outside the gates and from the quadrangle inside are the same. On the sweeping lawn in front of the facade are statues of two of the university's illustrious alumni—statesman Edmund Burke and poet Oliver Goldsmith. Other famous students include the philosopher George Berkeley (who gave his name to the northern California city), Jonathan Swift, Thomas Moore, Oscar Wilde, John Millington Synge, Henry Grattan, Wolfe Tone, Robert Emmet, Bram Stoker, Edward Carson, Douglas Hyde, and Samuel Beckett.

The 18th-century building on the left, just inside the entrance, is the chapel. There's an identical building opposite, which is the Examination Hall. The oldest buildings are the library in the far right-hand corner, completed in 1712, and a 1690 row of redbrick buildings known as the Rubrics, which contain student apartments.

Ireland's largest collection of books and manuscripts is housed in the **Trinity College Library.** There are 3 million volumes gathering dust here; about 1 km (½ mi) of new shelving has to be added every year to keep pace with acquisitions. The library is entered through the library shop. Its principal treasure is the Book of Kells, a beautifully illuminated manuscript of the Gospels dating from the 8th century. Only a few pages from the 682-page, 9th-century gospel are displayed at a time, but there is an informative exhibit that reproduces many of them. At peak hours you may have to wait in line to enter the library. Apart from the many treasures it contains, the aptly named Long Room is impressive in itself, stretching for 213 ft and housing 200,000 of the library's volumes, mostly manuscripts and old books. Originally it had a flat plaster ceiling, but the perennial need for more shelving resulted in a decision to raise the level of the roof and add the barrel-vaulted ceiling and the gallery bookcases. *Tel. 01/677–2941. Admission: IR£3.50. Open Mon.–Sat. 9:30–4:45, Sun. noon–4:30.*

6 The **Genealogical Office**—the starting point for ancestor tracing—also incorporates the Heraldic Museum, which features displays of flags, coins, stamps, silver, and family crests that highlight the uses and development of heraldry in Ireland. *2 Kildare St., tel. 01/661–8811. Museum admission free. Office weekdays 10–5, Sat. 10–12:30; guided tours by appointment. Museum Mon.–Wed. 10–8:30, Thurs.–Fri. 10–4:30, Sat. 10–12:30.*

7 The **National Gallery of Ireland** is the first in a series of important buildings on the west side of Merrion Square. It contains the country's finest collection of Old Masters—great treasures include Vermeer's incomparable *Woman Writing a Letter,* Gainsborough's *Cottage Girl,* and Caravaggio's *The Arrest of Christ.* Free guided tours are available on Saturday at 3 PM and on Sunday at 2:15, 3, and 4. *Merrion Sq. (West), tel. 01/661–5133. Admission free. Open Mon.–Sat. 10–5:30, Thurs. until 8:30, Sun. 2–5.*

8 The **National Library**'s collections include first editions of every major Irish writer. Temporary exhibits are held in the entrance hall, off the colonnaded rotunda. The main reading room, opened in 1890, has a dramatic domed ceiling. *Kildare St., tel. 01/661–8811. Admission free. Open Mon. 10–9, Tues.–Wed. 2–9, Thurs.–Fri. 10–5, Sat. 10–1.*

9 **Leinster House,** seat of the Irish parliament, is an imposing 18th-century building with two facades: its Merrion Square facade is designed in the style of a country house, and the other facade, in Kildare Street, is in the style of a town house. Visitors may be shown the house when Dáil Eireann (pronounced Dawl Erin), the parliament, is not in session. *Kildare St., tel. 01/618–3000. Tours: Mon., Fri. by prior arrangement. Dáil visitors' gallery: access with an introduction from a member of pParliament.*

Situated on the other side of Leinster House from the Na-
10 tional Library, the **National Museum** is most famous for its

spectacular collection of Irish artifacts from 6000 BC to the present, including the Tara Brooch, the Ardagh Chalice, the Cross of Cong, and a fabled hoard of Celtic gold jewelry. It also houses an important collection of Irish decorative arts and a replica of a small Viking boat. *Kildare St., tel. 01/660–1117. Admission free. Open Tues.–Sat. 10–5, Sun. 2–5.*

Legend has it that St. Patrick baptized many converts at a well on the site of **St. Patrick's Cathedral** in the 5th century. The building dates from 1190 and is mainly early English Gothic in style. At 305 ft, it is the longest church in the country. Its history has not always been happy. In the 17th century, Oliver Cromwell, dour ruler of England and no friend of the Irish, had his troops stable their horses in the cathedral. It wasn't until the 19th century that restoration work to repair the damage was begun. St. Patrick's is the national cathedral of the Protestant Church of Ireland and has had many illustrious deans. The most famous was Jonathan Swift, author of *Gulliver's Travels,* who held office from 1713 to 1745. Swift's tomb is in the south aisle. Memorials to many other celebrated figures from Ireland's past line the walls. *Patrick St., tel. 01/475–4817. Admission: IR£2. Open May and Sept.–Oct., weekdays 9–6, Sat. 9–5, Sun. 10–11 and 12:30–3; June–Aug., weekdays 9–6, Sat. 9–4, Sun. 9:30–3 and 4:15–5:15; Nov.–Apr., weekdays 9–6, Sat. 9–4, Sun. 10–11 and 12:30–3.*

Guided tours of the lavishly furnished state apartments in **Dublin Castle** run every half hour and provide one of the most enjoyable sightseeing experiences in town. Only fragments of the original 13th-century building survive; the elegant castle you see today is essentially an 18th-century building. The state apartments were formerly the residence of the English viceroys and are now used by the president of Ireland to entertain visiting heads of state. The state apartments are closed when in official use, so call first. *Castle St., off Dame St., tel. 01/677–7129. Admission to State Apartments: IR£3 including tour. Open weekdays 10–5, weekends 2–5.*

The **Guinness Brewery,** founded by Arthur Guinness in 1759 and covering 60 acres, dominates the area to the west of Christ Church. The brewery itself is closed to the public, but the Hop Store, part museum and part gift shop, puts on an 18-minute audiovisual show. After the show, visitors get two complimentary glasses (or one pint) of the famous black stout. *Guinness Hop Store, Crane St., tel. 01/453–3645. Admission: IR£5. Open Apr.—Sept., Mon.-Sat. 9:30–5, Sun. 10:30–4:30; Oct.-Mar., Mon.-Sat. 9:30–4, Sun. noon–4.*

⓮ **Old Jameson Distillery** is just behind St. Michan's. A 90-year-old warehouse has been converted into a museum to introduce visitors to the pleasures of Irish whiskey, or "holy water," as whiskey is known in Irish. There is a 40-minute guided tour of the old distillery, a 20-minute audiovisual tour, and a complimentary tasting. *Bow St., tel. 01/807–2355. Admission: IR£3.95. Open daily 9:30–5:30; tours every half hour.*

Off the River Liffey are two of Dublin's most famous landmarks, both of them the work of 18th-century architect James Gandon and both among the city's finest buildings.

⓯ The first is the **Four Courts,** surmounted by a massive copper-covered dome that gives it a distinctive profile. It is the seat of the High Court of Justice of Ireland. The building was completed between 1786 and 1802, then gutted during the "Troubles" of the 1920s and restored in 1932. You

⓰ will recognize the same architect's hand in the **Custom House,** farther down the Liffey. Its graceful dome rises above a central portico, itself linked by arcades to the pavilions at either end. The visitors center is open to the public. *Four Courts: Inns Quay, tel. 01/872–5555. Admission free. Open daily 10:30–1 and 2:15–4. Custom House: Custom House Quay, tel. 01/679–3377. Admission: IR£1.50. Open weekdays 9:30–5, weekends 2–5.*

Shopping

Although the rest of the country is well supplied with crafts shops, Dublin is the place to seek out more specialized items—antiques, traditional sportswear, haute couture, designer ceramics, books and prints, silverware and jewelry, and designer hand-knit items.

The city's most sophisticated shopping area is around **Grafton Street. St. Stephen's Green Center** contains 70 stores, large and small, in a vast Moorish-style glass-roof building on the Grafton Street corner. **Molesworth** and **Dawson streets** are the places to browse for antiques; **Nassau** and **Dawson streets,** for books; the smaller cross streets for jewelry, art galleries, and old prints. The pedestrian **Temple Bar** area, with its young, offbeat ambience, has a number of small art galleries, specialty shops (including music and books), and inexpensive and adventurous clothes shops. The area is further enlivened by buskers (street musicians) and street artists.

TWEEDS AND WOOLENS

Ready-made tweeds for men can be found at **Kevin and Howlin** (on Nassau St.). The **Blarney Woollen Mills** (on Nassau St.) has a good selection of tweed, linen, and woolen sweaters. **Dublin Woolen Mills** (at Ha'penny Bridge) has a good selection of hand-knits and other woolen sweaters at competitive prices.

Edinburgh/Leith, Scotland

Scotland and England *are* different—and let no Englishman tell you otherwise. Although the two nations have been united in a single state since 1707, Scotland retains its own marked political and social character, with, for instance, legal and educational systems quite distinct from those of England. Indeed, since July 1999 there has been once again a Scottish Parliament, which at present sits in the Assembly Hall on the Mound. And by virtue of its commanding geographic position, on top of a long-dead volcano, and the survival of a large number of outstanding buildings carrying echoes of the nation's history, Edinburgh ranks among the world's greatest capital cities.

The key to understanding Edinburgh is to make the distinction between the Old and New Towns. Until the 18th century, the city was confined to the rocky crag on which its castle stands, straggling between the fortress at one end and the royal residence, the Palace of Holyroodhouse, at the other. In the 18th century, during a civilizing time of expansion known as the "Scottish Enlightenment," the city fathers fostered the construction of another Edinburgh, one a little to the north. This is the New Town, whose elegant squares, classical facades, wide streets, and harmonious proportions remain largely intact and are still lived in today.

Currency

The British unit of currency is the pound sterling, divided into 100 pence (p). Bills are issued in denominations of 5, 10, 20, and 50 pounds (£). Coins are £2, £1, 50p, 20p, 10p, 5p, 2p, and 1p. Scottish banks issue Scottish currency, of which all coins and notes—with the exception of the £1 notes—are accepted in England. At press time, exchange rates were approximately £.63 to the U.S dollar and £.42 to the Canadian dollar.

Telephones

The United Kingdom's country code is 44. When dialing from outside the country, drop the initial zero from the area code. Other than on the street, the best place to find a bank of pay phones is in a hotel or large post office. The workings of coin-operated telephones vary, but there are usually instructions in each unit. Most take 10p, 20p, 50p, and £1 coins. Phone cards are also available; they can be bought in a number of retail outlets. Card phones, which are clearly marked with a special green insignia, will not accept coins. The cheapest way to make an overseas call is to dial it yourself—but be sure to have plenty of coins or phone cards close at hand. After you have inserted the coins or card, dial 00 (the international code), then the country code, area code, and the local number. To reach an **AT&T** long-distance operator, dial 0500/890011; **MCI**, 0800/890222; for **Sprint**, 0800/890877 (from a British Telecom phone) or 0500/890877 (from a Mercury Communications phone). To make a collect or other operator-assisted call, dial 155.

Shore Excursions

The following is a good choice in Edinburgh. It may not be offered by all cruise lines. Time and price are approximate.

City Tour. Survey Old Town and New Town, visiting Edinburgh Castle. Pass by sights such as Princes Street, St. Giles Cathedral, the Royal Mile, and Holyroodhouse Palace. *4 hrs. Cost: $48.*

Coming Ashore

Ships dock at Leith, the port for Edinburgh. It is about a 15-minute drive to Edinburgh from the pier.

Walking is the best way to tour the old part of the city. It can be tiring, so wear comfortable shoes. Taxis are easily found; there are stands throughout the downtown area, most at the west end of Princes Street, South St. David Street and North St. Andrew Street (both just off St. Andrew Sq.), Waverley Market, Waterloo Place, and Lauriston Place.

Exploring Edinburgh

Numbers in the margin correspond to points of interest on the Edinburgh map.

❶ Edinburgh Castle, the brooding symbol of Scotland's capital and the nation's martial past, dominates the city center. The castle's attractions include the city's oldest building—the 11th-century St. Margaret's Chapel; the Crown Room, where the Regalia of Scotland are displayed; Old Parliament Hall; and Queen Mary's Apartments, where Mary, Queen of Scots, gave birth to the future King James VI of Scotland (who later became James I of England). In addition, military features of interest include the Scottish National War Memorial and the Scottish United Services Museum. The Castle Esplanade, the wide parade ground at the entrance to the castle, hosts the annual Edinburgh Military Tattoo—a grand military display staged during an annual summer festival. *Castlehill, tel. 0131/668–8800. Admission: £6.50 Open Apr.–Sept., daily 9:30–5:15; Oct.–Mar., daily 9:30–4:15.*

❷ The Royal Mile, the backbone of the Old Town, starts immediately below the Castle Esplanade. It consists of a number of streets, running into each other—Castlehill, Lawnmarket, High Street, and Canongate—leading downhill to the Palace of Holyroodhouse, home to the Royal Family when they visit Edinburgh. Tackle this walk in leisurely style; the many original Old Town "closes," narrow alleyways enclosed by high tenement buildings, are rewarding to explore and give a real sense of the former life of the city.

❸ The Writers' Museum, housed in Lady Stair's House, is a town dwelling of 1622 that recalls Scotland's literary heritage with exhibits on Sir Walter Scott, Robert Louis Stevenson, and Robert Burns. *Lady Stair's Close, Lawnmarket, tel. 0131/529–4901. Admission free. Open Mon.–Sat. 10–5, Sun. during festival 2–5.*

A heart shape set in the cobbles of High Street marks the
❹ site of the 15th-century **Tolbooth,** the center of city life—
and original inspiration for Sir Walter Scott's novel *The Heart
of Midlothian*—until it was demolished in 1817. *High St.*

❺ **High Kirk of St. Giles,** often called St. Giles's Cathedral, dates
back to the 12th century; the impressive choir is from the
15th. *High St., tel. 0131/225–4363. Suggested donation:
£1. Open Mon.– Sat. 9–5 (7 in summer), Sun. 1–5 and for
services.*

❻ The **Palace of Holyroodhouse,** still the Royal Family's official residence in Scotland, came into existence originally
as a guest house for the Abbey of Holyrood, founded in
1128 by Scottish king David I. It was then extensively re-
modeled by Charles II in 1671. The state apartments, with
their collections of tapestries and paintings, can be visited.
*East end of Canongate, tel. 0131/556–7371, 0131/556–1096
(recorded information). Admission: £5.50. Open Apr.–
Oct., daily 9:30–5:15; Nov.–Mar., daily 9:30–3:45; closed
during royal and state visits.*

❼ The **National Gallery of Scotland,** on the Mound, the street
that joins the Old and New Towns, contains works by the
Old Masters and the French Impressionists and has a good
selection of Scottish paintings. This is one of Britain's best
national galleries and is small enough to be taken in easily
on one visit. *The Mound, tel. 0131/556–8921. Admission
free; charge for special exhibitions. Open Mon.–Sat. 10–
5, Sun. 2–5. Print Room weekdays 10–noon and 2–4 by
arrangement.*

To the east along Princes Street is the unmistakable soar-
❽ ing Gothic spire of the 200-ft **Scott Monument,** built in the
1840s to commemorate Sir Walter Scott (1771–1832), the
celebrated novelist of Scots history. Currently closed for renovation, the monument can only be viewed from outside.
Princes St., tel. 0131/529–4068.

Shopping
Princes Street may have uninspiring architecture and a
smattering of fast-food joints, but it's still one of the best
places to shop for tweeds, tartans, and knits, especially if
your time is limited. **Jenners** (48 Princes St.), opposite the

Edinburgh

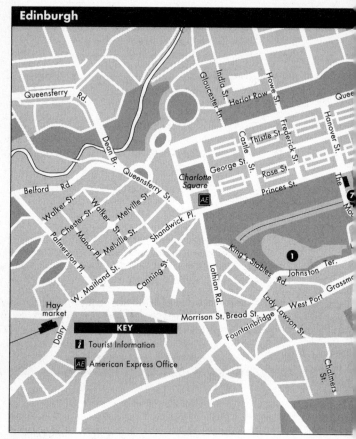

Queensferry Rd.

India St.

Gloucester Ln.

Heriot Row

Howe St.

Quee

Hanover St.

Castle St.

Thistle St.

Frederick St.

George St.

Rose St.

Dean Br.

Queensferry St.

Charlotte Square

Princes St.

Belford Rd.

AE

Walker St.

Chester St.

Walker St.

Melville St.

Shandwick Pl.

The No.

Palmerston Pl.

Manor Pl.

Melville St.

King's Stables Rd.

Johnston Ter.

W. Maitland St.

Canning St.

Lothian Rd.

West Port Grassm.

Hay-market

Lady Lawson St.

Morrison St.

Bread St.

Fountainbridge

Dalry

Chalmers St.

KEY

i Tourist Information

AE American Express Office

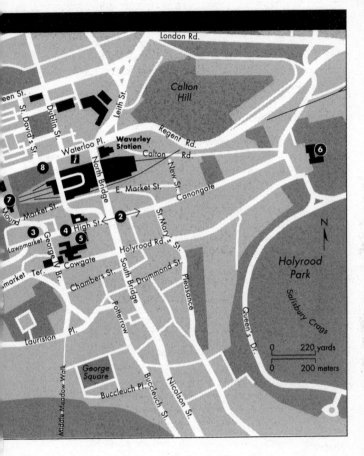

London Rd.

Calton
Hill

een St.

St. David's St.

Dublin St.

Leith St.

Waterloo Pl.

Regent Rd.

**Waverley
Station**

North Bridge

Calton Rd.

New St.

6

Mound

Market St.

E. Market St.

Canongate

7

3

Lawnmarket

George IV Br.

4

High St.

5

2

St. Mary's St.

Holyrood Rd.

market Ter.

Cowgate

Chambers St.

South Bridge

Drummond St.

Pleasance

Holyrood
Park

Queen's Dr.

Salisbury Crags

N

Lauriston Pl.

Potterrow

Middle Meadow Walk

George
Square

Buccleuch Pl.

Buccleuch St.

Nicolson St.

0   220 yards

0   200 meters

Scott Monument, is one of Edinburgh's last independent department stores; it has a wonderful Food Hall where you can find classic Scottish specialties like shortbreads and Dundee cakes. **George Street** is a good place to hit for smaller, upscale boutiques; the cross-streets Castle, Frederick, and Hanover are also well worth exploring.

Florence/Livorno, Italy

One of Europe's preeminent treasures, Florence draws visitors from all over the world. A port call in Florence is a visit to the birthplace of the Italian Renaissance, and the city bears witness to the proud spirit and unparalleled genius of its artists and artisans. Founded by Julius Caesar, the city has the familiar grid pattern common to all Roman colonies. Except for the major monuments, which are appropriately imposing, the buildings are low and unpretentious. It is a small, compact city of ocher and gray stone and pale plaster; its narrow streets open unexpectedly into spacious squares populated by strollers and pigeons. At its best, it has a gracious and elegant air, though it can at times be a nightmare of mass tourism. Plan, if you can, to visit Florence in early spring, late fall, or even winter to avoid the crowds. There is so much to see that it is best to savor a small part rather than attempt to absorb it all in a muddled vision.

Currency

The unit of currency in Italy is the lira (plural, lire). There are bills of 1,000, 2,000, 5,000, 10,000, 50,000, 100,000, and 500,000 lire (this largest bill being almost impossible to change, except in banks); coins are worth 50, 100, 200, 500, and 1,000 lire. In 1999 the euro began to be used as a banking currency, but the lira will still be the currency in use on a day-to-day basis. At press time, the exchange rate was about 1,822 lire to the U.S. dollar, 1,203 lire to the Canadian dollar, and 2,900 lire to the pound sterling. When your purchases run into hundreds of thousands of lire, beware of being shortchanged, a dodge that is practiced at ticket windows, toll booths, and cashiers' desks, as well as in shops and even banks. Always count your change before you leave the counter.

Telephones

The country code for Italy is 39. Do not drop the zero in the regional code when calling Italy. For all local calls, you must dial the regional area codes, even in cities. Most local calls cost 200 lire for two minutes. Pay phones take either 100-, 200-, or 500-lire coins or *schede telefoniche* (phone cards), purchased in bars, tobacconists, post offices, and TELECOM offices in either 5,000-, 10,000-, or 15,000-lire denominations. To place international calls, many travelers go to the Telefoni telephone exchange (usually marked TELECOM), where the operator assigns you a booth, can help place your call, and will collect payment when you have finished. To dial an international call, insert a phone card, dial 00, then the country code, area code, and phone number. For **AT&T USADirect,** dial access number tel. 172–1011; for **MCI Call USA,** access number tel. 172–1022; for **Sprint Express,** access number tel. 172–1877. You will be connected directly with an operator in the United States.

Shore Excursions

The following is a good choice in Florence. It may not be offered by all cruise lines. Time and price are approximate.

City and Coastal Tour. See many of Florence's major civic and religous sights on this whirlwind day of sightseeing—plus a stop along the way to see the Leaning Tower of Pisa. *10 hrs. Cost: $145, including lunch.*

Coming Ashore

Ships dock at Livorno, which is a little more than an hour from Florence. Most cruise lines sell bus transfers to Florence for independent sightseeing for about $70.

Once in the city, you can see most of Florence's major sights on foot, as they are packed into a relatively small central area. Wear comfortable shoes and wander to your heart's content: with the help of many landmarks, it is easy to find your way around in Florence, though the system of street addresses is unusual; commercial addresses (those with an *r* in them, meaning *rosso,* or red) and residential addresses are numbered separately (32/r might be next to or a block away from plain 32).

Taxis wait at stands. Use only authorized cabs, which are white with a yellow stripe or rectangle on the door. The meter starts at 4,000 lire. To call a taxi, phone 055/4798 or 055/4390. The meter starts at 4,500 lire, with extra charges for nights, holidays, or radio dispatch.

Exploring Florence

The best place to begin a tour of Florence is **Piazza del Duomo,** where the cathedral, bell tower, and baptistery stand in the rather cramped square.

The lofty **Duomo** (or Cattedrale of Santa Maria del Fiore) is one of the longest in the world. Its construction was begun in 1296 by master sculptor and architect Arnolfo di Cambio and took 140 years to complete. Inside, the church is cool and austere, a fine example of the architecture of the period. Among the sparse decorations, take a good look at the frescoes on the left wall and on the dome. These frescoes, however, take second place to the dome itself, Filippo Brunelleschi's (1377–1446) greatest architectural and technical achievement. It was the inspiration of such later domes as the one for St. Peter's in Rome and even the Capitol in Washington. Today, the dome stands for Florence in the same way that the Eiffel Tower symbolizes Paris. You can climb to the cupola gallery, 463 fatiguing steps up between the two skins of the double dome, for a fine view of Florence and the surrounding hills. *Piazza del Duomo, tel. 055/2302885. Admission to dome: 10,000 lire. Open Mon.–Sat. 10–5 (1st Sat. of month 10–3:30), Sun. 1–5. Cupola (entrance in left aisle of cathedral) open weekdays 9:30–7, Sat. 8:30–5 (1st Sat. of month 8:30–3:20).*

Next to the Duomo is Giotto's 14th-century **Campanile** (bell tower), richly decorated with colored marble and sculpture reproductions (the originals are in the Museo dell'Opera del Duomo). The 414-step climb to the top is less strenuous than that to the cupola of the Duomo. *Piazza del Duomo. Admission: 10,000 lire. Open Apr.– Oct., daily 9–6:50; Nov.–Mar., daily. 9–4:20.*

In front of the cathedral is the **Battistero** (baptistery), one of the city's oldest and most beloved edifices, where, since the 11th century, Florentines have baptized their children. The most famous of the baptistery's three portals is Ghiberti's east doors (facing the Duomo), dubbed the "gates of Paradise" by Michelangelo; luminous copies now replace the originals, which have been removed to the Museo dell'Opera del Duomo (Cathedral Museum). *Piazza del Duomo, tel. 055/ 2302885. Admission: 5,000 lire. Open Mon.–Sat. 1:30– 6:30, Sun. 8:30–1:30. Museo dell' Opera del Duomo: Piazza del Duomo 9, tel. 055/2302885. Admission: 10,000 lire. Open Mar.–Oct., Mon.–Sat. 9–7:30; Nov.–Feb., Mon.–Sat. 9–7.*

Along Via Calzaiuoli you'll come upon **Piazza della Signoria,** the heart of Florence and the city's largest square. In the center of the square a slab marks the spot of the 1497 "burning of the vanities," when reformist monk Savonarola urged the Florentines to burn their pictures, books, musical instruments, and other worldly objects. On the same spot, a year later, he was hanged and then burned at the stake as a heretic. Copies of several famous statues are found in the square or the adjoining Loggia dei Lanzi, including a copy of Michelangelo's *David* and a copy of Cellini's *Perseus Holding the Head of Medusa.*

The **Galleria degli Uffizi** (Uffizi Gallery) houses Italy's most important collection of paintings. The palace was built to house the administrative offices of the Medici, onetime rulers of the city ("uffizi" is Italian for "offices"). Later their fabulous art collection was arranged in the Uffizi Gallery on the top floor, which was opened to the public in the 17th century—making this the world's first public gallery of modern times. The emphasis is on Italian art of the Gothic and Renaissance periods. Make sure you see the works by Giotto, and look for the Botticellis in Rooms X–XIV, Michelangelo's *Holy Family* in Room XXV, and the works by Raphael next door. In addition to its art treasures, the gallery offers a magnificent close-up view of Palazzo Vecchio's tower from the little coffee bar at the end of the corridor. Notoriously long lines can be avoided by purchasing tickets in advance from Consorzio ITA. *Loggiato Uffizi 6, tel. 055/23885; Consorzio ITA (advance tickets), 055/ 2347941. Admission: 12,000 lire. Open Nov.–Mar., Tues.– Sat. 8:30–7, Sun. 8:30–1:50; Apr.–Oct., Mon.–Sat. 8:30– 10, Sun. 8:30–8.*

The **Galleria dell'Accademia** (Accademia Gallery) houses Michelangelo's famous *David*. Skip the works in the exhibition halls leading to the main attraction; they are of minor importance, and you'll gain a length on the tour groups. Michelangelo's statue is a tour de force of artistic conception and technical ability, for he was using a piece of stone that had already been worked on by a lesser sculptor. Take time to see the forceful *Slaves*, also by Michelangelo; the rough-hewn, unfinished surfaces contrast dramatically with the highly polished, meticulously carved *David*. Michelangelo left the *Slaves* "unfinished" as a symbolic gesture: to accentuate the figures' struggle to escape the bondage of stone. *Via Ricasoli 60, tel. 055/2388609. Admission: 12,000 lire. Open Nov.–Mar., Tues.–Sat. 8:30–7, Sun. 8:30–1:50; Apr.–Oct., Tues.–Sat. 8:30–10, Sun. 8:30–8.*

The remarkable **Cappelle Medicee** (Medici Chapels) contain the tombs of practically every member of the Medici family, and there were a lot of them, for they guided Florence's destiny from the 15th century to 1737. Cosimo I, a Medici whose acumen made him the richest man in Europe, is buried in the crypt of the Chapel of the Princes, and Donatello's tomb is next to that of his patron. The chapel upstairs is decorated in a dazzling array of colored marble. Michelangelo's New Sacristy, his tombs of Giuliano and Lorenzo de' Medici, include the justly famed statues of *Dawn* and *Dusk, Night* and *Day*. *Piazza Madonna degli Aldobrandini, San Lorenzo, tel. 055/2388602. Admission: 10,000 lire. Open daily 8:30–1:50. Closed 1st, 3rd, and 5th Mon. of month and 2nd and 4th Sun. of month.*

Don't be put off by the grim look of the Bargello, a fortresslike palace that served as residence of Florence's chief magistrate in medieval times, and later as a prison. It now houses Florence's **Museo Nazionale del Bargello** (National Museum), a treasure trove of Italian Renaissance sculpture. In a historically and visually interesting setting, it displays masterpieces by Donatello, Verrocchio, Michelangelo, and many other major sculptors. This museum is on a par with the Uffizi, so don't shortchange yourself on time. *Via del Proconsolo 4, tel. 055/238–8606. Admission: 8,000 lire. Open daily 8:30–1:50. Closed 1st, 3rd, and 5th Sun. and 2nd and 4th Mon. of month.*

The **Ponte Vecchio** (Old Bridge) is Florence's oldest bridge. It seems to be just another street lined with goldsmiths' shops until you get to the middle and catch a glimpse of the Arno flowing below. Spared during World War II by the retreating Germans (who blew up every other bridge in the city), it also survived the 1966 flood. It leads into the Oltrarno, which has its own charm and still preserves much of the atmosphere of old-time Florence, full of fascinating craft workshops. *East of Ponte Santa Trinita and west of Ponte alle Grazie.*

The church of **Santo Spirito** is important as one of Brunelleschi's finest architectural creations, and it contains some superb paintings, including a Filippino Lippi *Madonna.* Santo Spirito is the hub of a colorful neighborhood of artisans and intellectuals. An outdoor market enlivens the square every morning except Sunday; in the afternoon, pigeons, pet owners, and pensioners take over. *Piazza Santo Spirito, tel. 055/210030. Open Thurs.–Tues. 8:30–12 and 4–6; Wed. 8:30–12, Sun. 4–6.*

Shopping
Florence has quality leather goods, linens and upholstery fabrics, gold and silver jewelry, and cameos. Straw goods, gilded wooden trays and frames, hand-printed paper desk accessories, and ceramic objects make inexpensive gifts. Many shops offer fine old prints.

The most fashionable streets in Florence are **Via Tornabuoni** and **Via della Vigna Nuova.** Goldsmiths and jewelry shops can be found on and around the **Ponte Vecchio.**

The **monastery of Santa Croce** houses a leather-working school and showroom (Via San Giuseppe 5/r, Piazza Santa Croce 16). The entire Santa Croce area is known for its leather workshops and inconspicuous shops selling gold and silver jewelry at prices much lower than those of the elegant jewelers near Ponte Vecchio.

Outside the Church of San Lorenzo, you'll find yourself in the midst of the sprawling **Mercato di San Lorenzo** (San Lorenzo Market), dealing in everything and anything, including some interesting leather items. *Piazza San Lorenzo, Via dell'Ariento. Open Tues.–Sat. 8–7; June–Sept., 8–7.*

French Riviera and Monte Carlo

Few places in the world have the same pull on the imagination as France's fabled Riviera (also known as the Côte
d'Azur), the Mediterranean coastline stretching from St-
Tropez in the west to Menton on the Italian border. Cooled
by the Mediterranean in the summer and warmed by it in
winter, the climate is almost always pleasant. Avoid the area
in July and August, however, unless you love crowds.

Although the Riviera's coastal resorts seem to live exclu-
sively for the tourist trade and have often been ruined by
high-rise blocks, the hinterlands remain relatively untar-
nished. The little villages perched high on the hills behind
medieval ramparts seem to belong to another century. One
of them, St-Paul-de-Vence, is the home of the Maeght Foundation, one of the world's leading museums of modern art.
Artists, attracted by the light, have played a considerable
role in popular conceptions of the Riviera, and their presence is reflected in the number of modern art museums: the
Musée Picasso at Antibes, the Musée Renoir and the Musée
d'Art Moderne Mediterranée at Cagnes-sur-Mer, and the
Musée Jean Cocteau near the harbor at Menton.

The tiny principality of Monaco, which lies between Nice
and Menton, is included in this section, despite the fact that
it is a sovereign state. Although Monaco has its own army
and police force, its language, food, and way of life are
French.

Currency

The unit of French currency is the franc (fr), subdivided into
100 centimes. Bills are issued in denominations of 50, 100,
200, and 500 francs (frs.); coins are 5, 10, 20, and 50 centimes and 1, 2, 5, 10, and 20 francs. The small, copper-color
5-, 10-, and 20-centime coins have considerable nuisance
value, but they can be used for tips in bars and cafés. At
press time, the U.S. dollar bought 6.2 francs, the Canadian
dollar 4.1 francs, and the pound sterling 9.8 francs.

Telephones

The country code for France is 33. French phone numbers
have ten digits. All phone numbers have a two-digit prefix
determined by zone; for the southeast, the code is 04. (Drop

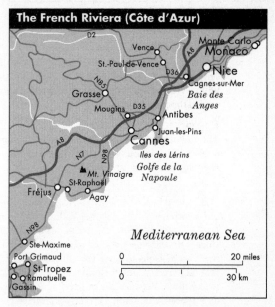

The French Riviera (Côte d'Azur)

the zero if you are calling France from a foreign country.) Though there is no frontier between France and Monaco, when dialing numbers from outside the country, even if calling from France, you must prefix the call with 377. Phone booths are plentiful; they are nearly always available at post offices, cafés, and métro stations. Some French pay phones take 1-, 2-, and 5-franc coins (1-fr. minimum), but most phones are now operated by *télécartes* (phone cards), which can be used for both local and international calls. The cards are sold in post offices, métro stations, and cafés sporting a red TABAC (tobacco) sign outside (cost: 49 frs. for 50 units; 97.50 frs. for 120 units). To call abroad, dial 00 and wait for the tone, then dial the country code, area code, and number. To reach an **AT&T** long-distance operator, dial 08–00–99–00–11; **MCI,** 08–00–99–00–19; **Sprint,** 08–00–99–00–87. Dial 12 for local operators.

Shore Excursions

The best way to spend time in the French Riviera is to wander the city streets, lunch at a café, or head to the beach.

Depending on where you're docked, your cruise line may offer excursions to other nearby towns.

Coming Ashore

Only small ships dock at St-Tropez or Monaco. Most larger ones will dock or drop anchor at Nice or Cannes, where you can hire a car, catch a train, or take a shore excursion to St-Tropez or Monaco.

Exploring the Riviera

The towns of the French Riviera are easily and best seen on foot. Only if you wish to travel between towns will you need additional transportation.

IN ST-TROPEZ

Old money never came to St-Tropez, but Brigitte Bardot did—with her director Roger Vadim in 1956 to film *And God Created Woman*. The town has never been the same since. Off-season is the time to come, but even in summer there are reasons to stay. The soft, sandy beaches are the best on the coast, and the pastel houses make it a genuinely pretty town. Between the old and new ports is the **Musée de l'Annonciade,** set in a cleverly converted chapel, which houses paintings by artists drawn to St-Tropez between 1890 and 1940—including Paul Signac, Matisse, Derain, and Van Dongen. *Quai de l'Épi, tel. 04–94–97–04–01. Admission: 30 frs. Open June–Sept., Wed.–Mon. 10–noon and 3–7; Oct.–May, Wed.–Mon. 10–noon and 2–6.*

A long climb up to the **Citadelle** (citadel) is rewarded by a splendid view over the Old Town and across the gulf to Ste-Maxime, a quieter, more working-class family resort with a decent beach.

IN CANNES

Cannes is for relaxing—strolling along the seafront on the **Croisette** and getting tanned on the beaches. Near the eastern end of La Croisette is the Parc de la Roserie, where some 14,000 roses nod their heads in the wind.

The **Palais des Festivals** is where the famous film festival is held each May, and it is near the Cannes harbor.

Only a few steps inland is the Old Town, known as the **Suquet,** with its steep, cobbled streets and its 12th-century watchtower. To reach it, take a right turn off rue Félix Faure onto rue St-Antoine and continue spiraling up through rue du Suquet to the top of a 60-m (197-ft) hill.

IN NICE

The **place Masséna** is the logical starting point for an exploration of Nice. This fine square was built in 1815 to celebrate a local hero: one of Napoléon's most successful generals.

The **Promenade des Anglais,** built by the English community here in 1824, is only a short stroll past the fountains and the **Jardin Albert Ier.** It now carries heavy traffic but still forms a splendid strand between town and sea.

Just up rue de Rivoli is the **Palais Masséna,** a museum of city history with eclectic treasures ranging from Garibaldi's death sheet to Empress Josephine's tiara. *65 rue de France, tel. 04–93–88–11–34. Admission 25 frs. Open Wed.–Mon. 10–noon and 2–6.*

Farther west, along rue de France and right up avenue des Baumettes, is the **Musée des Beaux-Arts Jules-Chéret,** Nice's fine-arts museum, built in 1878 as a palatial mansion for a Russian princess. The rich collection of paintings includes paintings by Sisley, Bonnard, and Vuillard; sculptures by Rodin; and ceramics by Picasso. *33 av. des Baumettes, tel. 04–92–15–28–28. Admission: 25 frs. Open May–Sept., Tues.–Sun. 10– noon and 2–6; Oct.–April, Tues.–Sun. 10–noon and 2–5.*

The narrow streets in the Old Town are the prettiest part of Nice: take the rue de l'Opéra to see the ornate **St-François-de-Paule** church (1750) and the **opera house.** At the northern extremity of the Old Town lies the vast **place Garibaldi**—all yellow-ocher buildings and formal fountains. Dominating Vieux Nice is the **Colline du Château** (Castle Hill), a romantic cliff fortified many centuries before Christ. It's fun to explore the ruins of the 6th-century castle and the surrounding garden; there's a lookout point on the stairs that gives you a stunning view of the bay.

The **Musée National Message Biblique Chagall** (Chagall Museum) houses a superb, life-affirming collection of Chagall's late works, including the 17 huge canvases of *The Message* *of the Bible,* which took 13 years to complete. *Av. du Dr-Ménard, tel. 04–93–53–87–20. Admission: 30 frs. (38 frs. in summer). Open July–Sept., Wed.–Mon. 10–6; Oct.–June, Wed.–Mon. 10–5.*

A 17th-century Italian villa amid Roman remains contains the **Musée Matisse** (Matisse Museum) with paintings and bronzes by Henri Matisse (1869–1954), who lived for nearly 40 years in Nice. *164 av. des Arènes-de-Cimiez, tel. 04–93–81–08–08. Admission 25 frs. Open Apr.–Oct., Wed.–Mon. 10–6; Nov.–Mar. 10–5.*

Next door to the Matisse museum, the **Musée Archéologique** displays findings from the Roman city that once flourished here. *Tel. 04–93–81–59–57. Admission: 25 frs. Open Apr.–Sept., Tues.–Sun. 10–noon and 2–6; Oct.–Mar., 10–1 and 2–5.*

IN MONACO

The Principality of Monaco covers just 473 acres and would fit comfortably inside New York's Central Park or a family farm in Iowa. The present ruler, Prince Rainier III, belongs to the Grimaldi dynasty; back in the 1850s, a Grimaldi named Charles III made a decision that turned Monaco into a giant blue chip. He opened a casino, and although it took over a decade to catch on, it turned the principality into a glittering watering hole for European society.

For more than a century Monaco's livelihood was centered in its splendid copper-roof **casino.** The oldest section dates from 1878 and was conceived by Charles Garnier, architect of the Paris opera house. It's as elaborately ornate as anyone could wish, bristling with turrets and gold filigree, and with masses of interior frescoes and bas-reliefs. There are lovely sea views from the terrace, and the gardens out front are meticulously tended. The main activity is in the American Room, where beneath the gilt-edged ceiling, busloads of tourists feed the one-armed bandits. *Pl. du Casino. Persons under 21 not admitted. Admission to European rooms, 50 frs; English Club and Monte-Carlo Sporting Club rooms, 100 frs; access to slot machines, free. Open daily noon–4 AM. Closed May 1.*

Monaco Town, the principality's old quarter, has many vaulted passageways and exudes an almost tangible medieval feeling. The magnificent **Palais du Prince** (Prince's Palace), a grandiose Italianate structure with a Moorish tower, was largely rebuilt in the last century. Here, since 1297, the Grimaldi dynasty has lived and ruled. The spectacle of the Changing of the Guard occurs each morning at 11:55; inside, guided tours take visitors through the state apartments and a wing containing the **Palace Archives** and **Musée Napoléon** (Napoleonic Museum). *Pl. du Palais, tel. 93–25–18–31. Palace admission: 30 frs; joint ticket with Musée Napoléon 40 frs. Open daily 9:30–6:30; Musée Napoléon and Palace Archives: Tues.–Sun. 9:30–6:30.*

Next to the St-Martin Gardens—which contain an evocative bronze monument in memory of Prince Albert I (Prince Rainier's great-grandfather, the one in the sou'wester and flying oilskins, benignly guiding a ship's wheel)—is the **Musée Océanographique** (Oceanography Museum and Aquarium). At this internationally renowned research institute founded by Prince Albert and run for years by underwater explorer Jacques Cousteau (1910–97), the aquarium is the undisputed highlight; here a collection of the world's fish and crustaceans—some colorful, some drab, some the stuff of nightmares—live out their lives in public. *Av. St-Martin, tel. 93–15–36–00. Admission: 60 frs. Open July–Aug., daily 9–8; Sept.–June, daily 9:30–7 (6 in winter).*

The Moneghetti area is the setting for the **Jardin Exotique** (Exotic Plants Garden), where 600 varieties of cacti and succulents cling to the rock face. Your ticket also allows you to explore the caves next to the gardens and to visit the adjacent **Musée d'Anthropologie Préhistorique** (Museum of Prehistoric Anthropology). *Blvd. du Jardin Exotique, tel. 93–15–80–06. Admission: 38 frs. Open mid-May–mid-Sept., daily 9–7; mid-Sept.–mid-May, daily 9–6.*

Beaches

IN CANNES

Many of Cannes's beaches are private, but that doesn't mean you can't use them, only that you must pay for the privilege.

IN ST-TROPEZ

The best beaches (*plages*) are scattered along a 5-km (3-mi) stretch reached by the Route des Plages (beach road). Close to town are the family-friendly **Plage des Greniers** and the **Bouillabaisse,** but most people prefer a 10-km (6-mi) sandy crescent at **Les Salins** and **Pampellone.** These beaches are about 4 km (3 mi) from town.

Gibraltar

The Rock of Gibraltar acquired its name in AD 711 when it was captured by the Moorish chieftain Tarik at the start of the Arab invasion of Spain. It became known as Jebel Tariq (Rock of Tariq), later corrupted to Gibraltar. After successive periods of Moorish and Spanish domination, Gibraltar was captured by an Anglo-Dutch fleet in 1704 and ceded to the British by the Treaty of Utrecht in 1713. This tiny British colony, whose impressive silhouette dominates the straits between Spain and Morocco, is a rock just 5⅗ km (3⅗ mi) long, ¾ km (½ mi) wide, and 1,394 ft high.

Currency
Gibraltar's official language is English and the currency is the British pound sterling. However, Spanish pesetas are generally accepted. At press time, exchange rates were approximately £.63 to the U.S dollar and £.42 to the Canadian dollar.

Shore Excursions
The following is a good choice in Gibraltar. It may not be offered by all cruise lines. Time and price are approximate.

The Rock. By taxi or cable car, you'll climb the 1,400-ft-high Rock of Gibraltar for a panoramic view of the town and harbor. Includes a visit to Ape's Den, home of Barbary apes. *1½–3½ hrs. Cost: $38.*

Coming Ashore
Cruise ships dock at Gibraltar's pier. From here, you can walk or take a taxi or shuttle to the center of town.

Since Gibraltar is just over 5 km (3 mi) long and only 1 km (½ mi) wide, getting around is not a major problem.

Exploring Gibraltar
Punta Grande de Europa (Europa Point) is the Rock's most southerly tip. Stop here to admire the view across the strait to the coast of Morocco, 22½ km (14 mi) away. You are standing on what in ancient times was called one of the two Pil-

Finally, a travel companion that doesn't snore on the plane or eat all your peanuts.

When traveling, your MCI WorldCom Card is the best way to keep in touch. Our operators speak your language, so they'll be able to connect you back home—no matter where your travels take you. Plus, your MCI WorldCom Card is easy to use, and even earns you frequent flyer miles every time you use it. When you add in our great rates, you get something even more valuable: peace-of-mind. So go ahead. Travel the world. MCI WorldCom just brought it a whole lot closer.

You can even sign up today at www.mci.com/worldphone or ask your operator to make a collect call to 1-410-314-2938.

EASY TO CALL WORLDWIDE

1 Just dial the WorldPhone access number of the country you're calling from.
2 Dial or give the operator your MCI WorldCom Card number.
3 Dial or give the number you're calling.

Argentina	
To call using Telefonica	0-800-222-6249
To call using Telecom	0-800-555-1002
Brazil	**000-8012**
France ◆	**0-800-99-0019**
Ireland	**1-800-55-1001**
United Kingdom	
To call using BT	0800-89-0222
To call using CWC	0500-89-0222
United States	**1-800-888-8000**

For your complete WorldPhone calling guide, dial the WorldPhone access number for the country you're in and ask the operator for Customer Service. In the U.S. call 1-800-431-5402.

◆ Public phones may require deposit of coin or phone card for dial tone.

EARN FREQUENT FLYER MILES

American Airlines
AAdvantage

Continental Airlines
OnePass

▲ Delta Air Lines
SkyMiles

✈ **MILEAGE PLUS.**
United Airlines

US AIRWAYS
D I V I D E N D   M I L E S

MCI WorldCom, its logo and the names of the products referred to herein are proprietary marks of MCI WorldCom, Inc. All airline names and logos are proprietary marks of the respective airlines. All airline program rules and conditions apply.

The first thing you need overseas is the one thing you forget to pack.

FOREIGN CURRENCY DELIVERED OVERNIGHT

Chase Currency To Go® delivers foreign currency to your home by the next business day*

It's easy—before you travel, call 1-888-CHASE84 for delivery of any of 75 currencies

Delivery is free with orders of $500 or more

Competitive rates— without exchange fees

You don't have to be a Chase customer—you can pay by Visa® or MasterCard®

◻ CHASE

THE RIGHT RELATIONSHIP IS EVERYTHING.®

1•888•CHASE84
www.chase.com

lars of Hercules (the second was just across the water, in Morocco—a mountain between the cities of Ceuta and Tangier.) Plaques explain the history of the gun installations here.

Jews' Gate is an unbeatable lookout point over the docks and the Bay of Gibraltar to Algeciras in Spain. From here you can gain access to the Upper Nature Preserve, which includes St. Michael's Cave (*see below*), the Apes' Den, the Great Siege Tunnel, and the Moorish Castle. *Engineer Rd. Admission to preserve, including all sights: £4.50, plus £2 per vehicle. Open daily 10–sunset.*

St. Michael's Cave, a series of underground chambers adorned with stalactites and stalagmites makes a wonderful setting for concerts, ballet, and drama.

Apes' Den, near the Wall of Charles V, is where you'll find the famous Barbary apes, a breed of cinnamon-colored, tailless monkeys, natives of the Atlas Mountains in Morocco. Legend holds that as long as the apes remain, the British will continue to hold the Rock. Winston Churchill himself issued orders for the maintenance of the ape colony when its numbers began to dwindle during World War II. The den is reachable by car or cable car. *Old Queen's Rd.*

The **Great Siege Tunnel** is found at the northern end of the Rock. These huge galleries were carved out during the Great Siege of 1779–83. Here, in 1878, the governor, Lord Napier of Magdala, entertained former president Ulysses S. Grant at a banquet in St. George's Hall. From here, the Holyland Tunnel leads out to the east side of the Rock above Catalan Bay.

The recently refurbished **Gibraltar Museum**'s exhibits recall the history of the Rock throughout the ages. *Bomb House La., tel. 9567/74289. Admission: £2. Open weekdays 10–6, Sat. 10–2.*

Greek Islands

The islands of the Aegean have colorful legends—the Minotaur in Crete; the lost continent of Atlantis, which some believe was Santorini; and the Colossus of Rhodes, to name a few. Each island has its own personality. Mykonos has

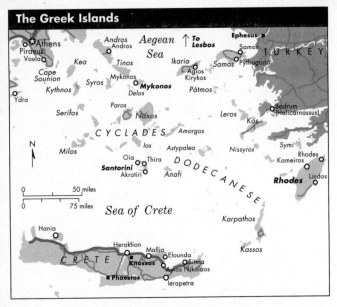

The Greek Islands

windmills, dazzling whitewashed buildings, hundreds of tiny red-domed churches and chapels on golden hillsides, and small fishing harbors. Visitors to volcanic Santorini sail into a vast volcanic crater and anchor near the island's forbidding cliffs. In Rhodes, a bustling modern town surrounds a medieval city with a castle.

Currency

The Greek monetary unit is the drachma (dr.). At press time, there were about 305 dr. to the U.S. dollar, 202 dr. to the Canadian dollar, and 485 dr. to the pound sterling.

Telephones

The country code for Greece is 30. When dialing Greece from outside the country, drop the first zero from the regional area code. Telephone kiosks are easy to find, although many can only be used for local calls. The easiest way to make a local or an international call is with a phone card, available at kiosks, convenience stores, or Hellenic Telecommunications Organization (OTE) offices. Go to an OTE office for convenience and privacy if you plan to make several international calls. For an **AT&T** long-distance operator, dial 00/800–1311; **MCI,** 00/800–1211; **Sprint,** 00/800–1411. For operator-assisted calls in English, dial 161 or 162.

Shore Excursions

The following excursions are good choices in the Greek Islands. They may not be offered by all cruise lines. Times and prices are approximate.

IN MYKONOS

The best way to explore Mykonos is on your own, wandering through the narrow whitewashed streets. Some lines may offer excursions to the neighboring island of Delos.

IN SANTORINI

Akrotiri & Wine Tasting. Visit the excavated town of Akrotiri, and then continue on your bus to a winery for a tasting. *4 hrs. Cost: $60.*

Oia. By motor coach, ride to the cliff-top village of Oia, where there will be time to wander through the town. *4 hrs. Cost: $30–$50.*

IN RHODES

Mount Philerimos and Rhodes Town. Visit the Church of Our Lady on the plateau of Philerimos and walk through the old walled portion of Rhodes Town to the Palace of Grand Masters. *4½ hrs. Cost: $49.*

Lindos. Drive 50 km (30 mi) to Lindos Village and up the summit of the Acropolis to see ruins and to shop in the village. *4 hrs. Cost: $45.*

IN LESBOS

Island Tour. Breeze through the island's highlights, including the Church of Taxiarches, Theofilos Museum, Theriade Museum, and Agiasso Village. *4 hrs. Cost: $36.*

Coming Ashore

Depending on which Greek Islands your ship visits—and how many port calls it makes—you may dock, tender, or both.

IN MYKONOS

Ships tender passengers to the main harbor area along the Esplanade in Mykonos Town.

IN SANTORINI

Ships drop anchor in the harbor off Thira or call at the port of Athinios. Passengers coming ashore below Thira can take the cable car to town, or, if you like a little more adventure, try the donkey service. Passengers who come ashore at Athinios will be met by buses and taxis. The bus ride into Thira takes about half an hour, and from there you can make connections to Oia.

IN RHODES

Ships dock at Mandraki Harbor, once the ancient port of Rhodes. Rhodes Town stretches in front of the port.

IN LESBOS

Cruise ships visiting Lesbos tender passengers to the main town of Mytilini, where most of the sights are clustered.

Getting Around

Most port cities in the Greek Islands are compact enough to explore on foot. There are, however, several outlying towns worth visiting; for these you'll need to hire a driver or rent a car.

IN MYKONOS

Mykonos Town is well suited to walking. Taxis and buses will take you to other points of interest. Motorbikes also can be rented.

IN SANTORINI

Buses and taxis will take you around town. Many people rent mopeds, but they're not recommended as a safe means of traveling about the island.

IN RHODES

It is possible to tour the island in one day only if you rent a car. Walking is advisable in Rhodes Town. Taxis can take you to other nearby sights and beaches.

IN LESBOS

A car is handy on Lesbos if you want to explore the island, and rentals cost around $75 a day. Bus service is relatively expensive and infrequent.

Exploring the Greek Islands

MYKONOS

The **archaeological museum** gives a sense of the island's history; the most significant local find is a 7th-century BC *pithos* (storage jar) showing the Greeks emerging from the Trojan Horse. *East end of port, tel. 0289/22325. Admission: 500 dr. Open Tues.–Sun. 8:30–3.*

The most beautiful of the island's churches is the **Church of Paraportiani.** The sloping, whitewashed conglomeration of four chapels, mixing Byzantine and vernacular idioms, has been described as a "confectioner's dream gone mad," and its position on a promontory facing the sea sets off the unique architecture. *Anargon St.*

Venetia (Little Venice) is a picturesque neighborhood where a few old houses have been turned into bars. In the distance across the water are the famous windmills. *Southwest end of the port.*

The **Old Folk Museum** is housed in an 18th-century house and features one bedroom furnished and decorated in the fashion of the period. On display are looms and lace-making devices, Cycladic costumes, old photographs, and Mykoniot musical instruments. *Near Little Venice, tel. 0289/22591 or 0289/22748. Admission free. Open Mon.–Sat. 4–8, Sun. 5:30–8.*

About 40 minutes by caique from Mykonos and its 20th-century holiday pleasures is the ancient isle of **Delos**—the legendary sanctuary of Apollo and Artemis. Its **Exedra ton Leonton** (Terrace of the Lions), a row of nine Naxian marble sculptures from the 7th century BC, overlooks the dried-up sacred lake. Worth seeing, too, are some of the houses of the Hellenistic and Roman periods, with their fine floor mosaics. The best of the mosaics from Delos's ruins are in the island's **archaeological museum.** *Boats leave Mykonos in morning and return at 1, depending on winds. Tel. 0289/22–259. Open Tues.–Sun. 8:30–3.*

SANTORINI

Santorini's volcano erupted violently about 1500 BC, destroying its Minoan civilization. At **Akrotiri,** on the south end of the island, the remains of a Minoan city buried by volcanic ash are being excavated. The site, once a prosperous town some claim to be the legendary Atlantis, is remarkably well preserved. Its charming frescoes are in Athens but the island wants them back. *13 km/8 mi from Fira, tel. 0286/ 81–366. Admission: 1,200 dr. Open Tues.–Sun. 8:30- -3.*

Though crowded in summer, tiny **Oia,** the serene town at the nothern tip pictured on dozens of advertisements for Greece, is famous for its marine sunset. Oia, 14 km (8½ mi) from Thira, has the usual souvenir and handicrafts shops and several reasonably priced jewelry shops. Be sure to try the local wines. The volcanic soil produces a unique range of flavors, from light and dry to rich and aromatic.

The capital, **Fira,** midway along the west coast of the east rim, is no longer just a picturesque town but a major tourist center, overflowing with discos, shops, and restaurants.

Archaia Thira (Ancient Thira), a cliff-top site on the east coast of the island, was founded before the 9th century BC; the well-preserved ancient town has a theater, agora, houses, fortifications, and temples. Though only foundations remain, it is very romantic; you can easily imagine its famed dances performed by naked youths. *Take taxi partway up Mesa Vouna then hike to summit, no phone. Admission free. Open Tues.–Sun. 8:30–3.*

The **Old Walled City,** near the harbor, was built by crusaders—the Knights of St. John—on the site of an ancient city. The knights ruled the island from 1309 until they were defeated by the Turks in 1522.

Within the fine medieval walls, on the Street of the Knights, stands the Knights' Hospital. Behind it, the **archaeological museum** houses ancient pottery and sculpture, including two voluptuous statues of Aphrodite. *Platia Mouseiou (Museum Square), reached by the wide staircase from the Hospital, tel. 0241/31048. Admission: 1,000 dr. Open Tues.–Fri. 8 AM–9 PM (winter until 2:40), weekends 8:30–3.*

Another museum that deserves your attention is the restored and moated medieval **Palati ton Ippoton** (Palace of the Knights). Destroyed in 1856 by a gunpowder explosion, the palace was renovated by the Italians as a summer retreat for Mussolini. Note its splendid Hellenistic and Roman floor mosaics. *Ippoton St., tel. 0241/23–359. Admission: 1,200 dr. Open May–Oct., Tues.–Fri. 8–7, weekends 8:30–3; Nov.–Apr., Tues.–Fri. 8:30–2:40, weekends 8:30–3.*

The walls of Rhodes's **Old Town** are among the greatest medieval monuments in the Mediterranean. For 200 years the knights strengthened them, making them up to 40 ft thick in places and curving the walls to deflect cannonballs. You can take a guided walk on about half of the 4-km (2½-mi) road along the top of the fortifications. *Old Town, tel. 0241/23–359. Tours Tues. and Sat. 2:45 (arrive at least 15 mins early).*

The enchanting village of **Lindos** is about 60 km (37 mi) down the east coast from Rhodes Town. Put on your comfortable shoes and walk up the winding path and steep stairs to the ruins of the ancient **Akropoli tis Archaias Lindou** (Acropolis of Lindos). The sight of its beautiful colonnade—part of the sanctuary to Athena Lindaia—with the sea far below, is unforgettable. Look for little St. Paul's Harbor, beneath the cliffs of the Acropolis; seen from above, it appears to be a lake, as rocks obscure its entrance. *Above town, tel. 0241/75–674. Admission: 1,000 dr. Open May–Oct., Tues.–Sun. 8–6; Nov.–Apr., Tues.–Sun. 8:30–2:40.*

LESBOS

In the main town of **Mytilini** there is a traditional Lesbos house, restored and furnished in 19th-century style, that people are permitted to visit. Call to arrange a time with owner Marika Vlachou. *Mitropleos 6, tel. 0251/28550. Admission free by appointment only.*

Above Mytilini looms the **stone fortress** built by the Byzantines above a 600 BC temple of Apollo. It was repaired by Francesco Gateluzzi of the famous Genoese family. Inside there's only a crumbling prison and a Roman cistern, but a visit is worth it for the fine views. *On pine-covered hill, tel. 0251/27297. Admission: 400 dr. Open daily sunrise–sunset.*

One of Greece's best art museums is at **Varia,** home of the early 20th-century painter Theofilos. Eighty of his paintings can be seen. *4 km/2½ mi south of Mytilini, tel. 0251/28179. Admission: 500 dr. Open Tues.– Sun. 10–1 and 4:30–8.*

The **Museum of Modern Art** includes Theriade's publications *Minotaure* and *Verve* and his collection of works, mostly lithographs, by Picasso, Matisse, Chagall, Roualt, Giacometti, and Miró. *Next to Varia, tel. 0251/23372. Admission: 600 dr. Open Tues.–Sun. 9–2 and 3–5.*

The 17th-century monastery **Taxiarchis Michail** is famous for its black icon of the archangel Michael. Visitors used to make a wish and press a coin to the archangel's forehead; if it stuck, the wish would be granted. Owing to wear and tear on the icon, the practice is now forbidden. *In town of Mandamados, 36 km/22½ mi northwest of Mytilini.*

At the foot of Mt. Olympos, the island's highest peak, sits **Agiassos** village. It remains a lovely settlement, with gray stone houses, cobblestone lanes, a medieval castle, and the church of Panayia Vrefokratousa. The latter was founded in the 12th century to house an icon believed to be the work of St. Luke.

Shopping

IN MYKONOS

Mykonos is the best of the Greek Islands for shopping. The main shopping street in Mykonos runs perpendicular to the harbor and is lined with jewelry stores, clothing, boutiques, cafés, and candy stores.

IN SANTORINI

For locally made items head to Oia, where you will find the best art galleries, antiques shops, craft shops, and stores that sell Byzantine reproductions. Boutiques abound in Thira as well.

IN RHODES

Many attractive souvenir and handicrafts shops are in the Old Town, particularly on Sokratous Street, and just outside the walls vendors sell decorative Rhodian pottery, local embroidery, sea sponges, and relatively inexpensive jewelry.

IN LESBOS

Lesbos is famous for its chestnuts, olive oil, and ouzo. Agiassos is known for its wood crafts.

Beaches

IN MYKONOS

Within walking distance of Mykonos Town are **Tourlos, Ayios Stefanos,** and **Ayios Ioannis. Psarou,** on the south coast, protected from wind by hills and surrounded by restaurants, offers a wide selection of water sports and is considered the finest beach.

IN SANTORINI

There is a red-sand beach below Akrotiri on the southwest shore. Long black-sand/volcanic beaches are found in Kamari and Perissa.

IN RHODES

Rhodes town and the more sheltered east coast have exquisite stretches of beach, but the west side can be choppy. **Elli** beach in town has fine sand. Much of the coast is developed, so you can reach the best beaches only through the hotels that occupy them. There also is a long nice stretch of beach between Haraki and Vlicha Bay.

IN LESBOS

Some of the most spectacular beaches are sandy coves in the southwest, including the stretch from Skala Eressou to Sigri. One of the island's best beaches is in **Vatera,** southwest of Agiassos on the southeast side of the island.

Helsinki, Finland

Helsinki is a city of the sea, built on peninsulas and islands along the Baltic shoreline. Streets curve around bays, bridges arch over the nearby islands, and ferries carry traffic to destinations farther offshore. The smell of the sea hovers over the city, while the huge ships that ply the Baltic constantly come and go from the city's harbors. Helsinki has grown dramatically since World War II; it now has a population of well over 500,000, accounting for more than ⅒th of Finland's population. The city covers a total of 1,140 square km (433 square mi), including some 315 islands, with at least 30% of the metropolitan area reserved for parks and other open spaces. Most of the city's sights, hotels, and restaurants, however, are on one peninsula—forming a compact hub of special interest to cruise passengers.

Currency

The unit of currency in Finland is the Finnish mark, divided into 100 penniä. There are bills of FIM 20, 50, 100, 500, and 1,000. Coins are 10 and 50 penniä and FIM 1, FIM 5, and FIM 10. At press time, the exchange rate was about FIM 5.6 to the U.S. dollar, FIM 3.7 to the Canadian dollar, and FIM 8.9 to the pound sterling. Finland is one of the "first wave" countries in the European Monetary Union project.

Telephones

The country code for Finland is 358. If calling from outside the country, drop the initial zero from the city code. Local calls can be made from public pay phones; have some FIM 1 and FIM 5 coins ready. Many pay phones only accept a phone card, the Sonera Kortti or HPY Kortti, available at post offices, R-kiosks, and some grocery stores. They come in increments of FIM 30, 50, 100, and 150. For directory assistance dial 118 or 10013 (English-speaking operator). You can dial North America directly from anywhere in Finland. To make a direct international phone call from Finland, dial 00, or 999, or 990, then the appropriate country code and phone number. For an **AT&T** long-distance operator, dial 9800–10010; **MCI,** 9800–10280; **Sprint,** 9800–10284.

Shore Excursions

The following is a good choice in Helsinki. It may not be offered by all cruise lines. Time and price are approximate.

Heart of Helsinki. Take in the major sights, including the Senate Square, the Esplanade, and other Helsinki landmarks on this quick tour of the town. *2½ hrs. Cost: $30.*

Coming Ashore

Ships calling at Helsinki dock harborside near Market Square. From here, you can easily spend the day exploring the city center.

The center of Helsinki is compact and best explored on foot. If you want to use public transportation, your best buy is the *Helsinki Kortti* (Helsinki Card), which gives unlimited travel on city public transportation, as well as free entry to many museums, a free sightseeing tour, and a variety of other discounts. A one-day pass costs FIM 135; you can buy it at some hotels and travel agencies, Stockmann's department store, and the Helsinki City Tourist Office. Street-cars can be very handy and route maps and schedules are posted at most downtown stops. Single tickets are sold on board for FIM 8 (one ride without transfers) or FIM 10 (one ride with transfers). Taxis are all marked TAKSI. The meters start at FIM 30, with the fare rising on a kilometer basis. A listing of all taxi companies appears in the white pages under *Taksi*—try to choose one that is located nearby, because they charge from point of dispatch. The main phone number for taxi service is 700–700.

Exploring Helsinki

Numbers in the margin correspond to points of interest on the Helsinki map.

① The **Kauppatori** (Market Square) is frequented by locals and tourists alike. Under bright orange tents you'll find stalls selling everything from colorful, freshly cut flowers to ripe fruit to vegetables trucked in from the hinterland to handicrafts made in small villages. Look at the fruit stalls—lots of strawberries, raspberries, blueberries, and, if you're lucky, cloudberries. Watching over it all is the unmissable, curvaceous Havis Amanda statue. *At South Harbor, harborside at Eteläranta and Pohjoisesplanadi. Market: open year-round, Mon.—Fri. 6:30–2, Sat. 6:30–3; June–Aug., also open Mon.–Fri. 3:30–8 and Sun. 9–4 (except on Midsummer).*

② On the Pohjoisesplanadi (North Esplanade) is the **Presidentinlinna** (President's Palace), built as a private home in 1818 and converted for use by the czars in 1843. It was the official residence of Finnish presidents from 1919 to 1993. It still houses the presidential offices and is the scene of official receptions. It is not open to the public except for pre-arranged tours on Wednesdays and Saturdays, 11 to 4. *Pohjoiseplanadi 1, tel. 09/601–966.*

In the district of **Katajanokka,** 19th-century brick warehouses have been converted into a complex of boutiques, arts-and-crafts studios, and restaurants. You'll find innovative designs at these shops, and the restaurants tend to offer lighter fare, which can make this a tempting area in which to stop for lunch.

Helsinki

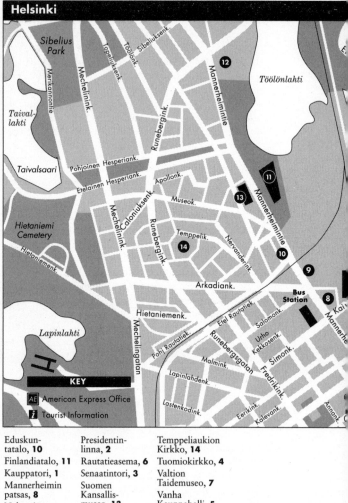

Sibelius Park

Töölönlahti

Taival-lahti

Taivalsaari

Hietaniemi Cemetery

Lapinlahti

KEY

AE American Express Office

i Tourist Information

Eduskunta-
tatalo, **10**

Finlandiatalo, **11**

Kauppatori, **1**

Mannerheimin
patsas, **8**

Nykytaiteen-
museo
(Kiasma), **9**

Presidentin-
linna, **2**

Rautatieasema, **6**

Senaatintori, **3**

Suomen
Kansallis-
museo, **13**

Suomen
Kansallis-
ooppera, **12**

Temppeliaukion
Kirkko, **14**

Tuomiokirkko, **4**

Valtion
Taidemuseo, **7**

Vanha
Kauppahalli, **5**

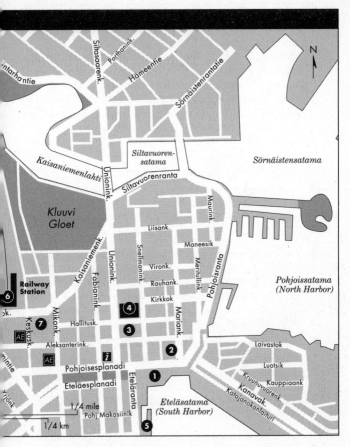

③
④ **Senaatintori** (Senate Square), the heart of neoclassical Helsinki, is dominated by the domed **Tuomiokirkko** (Lutheran cathedral). The square, designed by Carl Ludvig Engel, is a blend of Europe's ancient architectural styles. It has a dignified, stately air, enlivened in summer by sun worshipers who gather on the wide steps leading up to Tuomiokirkko and throughout the year by the bustle around the Kiseleff Bazaar on the square's south side. *Bordered by Aleksanterinkatu to south and Hallituskatu to north. Tuomiokirkko: Yliopistonkatu 7, tel. 09/6220–8610. Open June–Aug., weekdays 9–5, Sat. 9–7, Sun. 9–8; Sept.–May, weekdays 10–4, Sat. 10–7, Sun. 10–4.*

⑤ Worth taking a look at is the old brick **Vanha Kauppahalli** (Old Market Hall)—with its voluminous displays of meat, fish, and other gastronomic goodies. *Eteläranta, along the South Harbor. Open weekdays 8–8, Sat. 8– 3.*

⑥ The **Rautatieasema** (train station) and its square form the bustling commuting hub of the city. The station's huge red-granite figures are by Emil Wikström, but the solid building they adorn was designed by Eliel Saarinen, one of the founders of the early 20th-century National Romantic style. *Kaivokatu, tel. 09/7071.*

⑦ The **Valtion Taidemuseo** (Finnish National Gallery) houses both the Ateneum Museum of Finnish Art as well as major changing shows, an excellent bookshop, and a café. *Kaivokatu 2–4, tel. 09/173–361. Admission: FIM 15 (higher for special exhibits). Open Tues. and Fri. 9–6, Wed. and Thurs. 9–8, weekends 11–5.*

In front of the main post office, west of the railway station,
⑧ is the **Mannerheimin patsas** (statue of Marshal Mannerheim), gazing down Mannerheimintie, the major thoroughfare named in his honor. Perhaps no man in Finnish history is so revered as Baron Carl Gustaf Mannerheim, the military and political leader who guided Finland through much of the turbulent 20th century. When he died in Switzerland on January 28, 1951, his body was flown back to lie in state in the cathedral. For three days, young war widows, children, and soldiers filed past his bier.

Praised for the boldness of its curved steel shell, but also condemned for its encroachment on the territory of the Man

9 nerheim statue, the **Nykytaiteenmuseo (Kiasma)** (Museum of Contemporary Art) is one of the latest additions to Helsinki's varied architectural catalogue. It opened to the public in spring 1998 and displays a wealth of Finnish and foreign art from the 1960s to the present. Look for the "butterfly" windows and don't miss the view of Töölönlahti from the café. *Mannerheiminaukio 2, tel. 09/1733–6501. Admission: FIM 25. Open year-round Tues. 9–5, Wed.–Sun. 10–10.*

About 1 km (½ mi) along, past the colonnaded red-gran-
10 11 ite **Eduskuntatalo** (Parliament House), stands **Finlandiatalo** (Finlandia Hall; tel. 09/402–4246), one of the last creations of Alvar Aalto, and, farther up Mannerheimintie, the
12 **Suomen Kansallisooppera** (Finnish National Opera; tel. 09/ 4030– 2210), a striking example of Scandinavian architecture. If you can't make it to a concert there, take a guided tour (1 hour, FIM 350). Behind Finlandia Hall and the opera house lies the inland bay of Töölönlahti, and al-
13 most opposite the hall stands the **Suomen Kansallismuseo** (National Museum), another example of National Romantic exotica in which Eliel Saarinen played a part. The museum is closed for renovations until spring 2000, when it will reopen its archaeological, cultural, and ethnological collection to the public. *Mannerheimintie 34, tel. 09/405–0470.*

Tucked away in a labyrinth of streets to the west of the Opera
14 is the strikingly modern **Temppeliaukion Kirkko** (Temple Square Church). Carved out of solid rock and topped with a copper dome, this landmark is a center for church services and concerts. (From here it's only a short distance back to Mannerheimintie, where you can pick up any streetcar for the downtown area.) *Lutherinkatu 3, tel. 09/494–698. Open weekdays 10–8, Sat. 10–6, Sun. 12:00–1:45 and 3:15–5:45. Closed Tues. 12:45–2 PM and during weddings, concerts, and services.*

Shopping

Helsinki's prime shopping districts run along **Pohjoisesplanadi** (North Esplanade) and **Aleksanterinkatu** in the city center. Antiques shops cluster in the neighborhood behind Senate Square, called **Kruununhaka.** For one-stop shopping, hit **Stockmann's** (Aleksanterinkatu 52), a huge store filling an entire block, which was a target for Russian consumers before the fall of the Iron Curtain. The **Forum** (Mannerheimintie 20) is a modern, multistory shopping center with a wide variety of stores, including clothing, gifts, books, and toys. Some shops in the **Kiseleff Bazaar Hall** (Aleksanterinkatu 22–28) sell handicrafts, toys, and knitwear. **Kalevala Koru** (Unioninkatu 25) has jewelry based on ancient Finnish designs.

Along Pohjoisesplanadi and on the other side Eteläesplanadi, you will find Finland's design houses. **Hackman Arabia** (Pohjoisesplanadi 25) sells Finland's well-known Arabia china, Iittala glass, and other items. **Pentik** (Fabianinkatu 14) features tasteful pottery and household goods. **Aarikka** (Pohjoisesplanadi 27 and Eteläesplanadi 8) offers wooden jewelry, toys, and gifts. **Artek** (Eteläesplanadi 18) is known for its Alvar Aalto–designed home furnishings. **Marimekko** (Pohjoisesplanadi 2, Pohjoisesplanadi 31/Kämp Galleria, Mannerheimintie 20/Forum shopping center, and Eteläesplanadi 14) sells women's clothing, household items, and gifts made from its famous textiles.

Ibiza, Spain

Settled by the Carthaginians in the 5th century BC, Ibiza in the 20th century has been transformed by tourism. From a peasant economy, it became a wild, anything-goes gathering place for the international jet set and for the hippies of the 1960s—only to enter the 1990s with its principal resort, Sant Antoni, regarded as one of the most boorish, noisy, and brash on the Mediterranean. Recently, however, ecology-minded residents have begun to make headway in their push for development restrictions.

Currency

The unit of currency in Spain is the peseta (pta.). There are bills of 1,000, 2,000, 5,000, and 10,000 ptas. Coins are 1, 5, 25, 50, 100, 200, and 500 ptas. At press time, the exchange rate was about 156 ptas. to the U.S. dollar, 103 ptas. to the Canadian dollar, and 248 ptas. to the pound sterling.

Telephones

The country code for Spain is 34. Note that to call anywhere within the country—even locally—from any kind of phone, you need to dial the area code first; all provincial codes begin with a 9. Pay phones generally take the new, smaller 5- and 25-pta. coins; the minimum charge for short local calls is 25 ptas. Newer pay phones take only phone cards, which can be purchased at any tobacco shop in denominations of 1,000 or 2,000 ptas. International calls can be made from any pay phone marked TELÉFONO INTERNACIONAL. Use 50-pta. (or 100-pta. if the phone takes them) coins initially, then coins of any denomination to prolong your call. For lengthy international calls, go to the *telefónica,* a telephone office, where an operator assigns you a private booth and collects payment at the end of the call; this is the least expensive and by far the easiest way of phoning abroad. Dial 07 for international calls, wait for the tone to change, then dial the country code, area code, and the number. To reach an **AT&T** operator, dial 900/99–00–11; **MCI,** 900/99–00–14; **Sprint,** 900/99–00– 13.

Shore Excursions

The following is a good choice in Ibiza. It may not be offered by all lines. Time and price are approximate.

Sanctuaries of Ibiza. Explore Ibiza's Old World treasures from a 15th-century church to the fortified upper town. *4 hrs. Cost: $40.*

Coming Ashore

Ships calling at Ibiza dock in the harbor at Eivissa. You can explore the town on foot, but to see the outlying areas of the island you will need to take a taxi or bus.

Exploring Ibiza

Once a quiet fisherman's quarter, **Sa Penya,** part of the town of Eivissa, has been a tourist mecca since the 1960s; it is full of lively bars, restaurants, and flea markets.

Dalt Vila, the walled upper town, is entered through Las Tablas, its main gate. On each side of the gate stands a statue, Roman in origin; both are now headless.

Inside the upper town, a ramp continues to the right and opens onto a long, narrow plaza lined with cafés. A little way up Sa Carroza, a sign on the left points back toward the **Museu d'Art Comtemporani** (Museum of Contemporary Art), housed in the gateway's arch. *Ronda Pintor Narcis*

Putget s/n, tel. 971/30–27–23. Admission: 450 ptas. Open daily 10:30–1 and 6–8:30.

At the top of the hill Carrer Major lies the **cathedral,** which sits on the site of religious constructions from each of the cultures that have ruled Ibiza since the Phoenicians. Built in the 13th and 14th centuries and renovated in the 18th century, the cathedral has a Gothic tower and a baroque nave. The painted panels above a small vault adjoining the sacristy depict souls in purgatory being consumed by flames and tortured by devils while angels ascend to heaven. Go through the nave to the museum, which is well worth seeing. *Admission to museum: 300 ptas. Cathedral and museum open Sun.–Fri. 10–1 and 4–6:30, Sat. 10–1.*

The **Museu Dalt Vila** (Museum of Archaeology) in the upper town, across the plaza from the cathedral, has a collection of Phoenician, Punic, and Roman artifacts. *Plaça Catedral 3, tel. 971/301231. Admission: 400 ptas. Open Mon.–Sat. 10–1.*

A passageway leads between the cathedral and castle to the **Bastion of Sant Bernardo.** (There's a great view here of the wide bay.)

A Punic necropolis, with more than 3,000 tombs, has been excavated at **Puig des Molins.** Many of the artifacts can be seen at the Museu Puig d'Es Molins (Punic Archaeological Museum), adjacent to the site. *Via Romana 31, tel. 971/30–17–71. Admission: 400 ptas. Open Mon.–Sat. 10–1.*

Irish Coast and Cork

Hilly Cork is Ireland's second-largest city. The road to Cork City passes through the beautiful wooded glen of Glanmire and along the banks of the River Lee. In the center of Cork, the Lee divides in two, giving the city a profusion of picturesque quays and bridges. The name Cork derives from the Irish *corcaigh* (pronounced corky), meaning a marshy place. The city received its first charter in 1185 and grew rapidly in the 17th and 18th centuries with the expansion of its butter trade. It is now the major metropolis of the south, with a population of about 175,000. The main business and shopping center of Cork lies on the island created by the

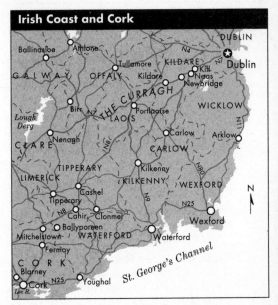

Irish Coast and Cork

two diverging channels of the Lee, and most places of interest are within walking distance of the center.

Currency

The unit of currency in Ireland is the pound, or punt (pronounced poont), written as IR£ to avoid confusion with the pound sterling. The currency is divided into 100 pence (written *p*). The North uses British currency; Irish punts are not accepted. Ireland is now a member of the European Monetary Fund (EMU) and since January 1, 1999, all prices have been quoted in pounds and euros. January 2002 is to see the introduction of the euro coins and notes and the gradual withdrawal of the local currency. The rate of exchange at press time was 74 pence to the U.S. dollar, 50 pence to the Canadian dollar, IR£1.18 to the British pound sterling.

Telephones

The country code for the Republic of Ireland is 353 and for Northern Ireland it's 44. When dialing from outside the country, drop the initial zero from the regional area code. There are pay phones in all post offices and most hotels and bars, as well as in street booths. Telephone cards are available at all post offices and most newsagents. Booths accepting cards are as common as coin booths. For calls to the United States and Canada, dial 001 followed by the area code; for calls to the United Kingdom, dial 0044 and then the area code (dropping the beginning zero). To reach an **AT&T** long-distance operator, dial 1–800/550–000; **MCI,** 1–800/551–001; **Sprint,** 1–800/552– 001.

Shore Excursions

The following are good choices in Cork. They may not be offered by all cruise lines. Times and prices are approximate.

Cork City and Blarney Tour. This is a good choice for passengers who want to visit Blarney. Upon reaching the village, you'll walk up the castle's steps to reach the famous Blarney Stone. The tour also includes highlights of Cork city. *4 hrs. Cost: $58.*

Cobh Island and Whiskey Distillery. Drive through the seaside resort town of Cobh, the countryside, and Cork to reach Midleton for a visit to the Jameson Irish Whiskey Heritage Center. *4 hrs. Cost: $43.*

Coming Ashore

Ships dock at the harbor of Cobh, which is around 24 km (15 mi) from the main district of Cork.

Once in the compact main district of Cork, the best way to see the city and soak in its full flavor is on foot.

Exploring Cork

Patrick Street is the focal point of Cork and its major shopping district (*see below*). In the hilly area to the north is the famous 120-ft **Shandon Steeple,** the bell tower of St. Anne's Church. It is shaped like a pepper pot and houses the bells immortalized in the song *The Bells of Shandon.* Visitors can climb the tower; read the inscriptions on the bells; and, on request, have them rung over Cork. *Church St. Admission: IR£1, with bell tower IR£1.50. Open May–Oct., Mon.–Sat. 9:30–5; Nov.–Apr., Mon.–Sat. 10–3:30.*

Cobh is an attractive hilly town dominated by its 19th-century **cathedral.** It was the first and last European port of call for transatlantic liners, one of which was the ill-fated

Titanic. Cobh has other associations with shipwrecks: It was from here that destroyers were sent out to search for survivors of the *Lusitania,* which was sunk by a German submarine off this coast on May 7, 1915. Cobh's maritime past and its links with emigration are documented in a IR£2 million heritage center known as the **Queenstown Project,** which opened in the town's old railway station in 1993. A suburban rail service leaves from Cork's Kent Station (021/506–766 for schedule) with stops in Cobh and Fota Island. *Queenstown Project: tel. 021/481-3591. Admission: IR£3.50. Open Feb.–Nov., daily 10– 6.*

Most visitors to Cork want to kiss the famous **Blarney Stone** in the hope of acquiring the "gift of the gab." Blarney itself, 8 km (5 mi) from Cork City, should not, however, be taken too seriously as an excursion. All that is left of Blarney Castle is its ruined central keep containing the celebrated stone. The stone is set in the battlements, and to kiss it, you must lie on the walk within the walls and lean your head back. Nobody knows how the tradition originated, but Elizabeth I is credited with giving the word *blarney* to the language when, commenting on the unfulfilled promises of Cormac MacCarthy, Lord Blarney of the time, she remarked, "This is all Blarney; what he says, he never means." *Blarney Castle, tel. 021/438-5252. Admission: IR£3. Open Mon.–Sat. 9 to sundown, Sun. 9–5:30.*

Shopping
Patrick Street is the main shopping area of Cork, and there you will find the city's two major department stores, **Roches** and **Brown Thomas.** The liveliest place in town to shop is just off Patrick Street, to the west, near the city-center parking lot, in the pedestrian-only **Paul Street** area. **Mendows & Byrne** of Academy Street stocks the best in modern Irish design, including tableware, ceramics, knitwear, handwoven tweeds, and high fashion.

At the top of Paul Street is the **Crawford Art Gallery,** which has an excellent collection of 18th- and 19th-century views of Cork and mounts adventurous exhibitions by modern artists. *Emmet Pl., tel. 021/427–3377. Admission free. Open weekdays 10–5, Sat. 9–1.*

Istanbul, Turkey

Turkey is one place to which the phrase "East meets West" really applies, both literally and figuratively. It is in Turkey's largest city, Istanbul, that the continents of Europe and Asia meet, separated only by the Bosporus, which flows 29 km (18 mi) from the Black Sea to the Sea of Marmara. For 16 centuries Istanbul, originally known as Byzantium, played a major part in world politics: first as the capital of the Eastern Roman Empire, when it was known as Constantinople, then as capital of the Ottoman Empire, the most powerful Islamic empire in the world, when it was renamed Istanbul.

Although most of Turkey's landmass is in Asia, Turkey has faced West politically since 1923, when Mustapha Kemal, better known as Atatürk, founded the modern republic. He transformed the remnants of the shattered Ottoman Empire into a secular state with a Western outlook. So thorough was this changeover—culturally, politically, and economically—that in 1987, 49 years after Atatürk's death, Turkey applied to the European Community (EC) for full membership. Currently, though, the country is experiencing an identity crisis that could lead to social and political upheavals, particularly over the role of Islam in public life and the recognition of minority rights.

Istanbul is noisy, chaotic, and exciting. Spires and domes of mosques and medieval palaces dominate the skyline. At dawn, when the muezzin's call to prayer rebounds from ancient minarets, many people are making their way home from the nightclubs and bars, while others are kneeling on their prayer rugs, facing Mecca. Day and night, Istanbul has a schizophrenic air to it. Women in jeans, business suits, or elegant designer outfits pass women wearing the long skirts and head coverings that villagers have worn for generations. Donkey-drawn carts vie with old Chevrolets and Pontiacs or shiny Toyotas and BMWs for dominance of the loud, narrow streets, and the world's most fascinating Oriental bazaar competes with Western boutiques for your time and attention.

Currency

The monetary unit is the Turkish lira (TL), which comes in bank notes of 50,000, 100,000, 250,000, 500,000,

1,000,000 and 5,000,000. Coins come in denominations of 5,000, 10,000, 25,000, 50,000, and 100,000. At press time, the exchange rate was 428,115 TL to the U.S. dollar, 282,817 TL to the Canadian dollar, and 681,048 TL to the pound sterling. These rates are subject to wide fluctuation, so check close to your departure date. Be certain to retain your original exchange slips when you convert money into Turkish lira—you will need them to reconvert the money. Because the value of Turkish currency can sometimes fall significantly over a very short period, it is advisable to change enough money for only a few days at a time.

Telephones

The country code for Turkey is 90. When dialing a number from outside the country, drop the initial zero from the local area code. All telephone numbers in Turkey have seven local digits plus three-digit city codes. Intercity calls are preceded by 0. Pay phones are blue, push-button models. Many take *jetons* (tokens), although increasingly, particularly in large cities, they are being replaced with phones that take phone cards or, to a lesser extent, credit cards. Tokens can be purchased for 7¢ at post offices and, for a couple of cents more, at street booths. Telephone cards are available at post offices. Multilingual directions are posted in phone booths. For all international calls dial 00, then dial the country code, area or city code, and the number. You can reach an international operator by dialing 132. To reach an **AT&T** long-distance operator, dial 00800-12277; **MCI,** 00800- 1177; **Sprint,** 00800–14477.

Shore Excursion

The following is a good choice in Istanbul. It may not be offered by all lines. Times and prices are approximate.

Bazaar Sights. Visit the major city sights, including the Hippodrome, Blue Mosque, and Hagia Sophia, and shop at the Grand Bazaar, which should be a must on anyone's list of things to do. 4½ hrs. Cost: $40.

Coming Ashore

Ships dock on the Bosporus in Istanbul on the European side of the city. Across the Galata Bridge lie the city's main attractions.

The best way to get around all the magnificent monuments in Sultanahmet in Old Istanbul is to walk; they're all within easy distance of one another. To get to other areas, you can take Dolmuş vehicles and metered taxis, which are plentiful, inexpensive, and more comfortable than city buses. A tram system runs from Topkapı, via Sultanahmet, to Sirkeci. Trams run the length of İstiklâl Caddesi from Taksim to Tünel and cost about 25¢.

Exploring Istanbul

Numbers in the margin correspond to points of interest on the Istanbul map.

OLD ISTANBUL (SULTANAHMET)

1 The number one attraction in Istanbul is **Topkapı Saray** (Topkapı Palace), on Seraglio Point in Old Istanbul, known as Sultanahmet. The palace, which dates from the 15th century, was the residence of a number of sultans and their harems until the mid-19th century. To avoid the crowds, try to get there by 9:30 AM, when the gates open. If you're arriving by taxi, tell the driver you want the Topkapı Saray in Sultanahmet, or you could end up at the remains of the former Topkapı bus terminal on the outskirts of town.

Sultan Mehmet II built the first palace in the 1450s, shortly after the Ottoman conquest of Constantinople. Over the centuries, sultan after sultan added ever more elaborate architectural fantasies, until the palace eventually ended up with more than four courtyards and some 5,000 residents, many of them concubines and eunuchs. Topkapı was the residence and center of bloodshed and drama for the Ottoman rulers until the 1850s, when Sultan Abdül Mecit moved with his harem to the European-style Dolmabahçe Palace, farther up the Bosporus coast.

2 In Topkapı's outer courtyard are the **Aya İrini** (Church of St. Irene), open only during festival days for concerts, and **3** the **Merasim Avlusu** (Court of the Janissaries), originally for members of the sultan's elite guard.

Adjacent to the ticket office is the **Bab-i-Selam** (Gate of Salutation), built in 1524 by Suleyman the Magnificent, who was the only person allowed to pass through it. In the towers on either side, prisoners were kept until they were executed beside the fountain outside the gate in the first courtyard.

In the second courtyard, amid the rose gardens, is the **Divan-i-Humayun,** the assembly room of the council of state, once presided over by the grand vizier (prime minister). The sultan would sit behind a latticed window, hidden by a curtain so no one would know when he was listening, although occasionally he would pull the curtain aside to comment.

One of the most popular tours in Topkapı is the **Harem,** a maze of nearly 400 halls, terraces, rooms, wings, and apartments grouped around the sultan's private quarters on the west side of the second courtyard. Forty rooms are restored and open to the public. Next to the entrance are the quarters of the eunuchs and about 200 of the lesser concubines, who were lodged in tiny cubicles, as cramped and uncomfortable as the main rooms of the harem are large and opulent. Tours begin every half hour; because of the crowds during the height of the tourist season, buy a ticket for the harem tour soon after entering the palace.

In the third courtyard is the **Hazine Dairesi** (Treasury), four rooms filled with jewels, including two uncut emeralds, each weighing 3½ kilograms (7.7 pounds), that once hung from the ceiling. Here, too, you will be dazzled by the emerald dagger used in the movie *Topkapı* and the 84-carat "Spoonmaker" diamond, which, according to legend, was found by a pauper and traded for three wooden spoons.

In the fourth and last courtyard of the Topkapı Palace are small, elegant summerhouses, mosques, fountains, and reflecting pools scattered amid the gardens on different levels. Here you will find the **Rivan Kiosk,** built by Murat IV in 1636 to commemorate the successful Rivan campaign. In another kiosk in the gardens, called the **İftariye** (Golden Cage), the closest relatives of the reigning sultan lived in strict confinement under what amounted to house arrest. The custom began during the 1800s after the old custom of murdering all possible rivals to the throne had been abandoned. The confinement of the heirs apparently helped keep the peace, but it deprived them of any chance to prepare themselves for the formidable task of ruling a great

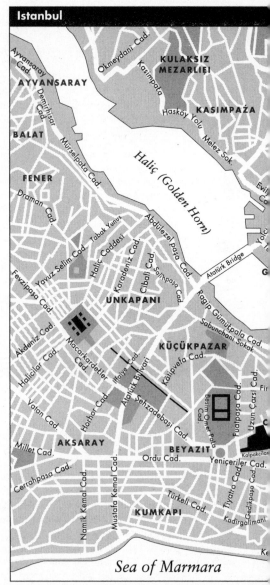

Istanbul

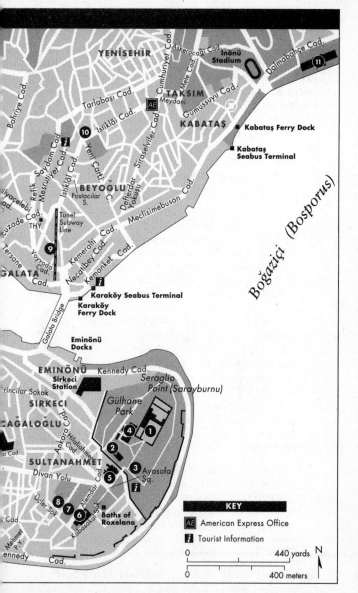

YENİSEHİR

Askerocağı Cad.

Cumhuriyet Cad.

Atele Cad.

İnönü Stadium

Dolmabahçe Cad.

Bahriye Cad.

Tarlabaşı Cad.

TAKSİM

İstiklâl Cad.

Taksim Meydani

Gümüşsuyu Cad.

AE

KABATAŞ

■ Kabataş Ferry Dock

Saydam Cad.

Meşrutiyet Cad.

Yeni Çarşı

10

i

■ Kabataş Seabus Terminal

Refik

İstiklâl Cad.

BEYOĞLU

Postacılar S.

Defterdar Yoksuu

Meclisimebusan Cad.

Sıraselviler Cad.

cuzade Cad.

ilyaçelebi ad.

THY

Tünel Subway Line

Kemeralti Cad.

Meclisimebusan Cad.

9

Necatibey Cad.

Voyvoda Cad.

GALATA Cad.

Kemanket Cad.

i

Boğaziçi (Bosporus)

Tersane Cad.

■ Karaköy Seabus Terminal

Galata Bridge

Karaköy Ferry Dock

Eminönü Docks

EMİNÖNÜ

Kennedy Cad.

Seraglio Point (Sarayburnu)

Sirkeci Station

rincilar Sokak

SİRKECİ

Gülhane Park

ÇAĞALOĞLU

ar Cad.

Ankara Cad.

Hilâliahmer Cad.

4
1

SULTANAHMET

2

Divan Yolu

3 Ayasofya Sq.

5

i

Üçler Sok.

8
7
6

Cad.

Alemdar Cad.

Kabasakal Sok.

Baths of Roxelana

Mehmet P. sl.

ennedy

Cad.

KEY	
AE	American Express Office
i	Tourist Information

0 — 440 yards

0 — 400 meters

N

empire. *Topkapı Palace, tel. 212/512–0480. Admission: $3.75, harem $1.50. Open Wed.–Mon. 9:30–4:30.*

To the left as you enter the outer courtyard of Topkapı Palace, a lane slopes downhill to three museums grouped together: the **Arkeoloji Müzesi** (Archaeological Museum), which houses a fine collection of Greek and Roman antiquities, including finds from Ephesus and Troy; the **Eski Şark Eserleri Müzesi** (Museum of the Ancient Orient), with Sumerian, Babylonian, and Hittite treasures; and the **Çinili Köşkü** (Tiled Pavilion), which houses ceramics from the early Seljuk and Osmanli empires. *Gülhane Park, tel. 212/520–7740. Admission: $2 includes all 3 museums. Open Tues.–Sun. 9:30–4:30; ticket office 9:30–4.*

❺ Just outside the walls of Topkapı Palace is **Aya Sofya** (Hagia Sophia, Church of the Divine Wisdom), one of the world's greatest examples of Byzantine architecture. Built in AD 532 under the supervision of Emperor Justinian, it took 10,000 men six years to complete. Aya Sofya is made of ivory from Asia, marble from Egypt, and columns from the ruins of Ephesus. The dome was the world's largest until the dome at St. Peter's Basilica was built in Rome 1,000 years later. Aya Sofya was the cathedral of Constantinople for 900 years, surviving earthquakes and looting Crusaders until 1453, when it was converted into a mosque by Mehmet the Conqueror. Minarets were added by succeeding sultans. Aya Sofya originally had many mosaics depicting Christian scenes, which were plastered over by Suleyman I, who felt they were inappropriate for a mosque. In 1935, Atatürk converted Aya Sofya into a museum. Shortly after that, American archaeologists discovered the mosaics, which were restored and are now on display.

According to legend, the **Sacred Column,** in the north aisle, "weeps water" that can work miracles. It's so popular that, over the centuries, believers have worn a hole through the marble and brass column with their constant caresses. You can stick your finger in it and make a wish. *Aya Sofya Meyd, Sultanahmet, tel. 212/522–1750. Admission: $4.50. Open Tues.–Sun. 9:30–4:30.*

❻ Across from Aya Sofya is the **Sultan Ahmet Cami** (Blue Mosque), with its shimmering blue tiles, 260 stained-glass windows, and six minarets, as grand and beautiful a monument to Islam as Aya Sofya was to Christianity. Mehmet Ağa, also known as Sedefkar (Worker of Mother of Pearl) built the mosque during the reign of Sultan Ahmet I in eight years, beginning in 1609, nearly 1,100 years after the completion of Aya Sofya. His goal was to surpass Justinian's masterpiece, and many believe he succeeded.

Press through the throngs and enter the mosque at the side entrance that faces Aya Sofya. Remove your shoes and leave them at the entrance. Immodest clothing is not allowed, but an attendant will lend you a robe if he feels you are not dressed appropriately. *Sultanahmet Meyd. Admission free. Open daily 9–5.*

The **Hünkar Kasri** (Carpet and Kilim museums) are in the mosque's stone-vaulted cellars and upstairs at the end of a stone ramp, where the sultans rested before and after their prayers. *Tel. 212/518–1330. Admission: $1.50. Call for hrs.*

7 The **Hippodrome** is a long park directly in front of the Blue Mosque. As a Roman stadium with 100,000 seats, it was once the focal point for city life, including chariot races, circuses, and public executions. Disputes between fans of rival chariot teams often degenerated into violence. In 531, 30,000 people died in the Hippodrome in what came to be known as the Nike riots. The monuments that can be seen today—the **Dikilitaş** (Egyptian Obelisk), the **Örme Sütun** (Column of Constantinos), and the **Yılanlı Sütun** (Serpentine Column) taken from the Temple of Apollo at Delphi in Greece—formed part of the central barrier around which the chariots raced. *Sultanahmet Meyd. Admission free. Open all hrs.*

On the western side of the Hippodrome is **Ibrahim Paşa Palace,** the grandiose residence of the son-in-law and grand vizier of Suleyman the Magnificent. Ibrahim Paşa was executed when he became too powerful for Suleyman's liking. **8** The palace now houses the **Türk Ve Islâm Eserleri Müzesi** (Museum of Turkish and Islamic Arts), which gives superb insight into the lifestyles of Turks of every level of society, from the 8th century to the present. *Atmeydanı 46, Sultanahmet, tel. 212/518–1385 or 212/518–1805. Admission: $2. Open Tues.–Sun. 9–4.*

NEW TOWN

New Town is the area on the northern shore of the Golden Horn, the waterway that cuts through Istanbul and divides Europe from Asia. The area's most prominent landmark is the **Galata Kulesi** (Galata Tower), built by the Genoese in 1349 as part of their fortifications. In this century, it served as a fire lookout until 1960. Today it houses a restaurant and nightclub and a viewing tower. *Büyük Hendek Cad., Galata, tel. 212/245–1160. Admission: $1. Open daily 9–8.*

⑩ North of the tower is the **Çiçek Pasajı** (Flower Arcade), off I stiklâl Caddesi, a lively blend of tiny restaurants, bars, and street musicians. Strolling farther on I stiklâl Caddesi is an experience in itself. The busy pedestrian road is lined with shops, restaurants, banks, and cafés in turn-of-the-century buildings. The restored original 19th-century tram still carries people from Tünel to Taksim Square. On the side streets you'll find Greek and Armenian churches, bars, and other establishments; in the narrow, poorer residential alleys, you'll see laundry hanging between the old buildings as you dodge through the children at play.

⑪ The **Dolmabahçe Sarayı** (Dolmabahçe Palace) was built in 1853 and, until the declaration of the modern republic in 1923, was the residence of the last sultans of the Ottoman Empire. It was also the residence of Atatürk, who died here in 1938. The palace, floodlit at night, is an extraordinary mixture of Hindu, Turkish, and European styles of architecture and interior design. Queen Victoria's contribution to the lavishness was a chandelier weighing 4½ tons. Guided tours of the palace take about 80 minutes. *Dolmabahçe Cad., tel. 212/258–5544. Admission: $10 for long tour, $5.50 for short tour. Open Apr.–Oct., Tues., Wed., and Fri.–Sun. 9–4; Nov.–Mar., Tues., Wed., and Fri.–Sun. 9–3.*

Shopping

The **Kapali Çarşişi** (Grand Bazaar) is what it sounds like: a smattering of all things Turkish—carpets, brass, copper, jewelry, textiles, and leather goods. A shopper's paradise, it lies about ½ km (¼ mi) northwest of the Hippodrome (*see* Exploring, *above*), a 15-minute walk or five-minute taxi ride. Also called the Covered Bazaar, this maze of 65 winding, covered streets hides 4,000 shops, tiny cafés, and restaurants. Originally built by Mehmet the Conqueror in the 1450s, it was ravaged by two modern-day fires, one in 1954 that virtually destroyed it, and a smaller one in 1974. In both cases, the bazaar was quickly rebuilt. It's filled with thousands of curios, including carpets, fabrics, clothing, brass ware, furniture, icons, and gold jewelry. *Yeniçeriler Cad. and Fuatpaşa Cad. Admission free. Open Apr.–Oct., Mon.–Sat. 8:30–7; Nov.–Mar., Mon.–Sat. 8:30–6:30.*

Tünel Square, a quick, short metro ride up from Karaköy, is a quaint group of stores with old prints, books, and artifacts.

BARGAINING

The best part of shopping in Turkey is visiting the *bedestans* (bazaars), all brimming with copper and brass items, hand-painted ceramics, alabaster and onyx goods, fabrics, richly colored carpets, and relics and icons trickling in from the former Soviet Union. The key word for shopping in the bazaars is "bargain." You must be willing to bargain, and bargain hard. It's great fun once you get the hang of it. As a rule of thumb, offer 50% less after you're given the initial price and be prepared to go up by about 25% to 30% of the first asking price. It's both bad manners and bad business to underbid grossly or to start bargaining if you're not serious about buying. Part of the fun of roaming through the bazaars is having a free glass of *çay* (tea), which vendors will offer you whether you're a serious shopper or just browsing. Outside the bazaars prices are usually fixed. Beware of antiques: chances are you will end up with an expensive fake, but even if you do find the genuine article, it's illegal to export antiques of any type.

Limassol, Cyprus

The Mediterranean island of Cyprus was once a center for the cult of Aphrodite, the Greek goddess who is said to have risen naked and perfect from the sea near what is now the beach resort of Paphos. Wooded and mountainous, with a 751-km-long (466-mi-long) coastline, Cyprus lies just off the southern coast of Turkey.

Cyprus's strategic position in the eastern Mediterranean has made it subject to regular invasions by powerful armies. Greeks, Phoenicians, Assyrians, Egyptians, Persians, Romans, Byzantines, Venetians, and British—all have ruled here and left their cultural mark.

Following independence from the British in 1960, the island became the focus of Greek-Turkish contention. Currently, some 80% of the population is Greek and 12.3% Turkish. Since 1974 Cyprus has been divided by a thin buffer zone—occupied by United Nations (UN) forces—between the Turkish Cypriot north and the Greek Cypriot south. The zone cuts right through the capital city of Nicosia. Talks aimed at uniting the communities into one bizonal federal state have been going on for years.

Currency

The monetary unit in the Republic of Cyprus is the Cyprus pound (C£), which is divided into 100 cents. There are notes of C£20, C£10, C£5, and C£1 and coins of 50, 20, 10, 5, 2, and 1 Cyprus cents. At press time the rate of exchange was C£0.54 to the U.S. dollar, C£0.36 to the Canadian dollar, and C£0.86 to the pound sterling.

Telephones

The country code for Cyprus is 357. Pay phones take either coins or Telecards; Telecards can be purchased at post offices, banks, souvenir shops, and kiosks. To reach an **AT&T** long-distance operator, dial 080–90010; **MCI**, 080– 90000; **Sprint,** 080–90001. Public phones may require a deposit of a coin or use of a phone card when you call these services.

Shore Excursions

The following are good choices in Limassol. They may not be offered by all cruise lines. Times and prices are approximate.

Paphos Castle. A drive along the southwest of Cyprus leads to vineyards, coastal scenery, and the Paphos castle for a tour. *4½ hrs. Cost: $35.*

Kolossi Castle and Curium Ruins. Visit a Crusader castle and Cyprus's Greek and Roman ruins after a drive through the countryside. *3 hrs. Cost: $36.*

Village Tour. Journey through the country to explore three quaint villages—Omodos, Platres, and Lania. *3½ hrs. Cost: $36.*

In case you want to see the world.

At American Express, we're here to make your journey a smooth one. So we have over 1,700 travel service locations in over 130 countries ready to help. What else would you expect from the world's largest travel agency?

do more AMERICAN EXPRESS

Travel

In case you want to be welcomed there.

We're here to see that you're always welcomed at establishments everywhere. That's why millions of people carry the American Express® Card – for peace of mind, confidence, and security, around the world or just around the corner.

do more

**To apply, call 1 800 THE-CARD
or visit www.americanexpress.com**

Cards

In case you're running low.

We're here to help with more than 190,000 Express Cash locations around the world. In order to enroll, just call American Express at 1 800 CASH-NOW before you start your vacation.

do more

Express Cash

And in case you'd rather be safe than sorry.

We're here with American Express® Travelers Cheques. They're the safe way to carry money on your vacation, because if they're ever lost or stolen you can get a refund, practically anywhere or anytime. To find the nearest place to buy Travelers Cheques, call 1 800 495-1153. Another way we help you do more.

do more

Travelers Cheques

Coming Ashore

Ships dock at Limassol, a commercial port and wine-making center on the south coast. The city is a bustling, cosmopolitan town. Luxury hotels, apartments, and guest houses stretch along 12 km (7 mi) of seafront. The nightlife is lively. In central Limassol, the elegant modern shops of Makarios Avenue contrast with those of the old part of town, where you'll discover local handicrafts.

Shared taxis accommodate four to seven passengers and are a cheap, fast, and comfortable way of traveling. Seats must be booked by phone, and passengers may embark/disembark anywhere within the town boundaries. The taxis run every half hour Monday–Saturday 5:45 AM–6:30 PM. Sunday service is less frequent and rides must be booked one day ahead. Drivers are bound by law to use and display a meter. In-town journeys range from C£1.65 to about C£4.25.

Exploring Limassol

Near the old port is **Limassol Fort,** a 14th-century castle built on the site of an earlier Byzantine fortification. According to tradition, Richard the Lionhearted married Berengaria of Navarre here in 1191. *Near old port, tel. 05/330132. Open weekdays 7:30–5, Sat. 9–5, Sun. 10–1.*

The **Cyprus Medieval Museum** at Limassol Fort displays a variety of medieval armor and relics. *Near old port, tel. 05/ 330132. Admission: C£1. Open weekdays 7:30–5, Sat. 9– 5, Sun. 10–1.*

For a glimpse of Cypriot folklore, visit the **Folk Art Museum** on St. Andrew's Street. The collection includes national costumes and fine examples of weaving and other crafts. *Agiou Andreou 253, tel. 05/362303. Admission: 50¢. Open Oct.– May, Mon.–Wed., Fri. 8:30–1:30 and 3:30–5:30, Thurs. 8:30–1:30; June–Sept., Mon.–Wed., Fri. 8:30–1:30 and 4– 6:30, Thurs. 8:30–1:30.*

The **Troodos Mountains,** north of Limassol, are popular in summer for their shady cedar and pine forests. Small, painted churches in the Troodos and Pitsilia foothills are rich examples of a rare indigenous art form. Asinou Church and St. Nicholas of the Roof, south of Kakopetria, are especially noteworthy. Be sure to visit the Kykko Monastery, whose prized icon of the Virgin is reputed to have been painted by St. Luke.

Kourion (Curium), west of Limassol, has numerous Greek and Roman ruins. There is an **amphitheater**, where actors occasionally present classical and Shakespearean drama. Next to the theater is the Villa of Eustolios, a summerhouse that belonged to a wealthy Christian. A nearby Roman stadium has been partially rebuilt. Three kilometers (2 miles) farther along the main Paphos road is the Sanctuary of Apollo Hylates (Apollo of the Woodlands), an impressive archaeological site. *Main Paphos Rd. Admission C£1. Open June–Sept., daily 7:30–7:30; Oct.–May, daily 8–4:45.*

Other places to visit include **Kolossi Castle,** a Crusader fortress of the Knights of St. John—constructed during the 13th century and rebuilt during the 15th—and the fishing harbor of **Latchi** on the west coast, 48 km (30 mi) north of Paphos. Near Latchi are the **Baths of Aphrodite,** where the goddess of love is said to have seduced swains. The wild and undeveloped Akamas Peninsula is perfect for a hike.

Lisbon, Portugal

Portugal's capital presents unending treats for the eye. Its wide boulevards are bordered by black-and-white mosaic sidewalks made of tiny cobblestones called *calçada.* Modern, pastel-color apartment blocks vie for attention with Art Nouveau houses faced with decorative tiles. Winding, hilly streets provide scores of *miradouros,* natural vantage points that offer spectacular views of the river and the city. The city center stretches north from the spacious Praça do Comércio, one of the largest riverside squares in Europe, to the Rossío, a smaller square lined with shops and sidewalk cafés. This district, known as the Baixa (Lower Town), is one of the earliest examples of town planning on a large scale. The Alfama, the old Moorish quarter, lies just east of the Baixa, and the Bairro Alto—an 18th-century quarter of restaurants, bars, and clubs—just to the west. About 5 km (3 mi) northeast of the center, the riverside Expo site has the Lisbon Oceanarium—Europe's largest aquarium—as its major attraction.

Lisbon is a hilly city, and places that appear to be close to one another on a map are sometimes on different levels.

Yet the effort is worthwhile—judicious use of trams, the funicular railway, and the majestic city-center vertical lift (also called the *elevador*) make walking tours enjoyable even on the hottest summer day.

Currency

The unit of currency in Portugal is the escudo, which can be divided into 100 centavos. Escudos come in bills of 500$00, 1,000$00, 2,000$00, 5,000$00, and 10,000$00. (In Portugal the dollar sign stands between the escudo and the centavo.) Owing to the complications of dealing with millions of escudos, 1,000$00 is always called a *conto,* so 10,000$00 is referred to as 10 contos. Coins come in denominations of 1$00, 2$50, 5$00, 10$00, 20$00, 50$00, 100$00, and 200$00. At press time the exchange rate was about 189$00 to the U.S. dollar, 125$00 to the Canadian dollar, and 300$00 to the pound sterling.

Telephones

The country code for Portugal is 351. When dialing from outside the country, drop the initial zero from the regional area code. Portugal has been updating its phone system since 1987, causing phone numbers to change throughout the country. The changes made up to press time have been incorporated, but a small percentage of the country's phone numbers are still slated to change. If you're trying to reach a number that has changed, your best bet is to get directory assistance through an international operator. Public telephones are easily found; older models accept coins, and PORTUGAL TELECOM card phones will accept plastic phone cards of 50 or 120 units (available at post and phone offices and most tobacconists and newsagents). International and collect calls can be made from most public telephones as well as from main post offices, which almost always have a supply of phone cabins—you'll be assigned a booth and payment will be collected at the end of the call. Access numbers to reach American long-distance operators are: for **AT&T,** 050–171288; **MCI,** 050–171234; **Sprint,** 050–171877.

Shore Excursions

The following are good choices in Lisbon. They may not be offered by all cruise lines. Times and prices are approximate.

Lisbon Highlights. If you'd rather not do a lot of walking, sign up for this tour of Lisbon's many moods. *3½ hrs. Cost: $41.*

Walking the City. Tour the Alfama district on foot, visiting St. George's Castle, Santa Justa elevator, Rossio Square, and Black Horse Square. *3 hrs. Cost: $43.*

Coming Ashore

Ships dock at the Fluvial terminal, adjacent to Praça do Comércio. Lisbon is a hilly city, and the sidewalks are paved with cobblestones, so walking can be tiring, even when you're wearing comfortable shoes.

Luckily, Lisbon's tram service is one of the best in Europe and buses go all over the city. A Tourist Pass for unlimited rides on the tram, bus, metro, or the Santa Justa elevator and Gloria and Bica funiculars costs 430$00 for one day's travel. Cabs can be easily recognized by a lighted sign on green roofs. There are taxi stands in the main squares, and you can usually catch one cruising by, though this can be difficult late at night. Taxis are metered and take up to four passengers at no extra charge. Rates start at 300$00, with an extra charge for luggage.

Exploring Lisbon

Numbers in the margin correspond to points of interest on the Lisbon map.

The Moors, who imposed their rule on most of the southern Iberian Peninsula during the 8th century, left their mark on Lisbon in many ways. The most visible examples are undoubtedly the imposing **Castelo de São Jorge** (St. George's Castle), set on one of the city's highest hills, and the Alfama, a district of narrow, twisting streets that wind their way up toward the castle. The best way to tour this area of Lisbon is to take a taxi to the castle and walk down.

Although the Castelo de São Jorge is Moorish in construction, it stands on the site of a fortification used by the Visigoths in the 5th century. The castle walls enclose the ruins of a Muslim palace that was the residence of the kings of Portugal until the 16th century; there is also a small village with a surviving church, a few simple houses, and souvenir shops. Inside the main gate are terraces offering

Lisbon

KEY

AE American Express Office

i Tourist Information

Tagus River

panoramic views of Lisbon; be wary of slippery footing. *Rua da Costa do Castelo, no phone. Admission free. Open Apr.–Sept., daily 9–9; Oct.–Mar., daily 9–7.*

2 **Alfama,** a warren of streets below St. George's Castle, is a jumble of whitewashed houses, with their flower-laden balconies and red-tile roofs resting on a foundation of dense bedrock. It's a notorious place for getting lost, but fortunately the area is relatively compact.

3 The **Museu de Artes Decorativas** (Museum of Decorative Arts), housed in an 18th-century mansion, puts on temporary exhibitions of its art and furniture; it also conducts workshops that teach threatened handicrafts—bookbinding, carving, and cabinetmaking. *Largo das Portas do Sol 2, tel. 01/886–2183. Admission: 800$00. Open Tues.–Sun. 10–5.*

4 The **Sé** (cathedral), founded in 1150 to commemorate the defeat of the Moors three years earlier, has an austere Romanesque interior enlivened by a splendid 13th-century cloister. The treasure-filled sacristy contains the relics of the martyr St. Vincent, carried—according to legend—from the Algarve to Lisbon in a ship piloted by ravens. *Largo da Sé, tel. 01/886–6752. Admission to cathedral free; cloister 100$00, sacristy 300$00. Cathedral open daily 9–noon and 2–6; sacristy open daily 10–1 and 2–6.*

5 **Rossío,** Lisbon's main square since the Middle Ages, is officially known as Praça Dom Pedro IV (whom the central statue commemorates). Renowned sidewalk cafés line the east and west sides of the square. *Praça Dom Pedro IV.*

6 In the **Parque Eduardo VII,** rare flowers, trees, and shrubs thrive in the *estufa fria* (cold greenhouse) and the *estufa quente* (hot greenhouse). *Parque Eduardo VII, tel. 01/388–2278. Admission to greenhouses: 95$00. Open Apr.–Sept., daily 9–6; Oct.–Mar., daily 9–5.*

7 The renowned **Fundação Calouste Gulbenkian** (Calouste Gulbenkian Foundation) is a cultural trust whose museum houses treasures collected by Armenian oil magnate Calouste Gulbenkian (1869–1955). There are superb examples of Greek and Roman coins, Persian carpets, Chinese porcelain, and paintings by such Old Masters as Rembrandt and Rubens, as well as Impressionist and pre-Raphaelite works. The complex also includes a good modern art museum and two concert halls that host music and ballet festivals in winter and spring. *Av. de Berna 45, tel. 01/795–0236. Admission: 500$00, free Sun. Open June–Sept., Tues., Thurs., Fri., and Sun. 10–5, Wed. and Sat. 2–7:30; Oct.–May, Tues.–Sun. 10–5.*

⑧ In the cozy, clublike lounge at the **Instituto do Vinho do Porto** (Port Wine Institute), you can sample Portugal's most famous beverage from the Institute's formidably well-stocked cellars. The five main types are white (an extra-dry aperitif, not for purists), tawny, ruby, late-bottled vintage, and vintage. *Rua S. Pedro de Alcântara 45, tel. 01/347–5707. Admission free. Prices of tastings vary, starting at 200$00. Open Mon.–Sat. 10–10.*

⑨ The plain exterior of the **Igreja de São Roque** (Church of St. Roque) belies its rich interior. Its flamboyant 18th-century Capela de São João Baptista (Chapel of St. John the Baptist) is adorned with rare stones and mosaics that resemble oil paintings. Adjoining the church is the Museu de Arte Sacra (Museum of Sacred Art). *Largo Trinidade Coelho, tel. 01/346–0361. Church and museum free. Church open daily 8:30–5; museum Tues.–Sun. 10–1 and 2–5.*

To see the best examples of that uniquely Portuguese, late-Gothic architecture known as Manueline, head for **Belém,** at the far southwestern edge of Lisbon.

The **Mosteiro dos Jerónimos** (Jerónimos Monastery), in the Praça do Império, was conceived and planned by King Manuel I at the beginning of the 16th century to honor the discoveries of Vasco da Gama. Construction began in 1502 and was financed by treasures brought back from the so-called *descobrimentos*—the "discoveries" made by the Portuguese in Africa, Asia, and South America. *Praça do Império, tel. 01/362- -0034. Admission to church free, to cloisters 400$00, free Sun. Open June–Sept., Tues.–Sun. 10–6:30; Oct.–May, Tues.–Sun. 10–1 and 2:30–5.*

The **Museu de Marinha** (Maritime Museum) is at the west end of the Mosteiro dos Jerónimos monastery. Its huge collection reflects Portugal's long seafaring tradition, and exhibits range from early maps, model ships, and navigational instruments to fishing boats and royal barges. *Praça do Império, tel. 01/362–0010. Admission: 300$00, free Sun. 10–1. Open Tues.–Sun. 10–6.*

The **Torre de Belém** (Belém Tower) is another fine example of Manueline architecture, with openwork balconies, loggia, and domed turrets. Although it was built in the early 16th century on an island in the middle of the Tagus River, today the tower stands near the north bank—the river's course has changed over the centuries. *Av. de India, tel. 01/301–6892. Admission: 400$00 June–Sept., 250$00 Oct.–May. Open June–Sept., Tues.–Sun. 10–6:30; Oct.–May, Tues.–Sun. 10–1 and 2:30–5.*

The stunning glass-and-stone **Oceanário de Lisboa** (Lisbon Oceanarium), rising from the river and reached by footbridge, is the largest aquarium in Europe. It contains 25,000 fish, seabirds, and mammals, and is the first aquarium to incorporate selected world ocean habitats (North Atlantic, Pacific, Antarctic, and Indian Ocean) within one complex. *Doca dos Olivais, Esplanada Dom Carlos I, tel. 01/891–7002, 01/891–7006, 01/891–7007, or 01/891–7008. Admission: 1,700$00. Open daily 10–6.*

Shopping

The **Baixa** (Rua Augusta between the Rossío and the River Tagus), one of Lisbon's main shopping and banking districts, features a small crafts market, some of the best shoe shops in Europe, glittering jewelry stores, and a host of delicatessens selling anything from game birds to *queijo da serra*—a delicious mountain cheese from the Serra da Estrela range north of Lisbon.

Downtown restoration is best exemplified by the beautifully renovated **Eden** building (Av. da Liberdade), an Art Deco triumph containing a Virgin Megastore, an aparthotel, and a small shopping center.

The *Feira da Ladra* (flea market) is held on Tuesday morning and all day Saturday in the Largo de Santa Clara behind the Church of São Vicente, near the Alfama district.

London/Southampton, England

Southampton—a traditional terminal port for transatlantic crossings and the starting point for many historic voyages, including that of the *Mayflower*—is the port for ships calling at London, a city with a vibrant artistic, cultural, and commercial life. Modern London began to evolve in the Middle Ages, more than 600 years ago, and still standing is much of the work of Christopher Wren, the master architect chiefly responsible for reconstruction after the disastrous Great Fire of 1666. Traditionally London has been divided between the City, to the east, where its banking and commercial interests lie, and Westminster to the west, the seat of the royal court and of government. Today the distinction between the two holds good, and even the briefest exploration will reveal each area's distinct atmosphere. It is also in these two areas that you will find most of the grand buildings that have played a central role in British history: the Tower of London and St. Paul's Cathedral, Westminster Abbey and the Houses of Parliament, Buckingham Palace, and the older royal palace of St. James's.

Currency

The British unit of currency is the pound sterling, divided into 100 pence (p). Bills are issued in denominations of 5, 10, 20, and 50 pounds (£). Coins are £2, £1, 50p, 20p, 10p, 5p, 2p, and 1p. At press time, exchange rates were approximately £.63 to the U.S dollar and £.42 to the Canadian dollar.

Telephones

The United Kingdom's country code is 44. If calling the United Kingdom from abroad, drop the initial zero from the area code. Other than on the street, the best place to find a bank of pay phones is in a hotel or large post office. The workings of coin-operated telephones vary, but there are usually instructions in each unit. Most take 10p, 20p, 50p, and £1 coins. Phone cards are also available; they can be bought in a number of retail outlets. Card phones, which are clearly marked with a special green insignia, will not accept coins. The cheapest way to make an overseas call is to dial it yourself—but be sure to have plenty of coins or phone cards close at hand (newsagents sell budget-rate international phone cards, such as First National and America First, which can be used from any phone by dialing an access number, then pin number). After you have inserted the coins or card, dial 00 (the international code), then the country code—for the United States, it is 1—followed by the area code and local number. To reach an **AT&T** long-distance operator, dial 0500/890011; **MCI,** 0800/890222; for **Sprint,** 0800/890877 (from a British Telecom phone) or 0500/890877 (from a Mercury Communications phone). To make a collect or other operator-assisted call, dial 155.

In order to facilitate expanded telephone access, British Telecom and other British telephone services are in the process of instituting new area codes for all London telephone numbers. The former London area codes of 0171 and 0181 are changing to 0207 and 0208, a procedure that began June 1999 and will continue until the official changeover April 22, 2000. Until that date London numbers can be accessed with parallel systems using both forms of area codes. Note that the new area codes will impact London's actual telephone numbers—for example, 0171/222–3333 will now become 020/7222-3333. 0800 numbers and national information numbers of 0345 will not change.

Shore Excursions

Most cruise lines use Southampton as an embarkation or disembarkation point. Your best bet is to add a few days to your cruise to visit London. You can either arrange your own package or book a line's pre- or post-cruise package.

The following is a good choice should you want to tour sights near Southampton. It may not be offered by all cruise lines. Time and price are approximate.

Salisbury and Stonehenge. An hour from Southampton lies Salisbury Cathedral, which was built in AD 1220. After a walk through town and lunch, continue to Stonehenge. *Full day. Cost: $90.*

Coming Ashore

Ships dock at the Southampton terminal. Southampton's attractions are a short drive from the pier; London is about an hour and a half from Southampton by bus. Places such as Winchester, Stonehenge, Salisbury, and Bath are not far from Southampton.

London, although not simple of layout, is a rewarding walking city, and this remains the best way to get to know its nooks and crannies. If you want, you can take "the tube," London's extensive Underground system, which is by far the most widely used form of city transportation. Trains run both beneath and above the ground out into the suburbs, and all stations are clearly marked with the London Underground circular symbol. (A SUBWAY sign refers to an under-the-street crossing.)

There are 10 basic lines—all named. The Central, District, Northern, Metropolitan, and Piccadilly lines all have branches, usually taking you to the outlying sections of the city, so be sure to note which branch is needed for your particular destination. Begun in the Victorian era, the Underground is still being expanded and improved. Autumn 1999 was the latest date for the opening of the Jubilee line extension: this state-of-the-art subway, when completed, will sweep from Green Park to London Bridge and Southwark, with connections to Canary Wharf and the Docklands and the much hyped Milennium Experience megadome, and on to the east at Stratford. A pocket map of the entire tube network is available free from most Underground ticket counters. One-day Travelcards are a good buy. These allow unrestricted travel on the tube, most buses, and British Rail trains in the Greater London zones and are valid weekdays after 9:30 AM, weekends, and all public holidays. The price is £3.80–£4.50

London's black taxis are famous for their comfort and for the ability of their drivers to remember the mazelike pattern of the capital's streets. Hotels and main tourist areas have ranks (stands) where you wait your turn to take one of the taxis that drive up. You can also hail a taxi if the flag is up or the yellow FOR HIRE sign is lighted. Fares start at £1.40; surcharges of 40p–60p are a tricky addition, used for extra passengers, bulky luggage, and the like. Note that fares are usually raised in April of each year. As for tipping, taxi drivers should get 10%–15% of the tab.

Exploring London

Numbers in the margin correspond to points of interest on the London map.

Westminster is the royal backyard—the traditional center of the royal court and of government. Here, within a kilometer or so of one another, are virtually all of London's most celebrated buildings (St. Paul's Cathedral and the Tower of London excepted). Generations of kings and queens and their offspring have lived here since the end of the 11th century—including the current monarch. The Queen resides at Buckingham Palace through most of the year; during summer periods when she visits her country estates, the palace is partially open to visitors.

❶ **Trafalgar Square** dates from about 1830. It is London's most famous and festive square—permanently alive with people, Londoners and tourists alike, roaring traffic, and pigeons, it remains London's "living room." Great events, such as New Year's, royal weddings, elections, and sporting triumphs, always see the crowds gathering. A statue of Lord Nelson, victor over the French in 1805 at the Battle of Trafalgar, at which he lost his life, stands atop a column. Stone lions guard the base of the column, which is decorated with four bronze panels depicting naval battles against France and cast from French cannons captured by Nelson. The bronze equestrian statue on the south side of the square is of the unhappy Charles I; he is looking down Whitehall toward the spot where he was executed in 1649.

❷ The **National Gallery** is generally ranked right after the Louvre as one of the world's greatest museums. Occupying the long neoclassical building on the north side of Trafalgar Square, it contains works by virtually every famous artist and school from the 14th to the 19th century. Its galleries overflow with masterpieces, including Jan van Eyck's *Arnolfini Marriage,* Leonardo da Vinci's *Burlington Virgin and Child,* Velásquez's *The Toilet of Venus* (known as "The Rokeby Venus"), and Constable's *Hay Wain.* The gallery is especially strong on Flemish and Dutch masters, Rubens and Rembrandt among them, and on Italian Renaissance works. *Trafalgar Sq., tel. 020/7747–2885. Admission free; charge for special exhibitions. Open Mon.– Sat. 10–6, Sun. 2–6; June–Aug., also Wed. until 9.*

At the foot of Charing Cross Road is a second major art collection, the **National Portrait Gallery,** which contains portraits of well-known (and not so well-known) Britons, including monarchs, statesmen, and writers. *2 St. Martin's Pl., at foot of Charing Cross Rd., tel. 020/7306–0055. Admission free. Open weekdays 10–5, Sat. 10–6, Sun. 2–6.*

❹ Buckingham Palace is the London home of the Queen and the administrative hub of the entire royal family. When the queen is in residence (normally on weekdays except in Jan., Aug., Sept., and part of June), the royal standard flies over the east front. Inside there are dozens of splendid state rooms used on such formal occasions as banquets for visiting heads of state. The private apartments of Queen Elizabeth and Prince Philip are in the north wing. Behind the palace lie some 40 acres of private gardens, a wildlife haven. The ceremony of the Changing of the Guard takes place in front of the palace at 11:30 daily, April through July, and on alternate days during the rest of the year. It's advisable to arrive early, since people are invariably stacked several deep along the railings, whatever the weather. Parts of Buckingham Palace are open to the public during August and September. The former chapel, bombed during World War II, rebuilt in 1961, is the site of the Queen's Gallery, which shows treasures from the vast royal art collections. Unfortunately, the gallery is closed for renovations until 2002. *Buckingham Palace Rd., tel. 020/7839–1377. Admission: £10. Open early Aug.–early Oct. (confirm specific dates, which are subject to the Queen's mandate), 9:30–4:15.*

❺ Parliament Square is flanked, on the river side, by the Palace of Westminster. Among the statues of statesmen long since dead are those of Churchill, Abraham Lincoln, and Oliver Cromwell, the Lord Protector of England during the country's brief attempt at being a republic (1648–60).

❻ Westminster Abbey is the most ancient of London's great churches and the most important, for it is here that Britain's monarchs are crowned. The main nave is packed with atmosphere and memories, as it has witnessed many splendid coronation ceremonies, royal weddings, and more recently, the funeral of Diana, Princess of Wales. The abbey dates largely from the 13th and 14th centuries, although Henry VII's Chapel, an exquisite example of the heavily decorated late-Gothic style, was not built until the early 1600s, and the twin towers over the west entrance are an 18th-

London

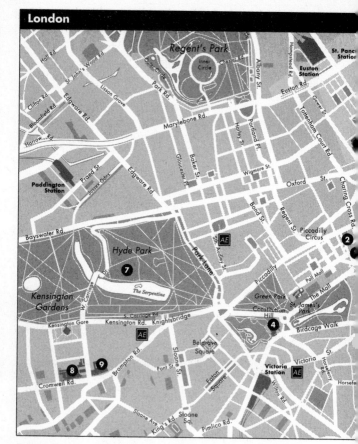

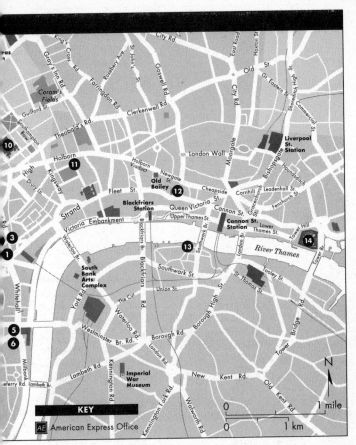

KEY

AE American Express Office

century addition. There is much to see inside, including the tomb of the Unknown Warrior, a nameless World War I soldier buried, in memory of the war's victims, in earth brought with his corpse from France; and the famous Poets' Corner, where England's great writers—Milton, Chaucer, Shakespeare, et al—are memorialized, and some are actually buried. Behind the high altar are the royal tombs, including those of Queen Elizabeth I; Mary, Queen of Scots; and Henry V. In the Chapel of Edward the Confessor stands the Coronation Chair. Among the royal weddings that have taken place here are those of the present Queen and most recently, in 1986, the (ill-starred) Duke and Duchess of York. The abbey tends to be packed with crowds, so try to come early in the morning. *Broad Sanctuary, tel. 020/7222–5152. Admission £5. Open Mon.—Sat. 9–3:45 (last admission Sat. 1:45). Closed Sun. except for religious services.*

❼ **Hyde Park,** which covers about 340 acres, was originally a royal hunting ground. The sandy track along the south side of the park, is **Rotten Row.** It was Henry VIII's royal path to the hunt—hence the name, a corruption of *route du roi.* It's still used by the Household Cavalry, the queen's guard. You can see them leave, in full regalia, plumed helmets and all, at around 10:30, or await the return of the exhausted ex-guard about noon. The neighboring **Kensington Gardens** are a little more formal than Hyde Park. First laid out as palace grounds, they adjoin Kensington Palace. There is boating and swimming in the Kensington's Serpentine, an S-shape lake formed by damming a stream that used to flow here. Refreshments are served at the lakeside tearooms, and the Serpentine Gallery (tel. 020/7402–6075) holds noteworthy exhibitions of modern art. *Bounded by the Ring, Bayswater Rd., Park La., and Knightsbridge.*

❽ The **Natural History Museum** is housed in an ornate late-Victorian building with striking modern additions. As in the Science Museum, its displays on topics such as human biology and evolution are designed to challenge visitors to think for themselves. *Cromwell Rd., 020/7938–9123; 0142/692–7654 recorded information. Admission: £6; free weekdays 4:30–5:50 and weekends 5–5:50. Open Mon.–Sat. 10–6, Sun. 2:30–6.*

⑨ The **Victoria and Albert Museum** (or V&A) originated in the 19th century as a museum of decorative art. It has extensive collections of costumes, paintings, jewelry, and crafts from every part of the globe; don't miss the sculpture court, the vintage couture collections, and the great Raphael Room. *Cromwell Rd., tel. 020/7938–8500. Suggested contribution: £5; free after 4:30, except Wed. Open Mon. noon–5:50, Tues.–Sun. 10–5:50.; Wed. late view 4:30–9:30.*

⑩ The **British Museum** ("Mankind's attic") houses a vast and priceless collection of treasures, including Egyptian, Greek, and Roman antiquities; Renaissance jewelry; pottery; coins; glass; and drawings from virtually every European school since the 15th century. It's best to pick out one section that particularly interests you—to try to see everything would be an overwhelming and exhausting task. Some of the highlights are the Elgin Marbles, sculptures that formerly decorated the Parthenon in Athens; the Rosetta stone, which helped archaeologists interpret Egyptian hieroglyphics; and a copy of the Magna Carta, the charter signed by King John in 1215 that is considered the foundation of English liberty. Changing the face of the museum just in time for the millennium, a vast, modern Great Court entrance, with new galleries and interactive attractions, is scheduled to open in Autumn 2000. *Great Russell St., tel. 020/7636–1555; 020/7580–1788 recorded information. Admission free (donation suggested). Open Mon.–Sat. 10–5, Sun. 2:30–6.*

⑪ **Sir John Soane's Museum,** on the border of London's legal district, is stuffed with antique busts and myriad decorative delights—it's an eccentric, smile-inducing 19th-century collection of art and artifacts in the former home of the architect of the Bank of England. *13 Lincoln's Inn Fields, tel. 020/7405–2107. Admission free. Open Tues.–Sat. 10–5; until 9 on the first Tues. of month.*

The City, the traditional commercial center of London, is the most ancient part of the capital, having been the site of the great Roman city of Londinium. Since those days, the City has been built and rebuilt several times, and today ancient and modern jostle each other elbow to elbow. The wooden buildings of the medieval City were destroyed in the Great Fire of 1666. There were further waves of reconstruction in the 19th century, and then again after World War II to repair the devastation wrought by air attacks. Modern developers in the 1980s contributed almost as much blight as the Blitz with the construction of ugly modern glass skyscrapers. Still, several of London's most famous attractions are here, along with the adjacent South Bank area, where Shakespeare's Globe Theatre, the new Tate Gallery of Modern Art, and the astonishing British Airways London Eye—the world's largest ferris wheel— have starring roles. Throughout all these changes, the City has retained its unique identity and character. The Lord Mayor and Corporation of London are still responsible for the government of the City, as they have been for many centuries. Commerce remains the lifeblood of the City, which is a world financial center rivaled only by New York, Tokyo, and Zurich. The biggest change has been in the City's population. Until the first half of the 19th century, many of the merchants and traders who worked in the City lived there, too. Today, despite its huge daytime population, scarcely 8,000 people live in the 677 acres of the City. Try, therefore, to explore the City on a weekday morning or afternoon. On weekends its streets are deserted, and many of the shops and restaurants, and even some of the churches, are closed.

⓬ **St. Paul's Cathedral** is London's symbolic heart. Its dome—the world's third largest—can be seen from many an angle in other parts of the city. Following the Great Fire, it was rebuilt by Sir Christopher Wren, the architect who was also responsible for designing 50 City parish churches to replace those lost in the disaster. St. Paul's is Wren's greatest work; fittingly, he is buried in the crypt under a simple Latin epitaph, composed by his son, which translates as: "Reader, if you seek his monument, look around you."

The greatest architectural glory of the cathedral is the dome. This consists of three distinct elements: an outer, timber-frame dome covered with lead; an interior dome built of brick and decorated with frescoes of the life of St. Paul by the 18th-century artist Sir James Thornhill; and, in-between, a brick cone that supports and strengthens both. There is a good view of the church from the Whispering Gallery, high up in the inner dome. The gallery is so called because of its remarkable acoustics, whereby words spoken on one side can be clearly heard on the other, 107 ft away. *St. Paul's Churchyard, Paternoster Sq., tel. 020/7236–4128. Admission: combined ticket £7.50. Cathedral open Mon.–Sat. 8:30–4; ambulatory, crypt, and galleries open Mon.–Sat. 9:30–4:15.*

⑬ Spectacular **Shakespeare's Globe Theatre** is a replica of Shakespeare's open-roofed Globe Playhouse (built in 1599; incinerated in 1613), where most of the playwright's great plays premiered. It stands 200 yards from the original site, overlooking the Thames. Built with authentic Elizabethan materials, down to the first thatched roof in London since the Great Fire, the theater stages its works in natural light (and sometimes rain), to 1,000 people on wooden benches in the "bays," plus 500 "groundlings," standing on a carpet of filbert shells and clinker, just as they did nearly four centuries ago. The theater season runs from June through September; throughout the year, you can tour the Globe through admission to the **New Shakespeare's Globe Exhibition,** which opened in September 1999 and is the largest ever to focus on the Bard. In addition, productions are now scheduled throughout the year in a second, indoor theater, built to a design of the 17th-century architect Inigo Jones. *New Globe Walk, Bankside (South Bank), tel. 0171/902–1500. Open daily 10–5. Call for performance schedule.*

⑭ The **Tower of London** is one of London's most famous sights and one of its most crowded, too. Come as early in the day as possible and head for the crown jewels, so you can see them before the crowds arrive. They are a breathtakingly splendid collection of regalia, precious stones, gold, and silver; the Royal Scepter contains the largest cut diamond in the world. The tower served the monarchs of medieval England as both fortress and palace.

Every British sovereign from William the Conqueror in the 11th century to Henry VIII in the 16th lived here, and it remains a royal palace, in name at least. The History Gallery is a walk-through display designed to answer questions about the inhabitants of the tower and its evolution over the centuries. Among other buildings worth seeing is the Bloody Tower. The little princes in the tower—the uncrowned boy-king Edward V and his brother Richard, duke of York, supposedly murdered on the orders of the duke of Gloucester, later crowned Richard III—certainly lived in the Bloody Tower, and may well have died here, too. Look for the ravens whose presence at the tower is traditional. It is said that if they leave, the tower will fall and England will lose her greatness. *Tower Hill, tel. 020/7709– 0765. Admission: £10.50. Open Mar.–Oct., Mon.–Sat. 9–5, Sun. 10–5; Nov.–Feb., Tues.–Sat. 9–4, Sun.–Mon. 10–4 (the Tower closes 1 hr after last admission time and all internal buildings close 30 mins after last admission). Yeoman Warder guides conduct tours daily from Middle Tower; no charge, but tip always appreciated. Subject to weather and availability of guides, tours conducted about every 30 mins until 3:30 in summer, 2:30 in winter.*

Shopping

Shopping is one of London's great pleasures. Different areas retain their traditional specialties. **Chelsea** centers on the King's Road; once synonymous with ultrafashion, it still harbors some designer boutiques, plus antiques and home-furnishings stores. **Covent Garden** is a something-for-every-one neighborhood, with clothing chain stores and top designers, stalls selling crafts, and shops selling gifts of every type—bikes, kites, herbs, beads, hats, you name it.

Regent Street has one of London's most pleasant department stores, Liberty, as well as Hamleys, the capital's toy mecca. Check out the cobbled streets in West Soho, behind Liberty, for handcrafted jewelry, designer gear, and stylish cafés. In **St. James's** the English gentleman buys the rest of his gear: handmade hats, shirts, and shoes, silver shaving kits, and hip flasks. Here is also the world's best cheese shop, Paxton & Whitfield. Nothing in this neighborhood is cheap, in any sense.

Kensington's main drag, **Kensington High Street,** is lined with small, classy boutiques, with some larger stores at the eastern end. Neighboring **Knightsbridge** has Harrods, of course, but also Harvey Nichols, the top clothes stop, and many expensive designers' boutiques along Sloane Street, Walton Street, and Beauchamp Place. Adjacent Belgravia is also a burgeoning area for posh designer stores.

Piccadilly is a busy street lined with some grand and very English shops (including Hatchards, the booksellers; Swaine, Adeney Brigg, the equestrian outfitters; and Fortnum and Mason, the department store that supplies the Queen's groceries). **Jermyn Street,** south of Piccadilly, is famous for upscale shops that sell accessories for the gentleman's wardrobe, from handmade shoes to bespoke hats (his suits come from nearby Savile Row). Shops along **Duke Street** and **Bury Street** specialize in paintings, the former in Old Masters, the latter in early English watercolors. Don't be put off by the exclusive appearance of these establishments—anyone is free to enter, and there is no obligation to buy.

There are three special shopping streets in Mayfair, each with its own specialties. **Savile Row** is the home of gentlemen's tailors. Nearby **Cork Street** has many dealers in modern and classical art. **Bond Street** (divided into two parts, Old and New, though both are some 300 years old) is the classiest shopping street in London, the home of haute couture, with such famous names as Gucci, Hermès, and Chanel, and costly jewelry from such shops as Asprey, Tiffany, and Cartier.

North of Kensington Gardens is the lively **Notting Hill** district, where the lively Portobello Road antiques and bric-a-brac market is held each Saturday (arrive early in the morning for the best bargains). The street is also full of regular antiques shops that are open most weekdays.

Napoli Coast, Italy

Campania (the region of Naples, the Amalfi coast, and the surrounding sun-drenched area) is where most people's preconceived ideas of Italy become a reality. You'll find lots of sun, good food that relies heavily on tomatoes and mozzarella, acres of classical ruins, and gorgeous scenery.

Currency
The unit of currency in Italy is the lira (plural, lire). There are bills of 1,000, 2,000, 5,000, 10,000, 50,000, 100,000, and 500,000 lire (this largest bill being almost impossible to change, except in banks); coins are worth 50, 100, 200, 500, and 1,000 lire. In 1999 the euro began to be used as a banking currency, but the lira will still be the currency in

use on a day-to-day basis. At press time, the exchange rate was about 1,822 lire to the U.S. dollar, 1,203 lire to the Canadian dollar, and 2,900 lire to the pound sterling. When your purchases run into hundreds of thousands of lire, beware of being shortchanged, a dodge that is practiced at ticket windows, toll booths, and cashiers' desks, as well as in shops and even banks. Always count your change before you leave the counter.

Telephones

The country code for Italy is 39. Do not drop the zero in the regional code when calling Italy. For all local calls, you must dial the regional area codes, even in cities. Most local calls cost 200 lire for two minutes. Pay phones take either 100-, 200-, or 500-lire coins or *schede telefoniche* (phone cards), purchased in bars, tobacconists, post offices, and TELECOM offices in either 5,000-, 10,000-, or 15,000-lire denominations. To place international calls, many travelers go to the Telefoni telephone exchange (usually marked TELECOM), where the operator assigns you a booth, can help place your call, and will collect payment when you have finished. To dial an international call, insert a phone card, dial 00, then the country code, area code, and phone number. For **AT&T USADirect,** dial access number tel. 172–1011; for **MCI Call USA,** access number tel. 172–1022; for **Sprint Express,** access number tel. 172–1877. You will be connected directly with an operator in the United States.

Shore Excursions

The following are good choices on the Napoli Coast. They may not be offered by all cruise lines. Times and prices are approximate.

IN NAPLES

Pompeii. It's a 45-minute motor-coach ride to the ruins at Pompeii, a place where time has stood still since AD 79, when Mount Vesuvius erupted. *4 hrs. Cost: $50.*

Herculaneum and Naples. The well-preserved ruins at Herculaneum and downtown Naples are the focus of this two-town tour. *3½ hrs. Cost: $53.*

IN SORRENTO

Excavations at Pompeii. Here's another chance to see the ruins at Pompeii. *4½ hrs. Cost: $50.*

IN CAPRI

Capri is a place to wander, not tour. Cruise lines will arrange round-trip tickets on the public jetfoil for passengers wishing to visit Capri.

IN AMALFI

Cruise lines often offer excursions featuring the Amalfi coast, from Naples or Sorrento. You can also arrange to hire a car, often through the ship's tour desk.

Coming Ashore

Ships calling on the Napoli Coast generally drop anchor offshore. Nearby towns are easily reached from the major ports of call.

IN NAPLES

Ships calling at Naples tender passengers ashore from Naples Bay. You'll probably do a lot of walking in Naples, since the buses are crowded and taxis get stalled in traffic. Keep a firm grip on your pocketbook and camera.

IN SORRENTO

Ships calling at Sorrento tender passengers to shore from the town's harbor. Sorrento is best explored on foot, since motor coaches must remain in designated areas.

IN CAPRI

The trip on the public jetfoil to Capri is about a 20-minute ride from Sorrento or about a 40-minute ride from Naples. A cog railway or bus service takes you up to the town of Capri from the marina.

IN AMALFI

Amalfi is within driving distance of Naples or Sorrento. Once in town, you will want to wander around on foot.

Exploring the Napoli Coast

NAPLES

The 17th-century **Palazzo Reale** (Royal Palace), built during the rule of the Bourbons, is still furnished in the lavish Baroque style that suited the Bourbons so well. *Piazza del Plebiscito, tel. 081/5808111. Admission: 8,000 lire. Open Thurs.–Fri. and Mon.–Tues. 9–2, weekends 9–7.*

Also known as the Maschio Angioino, the massive stone **Castel Nuovo** was built by the city's Aragon rulers in the

13th century; inside, the city's **Museo Civico** comprises mainly local artworks from the 15th to the 19th centuries, and there are also regular exhibitions. *Castel Nuovo, Piazza Municipio, tel. 081/7952003. Admission: 10,000 lire. Open Mon.–Sat. 9–7, Sun. 9–1.*

A favorite Neapolitan song celebrates the quiet beauty of the church of **Santa Chiara,** which was built in the early 1300s in Provençal Gothic style. Directly across from it are the oddly faceted stone facade and elaborate Baroque interior of the church **Gesù Nuovo** (Via Benedetto Croce). *Piazza Gesù Nuovo, tel. 081/5526209. Open Apr.–Sept., daily 8:30–noon and 4–7; Oct.–Mar., daily 8:30–noon and 4–6.*

The museum in the **Certosa di San Martino,** a Carthusian monastery restored in the 17th century, contains an eclectic collection of Neapolitan landscape paintings, royal carriages, and *presepi* (Christmas crèches). Check out the view from the balcony off Room 25. *Certosa di San Martino, tel. 081/5781769. Admission: 9,500 lire. Open Tues.–Sun. 9–2.*

The **Museo Archeologico Nazionale** (National Archaeological Museum) is dusty and unkempt, but it holds one of the world's great collections of antiquities. Greek and Roman sculptures, vividly colored mosaics, countless objects from Pompeii and Herculaneum, and an equestrian statue of the Roman emperor Nerva are all worth seeing. *Piazza Museo, tel. 081/440166. Admission: 12,000 lire. Open Aug.–Sept., Mon.–Sat. 9–10, Sun. 9–6; Oct.–July, Wed.–Mon. 9–2.*

The **Museo di Capodimonte,** housed in an 18th-century palace built by Bourbon king Charles III, is surrounded by a vast park that affords a sweeping view of the bay. The picture gallery is devoted to work from the 13th to the 18th centuries, including many familiar paintings by Dutch and Spanish masters, as well as by the great Italians. Other rooms contain an extensive collection of porcelain and majolica from the various royal residences, some produced in the Bourbons' own factory right here on the grounds. *Parco di Capodimonte, tel. 081/7441307. Admission: 9,500 lire. Open Tues.–Sun. 10–7.*

Near Naples is **Pompeii,** where an estimated 2,000 residents were entombed on that fateful August day when Mt. Vesuvius erupted in AD 79. The ancient city of Pompeii was much larger than nearby Herculaneum, and excavations have progressed to a much greater extent (though the remains are not as well preserved, owing to some 18th-century scavenging for museum-quality artwork, most of which you are able to see at Naples's Museo Archeologico Nazionale; *see above*). This prosperous Roman city had an extensive forum, lavish baths and temples, and patrician villas richly decorated with frescoes. It's worth buying a detailed guide of the site to give meaning and understanding to the ruins and their importance. Be sure to see the Villa dei Misteri, whose frescoes are in mint condition. Perhaps that is a slight exaggeration, but the paintings are so rich with detail and depth of color that one finds it difficult to believe that they are more than 1,900 years old. Have lots of small change handy to tip the guards at the more important houses so they will unlock the gates for you. *Pompeii Scavi, tel. 081/8610744. Admission: 12,000 lire. Open daily 9– 1 hr before sunset (ticket office closes 2 hrs before sunset).*

SORRENTO

Package tours have been stampeding here for years now, but truly, nothing can dim the delights of the marvelous climate and view of the Bay of Naples. The **Museo Correale,** an attractive 18th-century villa, houses an interesting collection of decorative arts (furniture, china, and so on) and paintings of the Neapolitan school. *Via Correale. Admission to museum and gardens: 8,000 lire. Open Wed.–Mon. 9–2.*

CAPRI

No matter how many day-trippers crowd onto the island, no matter how touristy certain sections have become, Capri remains one of Italy's loveliest places. Incoming visitors disembark at Marina Grande, from where you can take some time out for an excursion to the **Grotta Azzurra** (Blue Grotto). Be warned that this must rank as one of the country's all-time great rip-offs: motorboat, rowboat, and grotto admissions are charged separately, and if there's a line of boats waiting, you'll have little time to enjoy the grotto's marvelous colors. A cog railway or bus service takes you up to the deliberately commercial and self-consciously picturesque **Capri Town,** where you can stroll through the **Piazzetta,** a choice place from which to watch the action, and window-shop expensive boutiques.

To get away from the crowds, hike to **Villa Jovis,** one of the many villas that Roman emperor Tiberius built on the island, at the end of a lane that climbs steeply uphill. The walk takes about 45 minutes, with pretty views all the way and a final spectacular vista of the entire Bay of Naples and part of the Gulf of Salerno. *Villa Jovis, Via Tiberio, tel. 081/ 8370381. Admission: 4,000 lire. Open daily 9–1 hr before sunset.*

In Anacapri, the island's only other town, look for the little church of **San Michele,** where a magnificent hand-painted majolica-tile floor shows you an 18th-century vision of the Garden of Eden. (You'll need to take a bus or open taxi to Anacapri from Capri town.) *Off Via Orlandi. Open Easter–Oct., daily 9–7; Nov.–Easter, daily 10–3.*

Villa San Michele is the charming former home of Swedish scientist-author Axel Munthe; it's filled with stunning statuary, including a sphinx that looks out across the azure sea. *Via Axel Munthe, tel. 081/837401. Admission: 8,000 lire. Open May–Sept., daily 9–6; Nov.–Feb., daily 10:30–3:30; Mar., daily 9:30–4:30; Apr. and Oct., daily 9:30–5.*

AMALFI

The main historical attraction is the **Duomo** or Cathedral of St. Andrew, which shows a mix of Moorish and early-Gothic influences. The interior is a 10th-century Romanesque skeleton in an 18th-century Baroque dress. The cloisters, with whitewashed arches and palms, are worth a glance, and the small museum in the adjoining crypt could really inspire you to climb up all those stairs. *Tel. 089/ 871059. Open Apr.–Oct., daily 7:30 AM–8 PM; Nov.–Mar., daily 7:30–noon and 3–7. Cloisters and museum admission: 3,000 lire. Open Apr.–Oct., daily 9–9; Nov.–Mar., daily 10– 12:30 and 2:30–5:30.*

The village of **Ravello,** 8 km (5 mi) north of Amalfi, is not actually on the coast, but on a high mountain bluff overlooking the sea. The road up to it is a series of switchbacks, and the village itself clings precariously on the mountain spur. The village flourished during the 13th century and then fell into a tranquillity that has remained unchanged for the past six centuries.

The 11th-century **Villa Rufolo** in Ravello is where the composer Richard Wagner once stayed, and there is a Wagner festival every summer on the villa's garden terrace. It includes a Moorish cloister with interlacing pointed arches, beautiful gardens, an 11th-century tower, and a belvedere with a fine view of the coast. *Piazza del Duomo, tel. 089/857657. Admission: 4,000 lire. Open Apr.–Sept., daily 9–8; Oct.–Mar., daily 9–6 or sunset.*

At the entrance to the **Villa Cimbrone** is a small cloister that looks medieval but was actually built in 1917, with two bas-reliefs: one representing nine Norman warriors, the other illustrating the Seven Deadly Sins. Then, the long avenue leads through peaceful gardens scattered with grottoes, small temples, and statues to a belvedere and terrace, where, on a clear day, the view stretches out over the Mediterranean Sea. *Via Santa Chiara, tel. 089/857459. Admission: 6,000 lire. Open daily 8:30–1 hr before sunset.*

Norwegian Coast and Fjords

Norway's Far North, land of the summertime midnight sun, offers picturesque scenery and quaint towns. The fjords continue northward from Bergen all the way to Kirkenes, on Norway's border with Finland and Russia. Norway's Far North is for anyone eager to hike, climb, fish, bird-watch for seabirds, see Samiland (land of the Sami, or "Lapps"), or experience the unending days of nighttime sun in June and July.

The major towns north of Bergen are Ålesund, Trondheim, Bodø, Narvik, Tromsø, Hammerfest, and Kirkenes. The best way to reach these places is by ship, whether cruise ship or coastal ferry.

Currency

The unit of currency in Norway is the krone, written as Kr. on price tags but officially written as NOK (bank designation), NKr, or kr. The krone is divided into 100 øre. Bills of NKr 50, 100, 200, 500, and 1,000 are in general use. Coins are in denominations of 50 øre and 1, 5, 10, and 20 kroner. The exchange rate at press time was NKr 7.85 to the U.S. dollar, NKr 5.19 to the Canadian dollar, and NKr 12.48 to the pound sterling.

Telephones

The country code for Norway is 47. Public booths have either card phones or coin phones. Be sure to read the instructions; some phones require the coins to be deposited before dialing, some after. You can buy telephone cards at Narvesen kiosks or at the post office. The minimum deposit is NKr 2 or NKr 3, depending on the phone. International calls can be made from any pay phone. You will need to dial 00 for an international connection, then the country code, area code, and number. To reach an **AT&T** long-distance operator, dial 80019011.

Shore Excursions

The following are good choices in the towns along Norway's coast. They may not be offered by all cruise lines. Times and prices are approximate.

IN TRONDHEIM

City Tour. A visit to an open-air folk museum is the highlight of this tour, which also visits Nidaros Cathedral—built on the grave of St. Olav, who founded the city in AD 997. *3 hrs. Cost: $39.*

City View with Ringve Museum. You'll drive through the city on your way to the Ringve Museum of Musical Instruments, which is housed in a manor overlooking the fjord. *3 hrs. Cost: $45.*

IN BODØ

Tour of Kjerringoy. From Bodø, head off for Kjerringoy, which gained independence from Norway in 1800. Once there, you'll have time to wander the city's Central Square and streets. *Half day. Cost: $15.*

IN TROMSØ

Views of the City. Tour the Tromsø Museum before driving around the island of Tromsø. Pass Lake Prestvatn, where the Northern Lights Observatory is located, to reach Tromsø Bridge for a visit to Tromsdalen Church, known as the Arctic Cathedral. The tour includes a ride on the cable car to Mt. Storsteinen for panoramic views of the city. *3 hrs. Cost: $39.*

Northern Lights. Visit the Northern Lights Planetarium, which opened in 1989, where you'll see a film on a 360-

degree screen about, of course, the Aurora Borealis. A must for amateur astronomers. *3 hrs. Cost: $42.*

Coming Ashore

Ships calling at Tromsø, Bodø, and Trondheim dock in the harbor, which is the lifeline of all the towns along the Norwegian coast.

Attractions are close by the pier, and the best way to explore these ports is on foot.

Exploring Trondheim

This water-bound city has Scandinavia's two largest wooden buildings. One is the rococo **Stiftsgården** and the other is a student dormitory. Stiftsgården was built between 1774 and 1778 and became a royal palace in 1906. It is considered to be one of the highlights of Norwegian architecture although, strangely, the architect is unknown. *Muntkegt. 23, tel. 73/521311. Admission: NKr 30. Open June–mid-June, Tues.–Sat. 10–3, Sun. noon–5; late June–mid-Aug., Tues.– Sat. 10–5, Sun. noon–5; late Aug.–May, one day each month.*

Construction of Scandinavia's largest medieval building, **Nidaros Domkirke** (Nidaros Cathedral) was first started in 1070, but it was burned down several times and was not completed until 1969. The cathedral has attracted pilgrims for centuries. Norwegian kings were crowned here, and the crown jewels are still on display. *Kongsgårdgt. 2, tel. 73/ 538480. Admission: NKr 12. Open May–late June, 9–3; late June–late Aug., 9–6; late Aug.–late Sept., 9–3; late Sept.–Apr., 12–2:30.*

Exploring Bodø

Bodø was bombed by the Germans in 1940. The stunning, contemporary **Bodø Domkirke** (Bodø Cathedral), its spire separated from the main building, was built after the war. Inside are rich modern tapestries; outside is a war memorial.

The **Norsk Luftfarts Museum** (the Norwegian Aviation Museum) has an American U-2 spy plane, a Junkers JU 52, a Catalina anti-submarine aircraft, and the Mosquito Bomber, as well as other attractions. Try the flight simulator. *Olav V's Gt. Open Mid-June–mid-Aug., weekdays and Sun. 10– 8, Sat. 10–5; mid-Aug.–mid-June, Tues., Wed., Fri. 10–4, Thurs. 10–7, Sat. 10–5, Sun. 11–6.*

Exploring Tromsø

Be sure to see the spectacular **Ishavskatedral** (Arctic Cathedral), with its eastern wall made entirely of stained glass, across the long stretch of Tromsø bridge. Coated in aluminum, the bridge's triangular peaks make a bizarre mirror for the midnight sun. *Tel. 77/637611. Admission: NKr 10. Open June–Aug., Mon.–Sat. 10–6, Sun. 1:30–6. Times may vary according to church services.*

Be sure to walk around old Tromsø (along the waterfront) and visit the **Tromsø Museum,** which concentrates on science, the Sami, and northern churches. *Lars Thøringsvei 10, Folkeparken, tel. 77/645000; take Bus 28. Admission: NKr 20. Open June–Aug., daily 9–9; Sept.–May, weekdays 8:30–3:30, Sat. noon–3, Sun. 11–4.*

Oslo, Norway

Although it's one of the world's largest capital cities by land area, Oslo has only about 500,000 inhabitants. The foundations for modern Norwegian culture were laid here in the 19th century, during the period of union with Sweden, which lasted until 1905. Oslo blossomed at this time, and Norway produced its three greatest men of arts and letters: composer Edvard Grieg (1843–1907), dramatist Henrik Ibsen (1828–1906), and painter Edvard Munch (1863–1944). The polar explorers Roald Amundsen and Fridtjof Nansen also lived during this period.

In recent years the city has become more lively: shops are open later, and pubs, cafés, and restaurants are crowded at all hours. The downtown area is compact, but the city limits include forests, fjords, and mountains, giving Oslo a pristine airiness that complements its urban dignity. Explore downtown on foot, or if you've been here before, venture beyond via bus, streetcar, or train.

Currency

The unit of currency in Norway is the krone, written as Kr. on price tags but officially written as NOK (bank designation), NKr, or kr. The krone is divided into 100 øre. Bills of NKr 50, 100, 200, 500, and 1,000 are in general use. Coins are in denominations of 50 øre and 1, 5, 10, and 20 kroner. The exchange rate at press time was NKr 7.85 to the U.S. dollar, NKr 5.19 to the Canadian dollar, and NKr 12.48 to the pound sterling.

Telephones

The country code for Norway is 47. Public telephones accept small-denomination coins; for dialing instructions (in English), check the Oslo phone book. Public booths have either card phones or coin phones. Be sure to read the instructions; some phones require the coins to be deposited before dialing, some after. You can buy telephone cards at Narvesen kiosks or at the post office. The minimum deposit is NKr 2 or NKr 3, depending on the phone. International calls can be made from any pay phone. You will need to dial 00 for an international connection, then the country code, area code, and number. To reach an **AT&T** long-distance operator, dial 80019011.

Shore Excursions

The following are good choices in Oslo. They may not be offered by all cruise lines. Times and prices are approximate.

Sculpture and Skiing. See how master sculpter Gutav Vigeland has populated Frogner park with human figures made of stone, iron, and bronze, and the ski jump where in winter some of the world's top athletes compete, and where in summer you can get a great view of Oslo and the fjords. *3 hrs. Cost: $36.*

Munch Museum and Scandinavian Design. Art lovers won't want to miss this tour, which takes in the Munch Museum and the Museum of Scandinavian Design, with its diverse collection of arts and crafts from AD 600 to the present. *3 hrs. Cost: $34.*

Coming Ashore

Ships dock in Oslo's harbor. You can walk right into the main part of the city from the pier. The waterfront toward the central harbor is the heart of Oslo and head of the fjord. Aker Brygge, a quayside shopping and cultural center, with a theater, cinemas (including an IMAX film theater), and galleries among the shops, restaurants, and cafés, is a great place to hang out. You don't have to buy anything—just sit amid the fountains and statues and watch the activities.

A taxi is available if the roof light is on. There are taxi stands at Oslo Central Station and usually alongside Narvesen newsstands, or call 22388090; during peak hours, though, you may have to wait. The city also has a good bus and subway (T-bane) network. Tickets for either cost NKr 18; you can buy them at the stops. For NKr 40, the Dags Kort (Oneday Card) gives 24 hours' unlimited travel on all public transportation.

Exploring Oslo

Numbers in the margin correspond to points of interest on the Oslo map.

Oslo's main street, **Karl Johans Gate,** runs right through the center of town, from Oslo Central Station uphill to the Royal Palace. Half its length is closed to traffic, and it is in this section that you will find many of the city's shops and outdoor cafés.

❶ The **Slottet** (Royal Palace) is the king's residence. The neoclassical palace, completed in 1848, is as sober, sturdy, and unpretentious as the Norwegian character. The surrounding park is open to the public, though the palace is not. The changing of the guard happens daily at 1:30. When the king is in residence—signaled by a red flag—the Royal Guard strikes up the band. *Drammensvn. 1, tel. 22048700.*

❷ **Nasjonalgalleriet** (the National Gallery) is Norway's largest public gallery. It has a small but high-quality selection of paintings by European artists, but of particular interest is the collection of works by Scandinavian Impressionists. Here you can see Edvard Munch's most famous painting, *The Scream;* however, most of his work is in the Munch Museum *(see below). Universitetsgt. 13, tel. 22200404. Admission free. Open Mon., Wed., Fri. 10–6, Thurs. 10–8, Sat. 10–4, Sun. 11–4.*

❸ The **Historisk Museum** (Historical Museum) is in back of the National Gallery. In addition to displays of daily life and art from the Viking period, the museum has an ethnographic section with a collection related to the great polar explorer Roald Amundsen, the first man to reach the South Pole. *Frederiksgt. 2, tel. 22859964. Admission free. Open mid-May–mid-Sept., Tues.–Sun. 11–3; mid-Sept.–mid-May, Tues.–Sun. 12–3*

Don't Forget To Pack A Nikon.

PRONEA S

**The technology of a serious camera.
The spontaneity of a point-and-shoot.**

The Nikon Pronea S, the world's smallest and lightest SLR, is the easiest way to bring memories of your next vacation home with you. Serious camera technology. Three picture formats. Interchangeable zoom lenses. Point-and-shoot simplicity. At 15 ounces, it's ready to go anywhere you go. For more information, visit us at *www.nikonusa.com*

Distinctive guides packed with up-to-date expert advice and smart choices for every type of traveler.

Fodor's. For the world of ways you travel.

❹ The **Nationaltheatret** (National Theater) is watched over by the statues of Bjørnstjerne Bjørnson and Henrik Ibsen. Bjørnson was the nationalist poet who wrote Norway's anthem. Internationally lauded playwright Ibsen wrote *Peer Gynt* (he personally requested Edvard Grieg's musical accompaniment), *A Doll's House,* and *Hedda Gabler,* among others. He worried that his plays, packed with allegory, myth, and sociological and emotional angst, might not have appeal outside Norway. Instead, they were universally recognized and changed the face of modern theater. *Stortingsgt. 15, tel. 22412710.*

❺ The **Stortinget** (Parliament) is a bowfront, yellow-brick building that is open to visitors by request when Parliament is not in session: a guide will take you around the frescoed interior and into the debating chamber. *Karl Johans Gt. 22, tel. 22313050. Admission free. Guided tours July–Aug; public gallery, weekdays when parliament is in session.*

❻ **Oslo Domkirke** (cathedral), consecrated in 1697, is modest by the standards of those in some other European capital cities, but the interior is rich with treasures, such as the Baroque carved wooden altarpiece and pulpit. The ceiling frescoes by Hugo Lous Mohr were done after World War II. Look for arcades, small restaurants, and street musicians behind the cathedral. *Stortorvet 1. Admission free. Open weekdays 10–4.*

❼ **Akershus Slott,** a castle on the harbor, was built in 1299 but restored in 1527 by Christian IV of Denmark—Denmark then ruled Norway—after it was damaged by fire. He then laid out the present city of Oslo (naming it Christiania, after himself) around his new residence; Oslo's street plan still follows his design. Some rooms are open for guided tours, and the grounds form a park around the castle. *Festningspl., tel. 22412521. Admission: NKr 20. Guided tours May–Sept., Mon.–Sat. 11, 1, and 3, Sun. 1 and 3.*

❽ On the grounds of Akershus Slott are the **Forsvarsmuséet** and **Hjemmefrontmuseum** (the Norwegian Defense and Resistance museums). Both give you a feel for the Norwegian fighting spirit throughout history and especially during the German occupation, when the Nazis set up headquarters on this site and had a number of patriots ex-

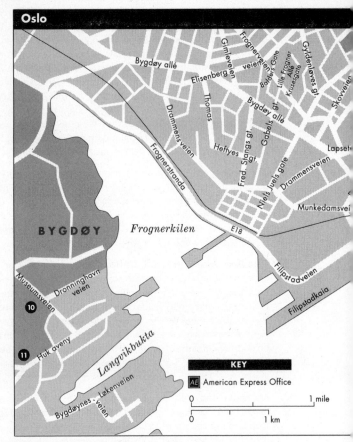

Oslo

BYGDØY

Frognerkilen

Langvikbukta

KEY

AE American Express Office

0   1 mile

0   1 km

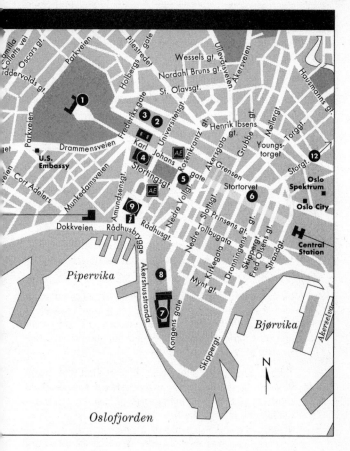

ecuted here. *Forsvarsmuséet: Festningspl., tel. 29093582. Admission free. Open June–Aug., weekdays 10–6, weekends 11–4; Sept.–May, weekdays 10–3, weekends 11–4. Hjemmefrontmuseum: Festningspl., tel. 23093138. Admission: NKr 20. Open mid-Apr.–mid-June, Mon.–Sat. 10–4, Sun. 11–4; mid-June–Aug., daily 11–5; Sept., Mon.–Sat. 10–4, Sun. 11–4; Oct.–mid-Apr., daily 11–4.*

❾ The large redbrick **Oslo Rådhus** (City Hall) is on the waterfront. Designed by architects Arnstein Arnesen and Magnus Paulsson, it opened officially in 1950. The friezes in the courtyard, depicting scenes from Norwegian folklore, pale in comparison to the marble-floored inside halls, where murals and frescoes bursting with color depict daily life, historical events, and Resistance activities in Norway. The elegant main hall has been the venue for the Nobel Peace Prize Ceremony since 1991. *Rådhuspl., tel. 22861600. Admission free. Open May–Aug., Mon.–Sat. 9–5, Sun. noon–5; Sept.–Apr., Mon.–Sat. 9–4. Sun. 12–4. Tours weekdays 10, noon, 2.*

From Rådhusbryggen (City Hall Wharf), you can board a ferry in the summertime for the seven-minute crossing of the fjord to the **Bygdøy** peninsula, where you'll find a complex of seafaring museums and some popular beaches. *Ferries run May–Sept., daily every ½ hr 8:15–5:45.*

Take the ferry from Rådhusbryggen (City Hall Wharf) and **❿** walk up a well-marked road to see the **Norsk Folkemuseum** (Norwegian Folk Museum), a large park where centuries-old historic farmhouses have been collected from all over the country and reassembled. A whole section of 19th-century Oslo was moved here, as was a 12th-century wooden stave church. *Museumsvn. 10, tel. 22/12–37–00. Admission: NKr 70. Open Jan.–mid-May, Mon.–Sat. 11–3, Sun. 11–4; mid-May–mid-June, daily 10–5; mid-June–Aug., daily 10–6; early Sept., daily 10–5; mid-Sept.–Dec., Mon.–Sat. 11–3, Sun. 11–4.*

⓫ **Vikingskiphuset** (Viking Ship Museum) contains 9th-century ships used by Vikings as royal burial chambers, which have been excavated from the shores of the Oslofjord. Also on display are the treasures and jewelry that accompanied the royal bodies on their last voyage. The ornate craftsmanship evident in the ships and jewelry dispels any notion that the Vikings were skilled only in looting and pillaging. *Huk aveny 35, tel. 22438379. Admission: NKr 30. Open Nov.–Mar., daily 11–3; Apr. and Oct., daily 11–4; May–Aug., daily 9–6; Sept., daily 11–5.*

⓬ In 1940, four years before his death, Munch bequeathed much of his work to the city of Oslo; the **Munch-Muséet** (Munch Museum) opened in 1963, the centennial of his birth. Although only a fraction of its 22,000 items—books, paintings, drawings, prints, sculptures, and letters—are on display, you can still get a sense of the tortured Expressionism that was to have such an effect on European painting. *Tøyengt. 53 (from Rådhuset take Bus 29 or take the T-bane from the Nationaltheatret to Tøyen, an area in northeast Oslo), tel. 22/67-37-74. Admission: NKr 50. Open June–Sept. 15, Tues.–Sat. 10–6, Sun. noon–6; Sept. 16–May, Tues., Wed., Fri, Sat. 10–4, Thurs. 10–6, Sun. noon–6.*

Shopping

Oslo has a wide selection of pewter, silver, glassware, sheepskin, leather, and knitwear. Prices on handmade articles are government-controlled.

Many of the larger stores are between Stortinget and the cathedral; much of this area is for pedestrians only. The **Basarhallene,** at the back of the cathedral, is an art and handicrafts boutique center. Oslo's newest shopping area, **Aker Brygge,** was once a shipbuilding wharf. Right on the waterfront, it is a complex of booths, offices, and sidewalk cafés. Also check out **Bogstadveien/Hegdehaugsveien,** which runs from Majorstua to Parkveien.

Paris/Le Havre, France

Le Havre is the port city for Paris, one of Europe's most treasured and beautiful cities. Most cruise passengers will find a day too little to truly explore the city. However, Paris is compact, and with the possible exception of the Bois de Boulogne and Montmartre, you can walk from one sight to the next. The city is divided in two by the River Seine, with two islands (Ile de la Cité and Ile St-Louis) in the middle. The south, or Left, Bank has a more intimate, bohemian flavor than the haughtier Right Bank. The east-west axis from Châtelet to the Arc de Triomphe, via the rue de Rivoli and the Champs-Elysées, is the principal thoroughfare for sightseeing and shopping on the Right Bank.

Currency

The unit of French currency is the franc (fr), subdivided into 100 centimes. Bills are issued in denominations of 50, 100, 200, and 500 francs (frs.); coins are 5, 10, 20, and 50 centimes and 1, 2, 5, 10, and 20 francs. The small, copper-color 5-, 10-, and 20-centime coins have considerable nuisance value, but they can be used for tips in bars and cafés. At press time, the U.S. dollar bought 6.2 francs, the Canadian dollar 4.1 francs, and the pound sterling 9.8 francs.

Telephones

The country code for France is 33. French phone numbers have ten digits. All phone numbers have a two-digit prefix determined by zone; for the southeast, the code is 04. (Drop the zero if you are calling France from a foreign country.) Phone booths are plentiful; they are nearly always available at post offices, cafés, and métro stations. Some French pay phones take 1-, 2-, and 5-franc coins (1-fr. minimum), but most phones are now operated by *télécartes* (phone cards), which can be used for both local and international calls. The cards are sold in post offices, métro stations, and cafés displaying a red TABAC (tobacco) sign outside (cost: 49 frs. for 50 units; 97.50 frs. for 120 units). To call abroad, dial 00 and wait for the tone, then dial the country code, area code, and number. To reach an **AT&T** long-distance operator, dial 08–00–99–00–11; **MCI**, 08–00–99–00–19; **Sprint**, 08–00–99–00–87. Dial 12 for local operators.

Shore Excursion

The following is a good choice from Le Havre. It may not be offered by all cruise lines. Time and price are approximate.

Paris. Journey by coach to Paris, where you will tour the Cathedral of Notre Dame, the Eiffel Tower, Place de la Concorde, and have time to shop. Glimpse the tree-lined Champs-Elysées and Arc de Triomphe, Place de l'Opera, and Pont Neuf. Includes lunch. *10–12 hrs. Cost: $165.*

Coming Ashore

Ships dock at Le Havre. The trip to Paris is approximately three hours each way. Cruise lines will typically sell transfers for around $100 to Paris for those who want to explore on their own.

Once you're in the city, you'll find that Paris's monuments and museums are within walking distance of one another. A river cruise is a pleasant way to get an overview. Even if you're stopping for a very short time, you may want to get a copy of the *Plan de Paris par Arrondissement,* a city guide available at most kiosks, with separate maps of each district, including the locations of métro stations and an index of street names.

The most convenient form of public transportation is the *métro*; buses are a slower alternative, though they do allow you to see more of the city. Maps of the métro/RER network are available free from any métro station. There are thirteen métro lines crisscrossing Paris and the nearby suburbs, and you are seldom more than a five-minute walk from the nearest station. It is essential to know the name of the last station on the line you take, since this name appears on all signs within the system. A connection (you can make as many as you please on one ticket) is called a *correspondance*. At junction stations, illuminated orange signs bearing the names of each line terminus appear over the corridors that lead to the various connections. Métro tickets cost 8 francs each, though a *carnet* (10 tickets for 52 frs.) is a far better value. Keep your ticket during your journey; you will need it to leave the RER system and in case you run into any green-clad inspectors when you are leaving the métro—they can be very nasty and will impose a big fine on the spot if you do not have a ticket.

Taxis are not terribly expensive but are not always easy to hail. There is no standard vehicle or color for Paris taxis, but all offer good value. Daytime rates (7 to 7) within Paris are about 2.80 fr. per km (½ mi), and nighttime rates are around 4.50 frs., plus a basic charge of 13 frs. Cruising cabs can be hard to find. There are numerous taxi stands, but these are not well marked. Taxis seldom take more than three people at a time.

Exploring Paris

Numbers in the margin correspond to points of interest on the Paris map.

❶ The most enduring symbol of Paris, and its historic and geographic heart, is the cathedral **Notre-Dame,** around the corner from Cité métro station. It was begun in 1163, making it one of the earliest Gothic cathedrals, although it was not finished until 1345. The south tower houses the great bell of Notre-Dame, as tolled by Quasimodo, Victor Hugo's fictional hunchback. The cathedral interior, with its vast proportions, soaring nave, and soft, multicolor light filtering through the stained-glass windows, is at its lightest and least crowded in the early morning. The 387-step climb up the towers is worth the effort for a perfect view of the famous gargoyles and the heart of Paris. *pl. du Parvis. Cathedral admission free. Towers admission: 32 frs. Cathedral open daily 8–7; treasury (religious and vestmental relics) Mon.–Fri. 9:30–6:30.*

❷ **Ste-Chapelle** (Holy Chapel) was built by Louis IX (1226–70) in the 1240s, to house what he believed to be Christ's Crown of Thorns, purchased from Emperor Baldwin of Constantinople. The lower chapel is low-ceilinged and brightly painted, and the upper one visually soars; its walls consist of little else but dazzling 13th-century stained glass. *In the Palais de Justice, Admission: 32 frs. Open daily 9:30–6:30; Oct.–Mar., daily 10–5.*

❸ **Sorbonne,** Paris's ancient university, is where students used to listen to lectures in Latin, which explains why the surrounding area is known as the Quartier Latin (Latin Quarter). The Sorbonne is the oldest university in Paris—indeed, one of the oldest in Europe—and has for centuries been one of France's principal institutions of higher learning. You can visit the main courtyard on rue de la Sorbonne and peek into the main lecture hall, a major meeting point during the tumultuous student upheavals of 1968. *rue de la Sorbonne.*

❹ The **Panthéon,** with its huge dome and elegant colonnade, is reminiscent of St. Paul's in London but dates from a century later (1758–89). The Panthéon was intended to be a church, but during the French Revolution it was earmarked as a secular hall of fame. Its crypt contains the remains of such national heroes as Voltaire, Rousseau, and Zola. The austere interior is ringed with Puvis de Chavannes's late-19th-century frescoes relating the life of Geneviève, patron saint of Paris, and contains a swinging model of the giant pendulum used here by Léon Foucault in 1851 to prove the earth's rotation. *pl. du Panthéon, tel. 01–44–32–18–00. Admission: 32 frs. Open daily 10–6:15.*

⑤ Rue de Navarre and rue Lacépède lead to the **Jardin des Plantes** (Botanical Gardens), which has occupied this site since the 17th century. The gardens have what is reputedly the oldest tree in Paris, an acacia Robinia (allée Becquerel) planted in 1636. Natural science enthusiasts will be in their element at the various museums, devoted to insects (Musée Entomologique), fossils and prehistoric animals (Musée Paléontologique), and minerals (Musée Minéralogique). The Grande Galerie de l'Evolution, with its collection of stuffed and mounted animals (some now extinct), is mind-blowing. Hothouses, a zoo, an aquarium, and a maze are also on the premises. *36 rue Geoffroy-St-Hilaire. Admission: 15–30 frs. Museums open Wed.–Mon. 10–5 (Musée Entomologique, 1–5). Grande Galerie de l'Évolution: Wed.–Mon. 10–6, Thurs. 10–10.*

⑥ You can hardly miss the sturdy pointed tower of **St-Germain-des-Prés,** the oldest church in Paris. It was built to shelter a relic of the true cross, brought back from Spain in AD 542. The chancel was enlarged and the church consecrated by Pope Alexander III in 1163 (the church tower dates from this period). Note the colorful nave frescoes by the 19th-century artist Hippolyte Flandrin, a pupil of Ingres. *Pl. St-Germain-des-Prés. Open weekdays 8– 7:30, weekends 8–9.*

⑦ In a stylishly converted train station, the **Musée d'Orsay**— devoted to the arts (mainly French) spanning the period 1848–1914—is one of the city's most popular sights. The main artistic attraction is the Impressionist collection: Renoir, Sisley, Pissarro, and Monet are all well represented. The post-Impressionists—Cézanne, van Gogh, Gauguin, and Toulouse-Lautrec—are on the top floor, and thought-provoking sculptures lurk at every turn. *1 rue Bellechasse, tel. 01–40–49–48–14. Admission: 40 frs, Sun. 30 frs. Open Tues.–Sat. 10–6; Thurs. 10–9:45; Sun. 9–6.*

Paris

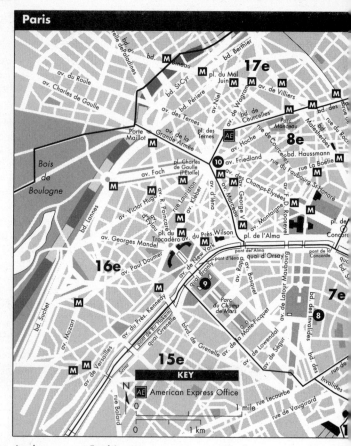

KEY

AE American Express Office

N

0 _____ 1 mile

0 _____ 1 km

Arc de
Triomphe, **10**

Eiffel Tower, **9**

Jardin des
Plantes, **5**

Louvre, **11**

Musée d'Orsay, **7**

Musée Rodin, **8**

Notre-Dame, **1**

Panthéon, **4**

Sorbonne, **3**

St-Germain-
des-Prés, **6**

Ste-Chapelle, **2**

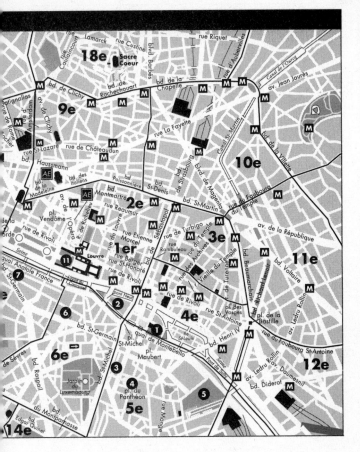

⑧ The **Musée Rodin** (Rodin Museum) is among the most charming of Paris's individual museums. This 18th-century mansion is filled with the vigorous sculptures of Auguste Rodin (1840–1917). You'll doubtless recognize the seated *Le Penseur* (*The Thinker*), with his elbow resting on his knee, and the passionate *Le Baiser* (*The Kiss*). The garden also has hundreds of rosebushes, with dozens of different varieties. *77 rue de Varenne, tel. 01–44–18–61–10. Admission: 28 frs, Sun. 18 frs; gardens only 5 frs. Sun. Open Tues.–Sun. 10–5.*

No one will want to miss Paris's most famous landmark, **⑨** the **Eiffel Tower** (Tour Eiffel). It was built by Gustave Eiffel for the World Exhibition of 1889. Such was Eiffel's engineering precision that even in the fiercest winds the tower never sways more than a few centimeters. Standing beneath it, you may have trouble believing that it nearly became 7,000 tons of scrap iron when its concession expired in 1909. Only its potential use as a radio antenna saved it—it now bristles with a forest of radio and television transmitters. The view from 1,000 ft up will enable you to appreciate the city's layout and proportions. *quai Branly, tel. 01–44–11–23–23. Admission: on foot, 14 frs; by elevator, 20–59 frs, depending on level. Open July–Aug., daily 9 AM–midnight; Sept.–June, Sun.–Thurs. 9 AM–11 PM.*

Looming over place Charles-de-Gaulle, known to Parisians **⑩** as "L'Étoile" (the Star), is the **Arc de Triomphe.** This 164-ft arch was planned by Napoléon to celebrate his military successes—but Napoléon had been dead for 15 years when the Arc de Triomphe was finally finished in 1836. From the top of the Arc you can see the "star" effect of Étoile's 12 radiating avenues and admire two special vistas: one down the Champs-Elysées toward place de la Concorde and the Louvre, and the other down avenue de la Grande Armée toward La Défense, a severe modern arch. France's Unknown Soldier is buried beneath the archway. Halfway up the Arc is a small museum devoted to its history. *Pl. Charles-de-Gaulle, tel. 01–43–80–31–31. Admission: 35 frs. Open Easter–Oct., daily 9:30 AM–11 PM; Oct.–Easter, daily 10 AM–10:30 PM.*

The **Champs-Elysées** is the site of colorful national ceremonies on July 14 and November 11; its trees are often decked with French tricolors and foreign flags to mark visits from heads of state. It is also where the cosmopolitan pulse of Paris beats strongest. The gracefully sloping 2-km (1¼-mi) boulevard was originally laid out in the 1660s by André Le Nôtre as a garden sweeping away from the Tuileries. There is not much sign of that as you stroll past the cafés, restaurants, airline offices, car showrooms, movie theaters, and chic arcades that occupy its upper half, although the avenue was spruced up in the early 1990s with wider sidewalks and an extra row of trees.

Once a royal palace and now the the world's largest and most famous museum, the **Louvre** has been given fresh purpose by a decade of expansion, renovation, and reorganization, symbolized by I. M. Pei's daring glass pyramid that now serves as the entrance to both the museum and an underground shopping arcade, the Carrousel du Louvre. The Louvre was begun as a fortress in 1200 (the earliest parts still standing date from the 1540s) and completed under Napoléon III in the 1860s. The museum's sheer variety can seem intimidating. The main tourist attraction is Leonardo da Vinci's *Mona Lisa* (known in French as *La Joconde*), painted in 1503. Be forewarned: her enigmatic smile is kept behind glass, invariably encircled by a mob of tourists. Turn your attention instead to some of the less-crowded rooms and galleries nearby, where Leonardo's fellow Italians are strongly represented: Fra Angelico, Giotto, Mantegna, Raphael, Titian, and Veronese. El Greco, Murillo, and Velázquez lead the Spanish; Van Eyck, Rembrandt, Frans Hals, Brueghel, Holbein, and Rubens underline the achievements of northern European art. English paintings are highlighted by works of Lawrence, Reynolds, Gainsborough, and Turner. Highlights of French painting include works by Poussin, Fragonard, Chardin, Boucher, and Watteau—together with David's *Oath of the Horatii,* Géricault's *Raft of the Medusa,* and Delacroix's *Liberty Guiding the People.* Famous statues include the soaring *Victory of Samothrace* and the eternally fascinating *Venus de Milo. Palais du Louvre (it's faster to enter through the Carrousel du Louvre mall on rue de Rivoli than through the pyramid), tel. 01–40–20–51–51. Admission: 45 frs., 26 frs. after 3 PM and Sun; free 1st Sun. of the month. Open Mon. and Wed. 9 AM–9:45 PM, Thurs.–Sun. 9–6.*

Shopping

The shopping opportunities in Paris are endless and geared to every taste. Perfume and designer clothing are perhaps the most coveted Parisian souvenirs. The elegant **Avenue Montaigne** is a showcase of international haute-couture houses; Prada and Dolce & Gabbana have joined Chanel, Dior, Nina Ricci, Valentino, and other exclusive spots. Rue du Faubourg-St-Honoré and the place des Victoires are also good places to hit.

The area surrounding St-Germain-des-Prés on the Left Bank is a mecca for specialty shops and boutiques, and has recently seen an influx of the elite names in haute couture. If you're on a tight budget, search for bargains along the streets around the foot of Montmartre or in the designer discount shops (Cacharel, Rykiel, Chevignon) along rue d'Alésia in Montparnasse. The most famous department stores in Paris are **Galeries Lafayette** and **Printemps,** on boulevard Haussmann. Others include **Au Bon Marché** on the Left Bank (métro: Sèvres-Babylone) and the **Samaritaine,** overlooking the Seine east of the Louvre (métro: Pont-Neuf).

Old prints are sold by *bouquinistes* (secondhand booksellers) in stalls along the Left Bank of the Seine. For state-of-the- art home decorations, the shop in the **Musée des Arts Décoratifs** in the Louvre (107 rue de Rivoli) is well worth visiting.

Reykjavik, Iceland

Iceland is anything but icy. Although glaciers cover about 10% of the country, summers are relatively warm, and winters are milder than those in New York. Coastal farms lie in green, pastoral lowlands where cows, sheep, and horses graze alongside raging streams. Distant waterfalls plunge from heather-covered mountains with great spiked ridges and snowcapped peaks. Iceland's chilly name can be blamed on Hrafna-Flóki, a 9th-century Norse settler who failed to plant enough crops to see his livestock through their first winter. Leaving in a huff, he passed a northern fjord filled with pack ice and cursed the country with a name that's kept tourism in cold storage for 1,100 years.

The second-largest island in Europe, Iceland is in the middle of the North Atlantic, where the warm Gulf Stream from the south meets cold currents from the north—just the right conditions for fish, which provide the nation with 80% of its export revenue. Beneath some of the country's glaciers are burning fires that become visible during volcanic eruptions—fires that heat the country's hot springs and geysers. The springs, in turn, provide hot water for public swimming pools and heating for most homes and buildings, helping to keep the air smogless.

Currency

The Icelandic monetary unit is the króna (plural, krónur), which is equal to 100 aurar and is abbreviated kr locally and IKr internationally. At press time, the rate of exchange was IKr 73 to the U.S. dollar, IKr 48 to the Canadian dollar, and IKr 116 to the pound sterling.

Telephones

The country code for Iceland is 354. All phone numbers in Iceland have seven digits; there are no city codes. Pay phones take IKr 10 and IKr 50 coins and are found in hotels, some shops, and post offices; bus station pay phones have become targets for vandals and may be nonfunctional. Phone cards cost IKr 500 and are sold at post offices, hotels, and some stores. For operator assistance with local calls dial 119; for information dial 118. For assistance with overseas calls, dial 115; for direct international calls dial 00. To reach a long-distance operator in the United States from Iceland, use the following international access codes: for **AT&T** dial 800–9001; **MCI**, 999–002; **Sprint**, 800–9003.

Shore Excursions

The following are good choices in Iceland. They may not be offered by all cruise lines. Times and prices are approximate.

Golden Circle. Iceland's natural wonders are the focus of this tour, which visits Thingvellir National Park, Gulifoss (the Golden Waterfall), and Strokkur Geyser. You'll also see the second-largest glacier in Iceland and postglacial lava fields. *5 hrs. Cost: $75.*

City Sights. Reykjavík's naturally heated outdoor swimming pool is a highlight of a half day of sightseeing, which also visits the Arabaer Folk Museum and the National Museum and drives by the University, Old Town, the Parliament, the Cathedral, and residential areas. *3 hrs. Cost: $38.*

Coming Ashore

Ships calling in Iceland berth at the dock in Reykjavík. The most interesting sights are in the city center, within easy walking distance of one another.

Getting Around

The center of Reykjavík is served by two main bus stop zones: Lækjatorg and Hlemmur bus station. Buses run from 7 AM to midnight. The flat fare for Reykjavík and suburbs is IKr 120. Taxi rates start at about IKr 300; few in-town taxi rides exceed IKr 700. The best taxis to call are Hreyfill (tel. 588–5522), BSR (tel. 561–0000 or 561–1720), and Bæjarleiðir (tel. 553–3500).

Exploring Reykjavík

The heart of Reykjavík is **Austurvöllur** (East Field), a small square in Old Midtown. The 19th-century Alþingishús (Parliament House), one of the oldest stone buildings in Iceland, faces the square. In the center of the square is a statue of Jón Sigurðsson (1811–79), the national hero who led Iceland's fight for independence, which it achieved fully in 1944.

Next to Alþingi is the **Dómkirkjan** (Lutheran cathedral), a small, charming stone church. Behind it is Tjörnin Lake, next to Reykjavík City Hall. One corner of the lake is fed by warm water that does not freeze, making it a haven for birds year-round. *Austurvöllur, tel. 551–2113. Open Mon. and Tues.–Fri. 9–5, Wed. 10–5, unless in use for services.*

Overlooking Tjörnin stands the **Listasafn Íslands** (National Gallery), which houses a collection of Icelandic art. *Fríkirkjuvegur 7, tel. 562–1000. Admission: IKr 300; free Wed. Open Tues.–Sun. noon–6.*

At Lækjartorg square, on the right, is the **Bernhöftstorfa** district, a small hill with colorful two-story wooden houses from the mid-19th century, where no modernizing efforts have been made. For a century and a half, the largest building has housed the oldest educational institution in the country, Menntaskólinn í Reykjavík; many of the college's graduates have shaped political and social life in Iceland. *Corner of Amtmannsstígur and Lækjargata.*

Leading west out of Lækjartorg square is Austurstræti, a semipedestrian shopping street with the main post office on the right. From here you can take Bus 100 (or Bus 10 from the bus station) for a 20-minute ride to the **Arbæjarsafn** (Open-Air Museum), a "village" of relocated 18th- and 19th-century houses. *Árbær, Bus 10 from Hlemmur bus station, tel. 577–1111. Open June–Aug., Tues.–Sun. 10–6, and by appointment.*

At the **Ásmundur Sveinsson Sculpture Museum,** some originals by this socialist realist sculptor (1896–1982) are exhibited in the museum's gallery and studio as well as in the surrounding garden, which is accessible at all times free of charge. *v/Sigtún, 5-min ride from Hlemmur Station on Bus 5, tel. 553–2155. Admission: IKr 400. Open June–Sept., daily 10–4; Oct.–May, daily 1–4.*

The **Náttúrufræðistofnun** (Museum of Natural History) has one of the last great auks on display plus several exhibits on Icelandic natural history. *Hlemmtorg, Hverfisgata 116, tel. 562–9822. Admission: IKr 300. Open Tues., Thurs., and weekends 1:30–4.*

The **Hallgrímskirkja** (Hallgrim's Church) has a 210-ft graystone tower that dominates the skyline. Open to the public, it offers a panoramic view of the city and its spacious suburbs. The church, which took more than 40 years to build, was completed in the 1980s. *Top of Skólavörðustígur, tel. 551–0745. Admission to tower: IKr 200. Open May–Sept., daily 9–6; Oct.–Apr., daily 10–6.*

The **Listasafn Einars Jónssonar** (National Gallery of Einar Jónsson) is devoted to the works of Iceland's leading early-20th-century sculptor (1874–1954). His monumental sculptures have a strong symbolic and mystical content. The sculpture garden is always open. *Njarðargata, tel. 551–3797. Admission: IKr 200. Open June– mid-Sept., Tues.–Sun 1:30–4; mid-Sept.–Nov. and Feb.–May, weekends 1:30–4.*

At the campus of the **University of Iceland** (founded 1911) is the outstanding þhjóðminjasafn (National Museum). On display are Viking artifacts, national costumes, weaving, wood carving, and silver works. The exhibitions in the main building of the museum are closed for renovations until 2001. *Suðurgata 141, tel. 530–2200. Admission: IKr 300. After June 2000: Open Mid-May–mid-Sept., Tues.–Sun. 11–5; late Sept.–early May, Tues., Thurs., and weekends noon–5.*

Shopping

Many of the shops that sell the most attractive Icelandic woolen goods and arts and crafts are on Aðalstræti, Hafnarstræti, and Vesturgata streets. At the **Handknitting Association of Iceland** (Skólavörðustígur 9, tel. 552–1890), you can buy high-quality hand-knits through a knitters' cooperative. **Rammagerðin** (Hafnarstræti 19, tel. 551–7910) stocks a wide range of Icelandic-made clothes and souvenirs. On weekends, try the **flea market** (Harborside Kolaportið in the rear of the Customs House on Geirsgata) between 11 and 5.

Rome/Civitavecchia, Italy

Civitavecchia is the port city for Rome, where antiquity is taken for granted. Successive ages have piled the present on top of the past—building, layering, and overlapping their own particular segments of Rome's more than 2,500 years of history to form a remarkably varied urban complex. Most of the city's major sights are in the *centro storico* (historic center), which is between the long, straight Via del Corso and the Tiber River. At its heart lies ancient Rome, where the Forum and Colosseum stand. It was around this core that the other sections of the city grew up through the ages: medieval Rome, which covered the horn of land that pushes the Tiber toward the Vatican and extended across the river into Trastevere; and Renaissance Rome, which was erected upon medieval foundations and extended as far as the Vatican, creating beautiful villas on what was then the outskirts of the city.

Currency

The unit of currency in Italy is the lira (plural, lire). There are bills of 1,000, 2,000, 5,000, 10,000, 50,000, 100,000, and 500,000 lire (this largest bill being almost impossible to change, except in banks); coins are worth 50, 100, 200, 500, and 1,000 lire. In 1999 the euro began to be used as a banking currency, but the lira will still be the currency in use on a day-to-day basis. At press time, the exchange rate was about 1,822 lire to the U.S. dollar, 1,203 lire to the Canadian dollar, and 2,900 lire to the pound sterling. When your purchases run into hundreds of thousands of lire, beware of being shortchanged, a dodge that is practiced at ticket windows and cashiers' desks, as well as in shops and even banks. Always count your change before you leave the counter.

Telephones

The country code for Italy is 39. Do not drop the zero in the regional code when calling Italy. For all local calls, you must dial the regional area codes, even in cities. Most local calls cost 200 lire for two minutes. Pay phones take either 100-, 200-, or 500-lire coins or *schede telefoniche* (phone cards), purchased in bars, tobacconists, post offices, and TELECOM offices in either 5,000-, 10,000-, or 15,000-lire denominations. To place international calls, many travelers go to the Telefoni telephone exchange (usually marked TELECOM), where the operator assigns you a booth, can help place your call, and will collect payment when you have finished. To dial an international call, insert a phone card, dial 00, then the country code, area code, and phone number. For **AT&T USADirect**, dial access number tel. 172–1011; for **MCI Call USA**, access number tel. 172–1022; for **Sprint Express**, access number tel. 172–1877. You will be connected directly with an operator in the United States.

Shore Excursion

Due to the limited amount of time you will have in the city and its wealth of sights, it is a good idea to select a tour in Rome. The following is a good choice in Rome. It may not be offered by all cruise lines. Time and price are approximate.

Highlights and History. An excellent choice for first-time visitors who want to span Rome's more than 2,500 years of history. Highlights include the Colosseum, the Vatican Museums, St. Peter's Basilica, and the Forum. Travel is by motor coach. *11 hrs. Cost: $160.*

Coming Ashore

Ships dock at Civitavecchia, about one hour and 45 minutes from Rome by bus. Cruise lines usually will sell bus transfers to Rome for those who want to explore independently.

The layout of the centro is highly irregular, but several
landmarks serve as orientation points to identify the areas
that most visitors come to see: the Colosseum, Pantheon,
Piazza Navona, St. Peter's Basilica, the Spanish Steps, and
the Terme di Caracalla. You'll need a good map to find your
way around; newsstands offer a wide choice. The important thing is to relax and enjoy Rome. Don't try to see everything, but do take time to savor its pleasures. If you are in
Rome during a hot spell, do as the Romans do: sightsee a
little, take a break during the hottest hours, then resume
sightseeing.

The best way to see Rome once you arrive is to choose an
area or a sight that you particularly want to see, reach it
by bus or metro, then explore the area on foot. Wear comfortable, sturdy shoes, preferably with thick rubber soles
to cushion you against the cobblestones. You can buy trans-
portation-route maps at newsstands and at ATAC (bus
company) information and ticket booths. The metro provides the easiest and fastest way to get around, although
its stops are limited. A BIG tourist ticket, valid for one day
on all public transport, costs 6,000 lire. Taxis wait at stands
and, for a small extra charge, can also be called by telephone.
The meter starts at 4,500 lire. Use the yellow or the newer
white cabs only, and be very sure to check the meter. To
call a cab, phone 06/3570, 06/5551, 06/4994, or 06/88177.

Exploring Rome

*Numbers in the margin correspond to points of interest on
the Rome map.*

❶ In the valley below the Campidoglio is the **Foro Romano**
(Roman Forum). Once only a marshy hollow, the forum
became the political, commercial, and social center of
Rome, studded with public meeting halls, shops, and temples. As Rome declined, these monuments lost their importance and eventually were destroyed by fire or the
invasions of barbarians. Rubble accumulated (though much
of it was carted off later by medieval home builders as construction material), and the site reverted to marshy pas-
tureland; sporadic excavations began at the end of the 19th
century. You don't really have to try to make sense of the
mass of marble fragments scattered over the area of the
Roman Forum. Just consider that 2,000 years ago this was

the center of the Mediterranean world. Wander down the Via Sacra and climb the Palatine Hill, where the emperors had their palaces and where 16th-century cardinals strolled in elaborate Italian gardens. From the belvedere you have a good view of the Circus Maximus. *Entrances at Via dei Fori Imperiali and Piazza del Colosseo, tel. 06/6990110. Admission free for Forum. Open Mon.–Sat. 9–2 hrs before sunset, Sun. 9–1.*

 Rome's most famous ancient ruin, the **Colosseo** (Colosseum), was inaugurated in AD 80 with a program of games and shows that lasted 100 days. On opening day alone 5,000 wild animals perished in the arena. The Colosseum could hold more than 50,000 spectators; it was faced with marble, decorated with stuccos, and had an ingenious system of awnings to provide shade. Gladiators would stand before the imperial box to salute the emperor, calling *"Ave, imperator, morituri te salutant"* (Hail, emperor, men about to die salute thee). The Colosseum, by the way, takes its name from a colossal, 118-ft statue of Nero that stood nearby. *Piazza del Colosseo, tel. 06/7004261. Admission 10,000 lire. Open Mon.–Sat. 9–2 hours before sunset, Sun. 9–1.*

 The **Terme di Caracalla** (Baths of Caracalla), numbered among ancient Rome's most beautiful and luxurious, were inaugurated by Caracalla in AD 217 and used until the 6th century. An ancient version of a swanky athletic club, the baths were open to the public; citizens could bathe, socialize, and exercise in huge pools and richly decorated halls and libraries, now towering ruins. *Via delle Terme di Caracalla, tel. 06/5758626. Admission: 10,000 lire. Open Apr.–Sept., Tues.–Sat. 9–6, Sun.–Mon. 9–1; Oct.–Mar., Tues.–Sat. 9–3, Sun.–Mon. 9–1.*

 The 200-year-old **Scalinata di Spagna** (Spanish Steps), named for the Spanish Embassy to the Holy See (the Vatican), opposite the American Express office, are a popular rendezvous, especially for the young people who throng this area. The steps are banked with blooming azaleas from mid-April to mid-May. *Piazza di Spagna and Piazza Trinità dei Monti.*

⑤ Fontana di Trevi (Trevi Fountain) is a spectacular fantasy of mythical sea creatures and cascades of splashing water.

Rome

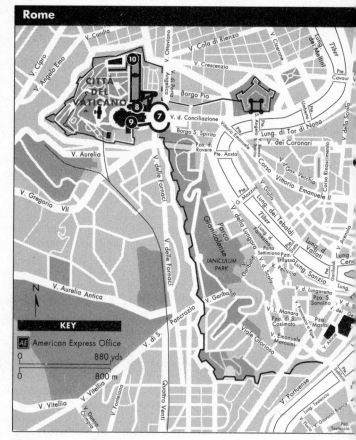

Legend has it that visitors must toss a coin into the fountain to ensure their return to Rome, but you'll have to force your way past crowds of tourists and aggressive souvenir vendors to do so. The fountain as you see it was completed in the mid-1700s, but there had been a drinking fountain on the site for centuries. Pope Urban VIII (1568–1644) almost sparked a revolt when he slapped a tax on wine to cover the expenses of having the fountain repaired. *Piazza di Trevi.*

❻ In the crypt of the church of **Santa Maria della Concezione,** skeletons and scattered bones of some 4,000 dead Capuchin monks are arranged in decorative motifs—a macabre practice peculiar to the Baroque age. *Via Veneto 27, tel. 06/4871185. Admission free, but donations encouraged. Open Fri.–Wed. 9–12, 3–6.*

Via della Conciliazione, the broad avenue leading to St. Peter's Basilica, was created by Mussolini's architects by razing blocks of old houses. This opened up a vista of the basilica, giving the eye time to adjust to its mammoth dimensions and thereby spoiling the effect Bernini sought when he enclosed his vast square (which is really oval) in the embrace of huge quadruple colonnades. In **Piazza San Pietro** ❼ (St. Peter's Square), which has held up to 400,000 people at one time, look for the stone disks in the pavement halfway between the fountains and the obelisk. From these points the colonnades seem to be formed of a single row of columns all the way around.

When you enter St. Peter's Square (completed in 1667), you are entering Vatican territory. Since the Lateran Treaty of 1929, **Vatican City** has been an independent and sovereign state, which covers about 108 acres and is surrounded by thick, high walls. Its gates are watched over by the Swiss Guards, who still wear the colorful dress uniforms designed by Michelangelo. The sovereign of this little state is John Paul II, 264th pope of the Roman Catholic Church.

At noon on Sunday the pope appears at his third-floor ❽ study window in the **Vatican Palace,** to the right of the basilica, to bless the crowd in the square. (Note: Entry to St. Peter's, the Vatican Museums, and all other sites within Vatican City, e.g., the Gardens, is barred to those wearing

shorts, miniskirts, sleeveless T-shirts, and otherwise revealing clothing. Women should carry scarves to cover
bare shoulders and upper arms or wear blouses that come
to the elbow. Men should dress modestly, in slacks and shirts.)

❾ Basilica di San Pietro (St. Peter's Basilica) is one of Rome's
most impressive sights. It takes a while to absorb the sheer
magnificence of it, however, and its rich decoration may
not be to everyone's taste. Its size alone is overwhelming,
and the basilica is best appreciated when it serves as the
lustrous background for ecclesiastical ceremonies thronged
with the faithful. The original basilica was built in the
early 4th century AD by the emperor Constantine, over an
earlier shrine that supposedly marked the burial place of
St. Peter. After more than a thousand years, the old basilica was so decrepit it had to be torn down. The task of building a new, much larger one took almost 200 years and
employed the architectural genius of Alberti, Bramante,
Raphael, Peruzzi, Antonio Sangallo the Younger, and
Michelangelo, who died before the dome he had planned
could be completed. The structure was finally finished in
1626. The basilica is full of extraordinary works of art.
Among the most famous is Michelangelo's *Pietà* (1498), seen
in the first chapel on the right just as you enter the basilica. It is the earliest and best known of Michelangelo's
four Pietàs; two others are in Florence, and the fourth, the
Rondanini Pietà, is in Milan.

At the end of the central aisle is the bronze statue of **St. Peter,**
its foot worn by centuries of reverent kisses. The bronze
throne above the altar in the apse was created by Bernini
to contain a simple wood and ivory chair once believed to
have belonged to St. Peter. Bernini's bronze *baldacchino*
(canopy) over the papal altar was made with metal stripped
from the portico of the Pantheon at the order of Pope
Urban VIII, from the powerful Roman Barberini family. His
practice of plundering ancient monuments for material to
implement his grandiose schemes inspired the famous quip,
"Quod non fecerunt barbari, fecerunt Barberini" ("What
the barbarians didn't do, the Barberini did").

As you stroll up and down the aisles and transepts, observe
the fine mosaic copies of famous paintings above the al-
tars, the monumental tombs and statues, and the fine stuc-

cowork. Stop at the **Museo Storico** (Historical Museum), which contains some priceless liturgical objects. *Apr.–Sept., daily 9–6; Oct.–Mar., daily 9–5.*

The entrance to the so-called **Grotte Vaticane** (Vatican Grottoes), or crypt, is in one of the huge piers at the crossing. It's best to leave this visit for last, as the crypt's only exit takes you outside the church. The crypt contains chapels and the tombs of many popes. It occupies the area of the original basilica, over the necropolis, the ancient burial ground where evidence of what may be St. Peter's burial place has been found. To see the roof and dome of the basilica, take the elevator or climb the stairs in the courtyard near the exit from the Vatican Grottoes. From the roof you can climb a short interior staircase to the base of the dome for an overhead view of the interior of the basilica. Only if you are in good shape should you attempt the very long, strenuous, and claustrophobic climb up the narrow stairs to the balcony of the lantern atop the dome, where the view embraces the Giardini Vaticani (Vatican Gardens) as well as all of Rome.

Free 60-minute tours of St. Peter's Basilica are offered in English daily (around 10 AM and 3 PM, and at 2:30 PM Sun.) by volunteer guides. They start at the information desk under the basilica portico. *St. Peter's Basilica, tel. 06/69884466. Open Apr.–Sept., daily 7–7; Oct.–Mar., daily 7–6, closed during ceremonies in the piazza. Museo Storico: admission: 8,000 lire. Open Apr.–Sept., daily 9–6; Oct.–Mar., daily 9–5. Roof and dome: entrance in courtyard to the left as you leave basilica. Admission: 6,000 lire for elevator, 5,000 lire for stairs. Open Apr.–Sept., daily 8–6; Oct.–Mar., daily 8–5. Vatican Grottoes: admission free. Open Apr.–Sept., daily 7–6; Oct.–Mar., daily 7–5.*

❿ The collections in the **Musei Vaticani** (Vatican Museums) cover nearly 8 km (5 mi) of displays. If you have time, allow at least half a day for Castel Sant'Angelo and St. Peter's and another half day for the museums. Posters at the museum entrance plot out a choice of four color-coded itineraries; the shortest takes about 90 minutes, the longest more than four hours, depending on your rate of progress.

No matter which tour you take, it will include the famed **Cappella Sistina** (Sistine Chapel). In 1508, Pope Julius II

(1443–1513) commissioned Michelangelo to fresco the more than 10,000 square ft of the chapel's ceiling. For four years Michelangelo dedicated himself to painting over fresh plaster, and the result was his masterpiece. Completed cleaning operations have removed centuries of soot and revealed its original and surprisingly brilliant colors. On the wall over the altar is Michaelangelo's *Last Judgement,* painted about 30 years after the ceiling was completed.

You can try to avoid the tour groups by going early or late, allowing yourself enough time before the closing hour. In peak season, the crowds definitely detract from your appreciation of this outstanding artistic achievement. To make sense of the figures on the ceiling, buy an illustrated guide or rent a taped commentary. A pair of binoculars and a mirror to reflect the ceiling also help.

The Vatican collections are so rich that unless you are an expert in art history, you will probably want only to skim the surface, concentrating on pieces that strike your fancy. Some of the highlights that might be of interest include the Egyptian collection and the *Laocoön,* the *Belvedere Torso,* which inspired Michelangelo, and the *Apollo Belvedere.* The *Stanze di Raffaello* (Raphael Rooms) are decorated with masterful frescoes, and there are more Raphaels in the *Pinacoteca* (Picture Gallery). At the Quattro Cancelli, near the entrance to the Picture Gallery, a rather spartan cafeteria provides basic nonalcoholic refreshments. *Viale Vaticano, tel. 06/69883041. Admission: 15,000 lire; free last Sun. of month. Open Easter wk and mid-Mar.–Oct., weekdays 8:45–3:45, Sat. 8:45–12:45; Nov.–mid-Mar. , Mon.–Sat. 8:45–12:45; last Sun. of month 8:45–12:45. Closed religious holidays (Jan. 1 and 6, Feb. 11, Mar. 19, Easter Sun. and Mon., May 1, Ascension Thurs., Corpus Christi, June 29, Aug. 15 and 16, Nov. 1, Dec. 8, Dec. 25 and 26) and Sun., except last Sun. of month.*

Originally built in 27 BC by Augustus's general Agrippa and ⓫ rebuilt by Hadrian in the 2nd century AD, the **Pantheon** is one of Rome's finest, best-preserved, and perhaps least appreciated ancient monuments. You don't have to look far past the huge columns of the portico and the original bronze doors to find the reason for its astounding architectural harmony: the diameter of the soaring dome is exactly equal to the height of the walls. The hole in the ceiling is intentional: the oculus at the apex of the dome signifies the "all-seeing eye of heaven." Romans and tourists alike pay little attention to it, and on summer evenings it serves mainly as a backdrop for all the action in the square. In ancient times the entire interior was encrusted with rich decorations of gilt bronze and marble. *Piazza della Rotonda, tel. 06/68300230. Admission: free. Open Mon.–Sat. 9–6:30, Sun. 9–1.*

Shopping

Shopping is part of the fun of being in Rome. The best buys are leather goods of all kinds, from gloves to handbags and wallets to jackets; silk goods; and high-quality knitwear. Shops are generally closed on Sunday and on Monday morning from September to mid-June; from mid-June through August, they close on Saturday afternoon as well. **Via Condotti,** directly across from the Spanish Steps, and the streets running parallel to Via Condotti, as well as its cross streets, form the most elegant and expensive shopping area in the city. Romans themselves do much of their shopping along **Via Cola di Rienzo** and **Via Nazionale.** For minor antiques, **Via dei Coronari** and other streets in the Piazza Navona area are good. The most prestigious antiques dealers are situated in **Via del Babuino** and its environs. The open-air markets at **Campo de' Fiori** and in many neighborhoods throughout the city provide an eyeful of local color.

Seville, Spain

Seville (Sevilla)—Spain's fourth-largest city and the capital of Andalucía—is one of the most beautiful and romantic cities in Europe. Here in this city of the sensuous Carmen and the amorous Don Juan, famed for the spectacle of its Holy Week processions and April Fair, you'll come close to the spiritual heart of Moorish Andalucía. The downside to a visit to Seville is that petty crime, much of it directed against tourists, is rife. Take only the minimum amount of cash with you when going ashore.

Currency

The unit of currency in Spain is the peseta (pta.). There are bills of 1,000, 2,000, 5,000, and 10,000 ptas. Coins are 1,

5, 25, 50, 100, 200, and 500 ptas. At press time, the exchange rate was about 156 ptas. to the U.S. dollar, 103 ptas. to the Canadian dollar, and 248 ptas. to the pound sterling.

Telephones

The country code for Spain is 34. Note that to call anywhere within the country—even locally—from any kind of phone, you need to dial the area code first; all provincial codes begin with a 9. Pay phones generally take the new, smaller 5- and 25-pta. coins; the minimum charge for short local calls is 25 ptas. Newer pay phones take only phone cards, which can be purchased at any tobacco shop in denominations of 1,000 or 2,000 ptas. International calls can be made from any pay phone marked TELÉFONO INTERNACIONAL. Use 50-pta. (or 100-pta. if the phone takes them) coins initially, then coins of any denomination to prolong your call. For lengthy international calls, go to the *telefónica*, a telephone office, where an operator assigns you a private booth and collects payment at the end of the call; this is the least expensive and by far the easiest way of phoning abroad. Dial 07 for international calls, wait for the tone to change, then dial the country code (1 for the United States, 0101 for Canada, or 44 for the United Kingdom). For the operator and directory information for any part of Spain, dial 1003 (some operators speak English). To reach an **AT&T** operator, dial 900/99–00–11; **MCI,** 900/99–00–14; **Sprint,** 900/99–00–13.

Shore Excursions

The following is a good choice in Seville. It may not be offered by all cruise lines. Time and price are approximate.

Survey of Seville. Travel through Seville's past and present on this comprehensive excursion that explores the city's religious, ethnic, and historical diversity. *8½ hrs. Cost: $129.*

Coming Ashore

Ships dock at Cádiz for Seville. The drive to and from Seville is around two hours each way.

Once in the city, you can walk from some sights to others; hop a cab or even take a horse-drawn carriage to reach other areas.

Exploring Seville

Numbers in the margin correspond to points of interest on the Seville map.

❶ A must is a visit to the **cathedral,** begun in 1402, a century and a half after Ferdinand III liberated Seville from the Moors. This great Gothic edifice, which took just over a century to build, is traditionally described in superlatives. It's the biggest and highest cathedral in Spain, the largest Gothic building in the world, and the world's third-largest church after St. Peter's in Rome and St. Paul's in London. As if that weren't enough, it boasts the world's largest carved wooden altarpiece. Despite such impressive statistics, the inside can be dark and gloomy, with too many overly ornate Baroque trappings. You may want to pay your respects to Christopher Columbus, whose mortal vestiges are said to be enshrined in a flamboyant mausoleum in the south aisle. Borne aloft by statues representing the four medieval kingdoms of Spain, it's to be hoped the great voyager has found peace at last, after the transatlantic quarrels that carried his body from Valladolid to Santo Domingo and from Havana to Seville. *Plaza Virgen de los Reyes, tel. 95/456–3321. Admission to cathedral and Giralda* (see below): *700 ptas.; free Sun. Open Mon.–Sat. 10:30– 5, Sun. 2–6, and for mass.*

Every day the bell that summons the faithful to prayer rings out from a Moorish minaret, a relic of the Arab mosque whose admirable tower of Abu Yakoub the Sevillians could not bring themselves to destroy. Topped in 1565–68 by a bell tower and weather vane and called the
❷ **Giralda,** this splendid example of Moorish art is one of the marvels of Seville. In place of steps, 35 gently sloping ramps climb to the viewing platform 230 ft high. St. Ferdinand is said to have ridden his horse to the top to admire the view of the city he had conquered. Seven centuries later your view of the Golden Tower and shimmering Guadalquivir will be equally breathtaking. *Plaza Virgen de los Reyes, tel. 95/456–3321. Open Mon.–Sat. 10:30–5, Sun. 2–6.*

❸ The high, fortified walls of the Moorish **Alcázar** belie the exquisite delicacy of the palace's interior. It was built by Pedro the Cruel—so known because he murdered his stepmother and four of his half-brothers—who lived here with his mis-

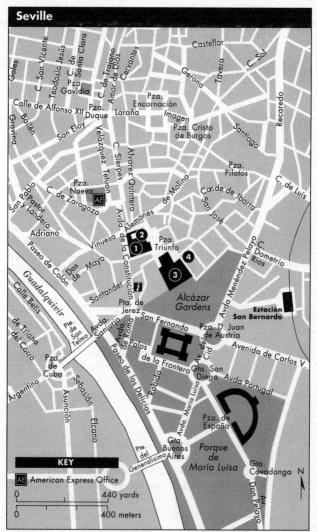

Seville

Alcázar, **3**
Barrio de
Santa Cruz, **4**
Cathedral, **1**
Giralda, **2**

tress María de Padilla from 1350 to 1369. Don't mistake this for a genuine Moorish palace, as it was built more than 100 years after the reconquest of Seville; rather, its style is Mudéjar—built by Moorish craftsmen working under orders of a Christian king. The palace centers around the beautiful **Patio de las Doncellas** (Court of the Damsels), whose name pays tribute to the annual gift of 100 virgins to the Moorish sultans whose palace once stood here. *Plaza del Triunfo, tel. 95/450–2324. Palace and gardens admission: 600 ptas. Open Tues.–Sat. 9:30–5, Sun. 9:30–1:30.*

④ The **Barrio de Santa Cruz,** with its twisting alleyways, cobbled squares, and whitewashed houses, is a perfect setting for an operetta. Once the home of Seville's Jewish population, it was much favored by 17th-century nobles, and today boasts some of the most expensive properties in Seville. All the romantic images you've ever had of Spain will come to life here: every house gleams white or deep ocher yellow, wrought-iron grilles adorn the windows, and balconies and patios are bedecked with geraniums and petunias. Ancient bars nestle side by side with antiques shops.

Stockholm, Sweden

The city of Stockholm, built on 14 small islands among open bays and narrow channels, is a handsome, cultivated place, full of parks, squares, and airy boulevards; yet it is also a bustling, modern metropolis. Glass-and-steel skyscrapers abound, but in the center you are never more than five minutes' walk from twisting, medieval streets and water views.

Currency

The unit of currency in Sweden is the krona (plural, kronor), which is divided into 100 öre and is written as SKr, SEK, or kr. Coins come in values of 50 öre and 1, 5, or 10 kronor; bills come in denominations of 20, 100, 500, and 1,000 kronor. At press time, the exchange rate was SKr 8.29 to the U.S. dollar, SKr 5.48 to the Canadian dollar, and SKr 13.18 to the pound sterling.

Telephones

The country code for Sweden is 46. When dialing from outside the country, drop the initial zero from the regional area code. Sweden has plenty of pay phones; to use them you'll need either SKr 1, SKr 5, or SKr 10 coins, since a local call costs SKr 2. You can also purchase a *telefonkort* (telephone card) from a Telebutik, hospital, or *Pressbyrån* store for SKr 35, SKr 60, or SKr 100. International calls can also be made from any pay phone. For calls to the United States and Canada, dial 009, then 1 (the country code), then wait for a second dial tone before dialing the area code and number. You can make calls from Telebutik offices. To reach an **AT&T** long-distance operator, dial 020/795611; **MCI,** 020/795922; **Sprint,** 020/799011.

Shore Excursions

The following are good choices in Stockholm. They may not be offered by all lines. Times and prices are approximate.

City and Vasa Museum. Visit City Hall and Golden Hall, the site of the Nobel Prize banquet. Pass the Senate Building and Royal Opera House on the way to the Vasa Ship Museum. *3½ hrs. Cost: $44.*

Royal Palace and Millesgarden. A complete tour of the royal residence precedes a visit to Millesgarden, the home, studio, and gardens of Sweden's famous modern sculptor, Carl Milles. In between, you'll stroll the streets of Old Town and drive through Stockholm Center past the Royal Opera House. *3 hrs. Cost: $44.*

Coming Ashore

Ships berth at Stockholm's pier within view of the Royal Palace in Old Town.

The most cost-effective way of getting around Stockholm is to buy a Stockholmskortet (Key to Stockholm card). Besides unlimited transportation on city subway, bus, and rail services, it offers free admission to 70 museums and several sightseeing trips. The card costs SKr 199 for 24 hours. It is available from the tourist information centers at Sweden House and the Kaknäs TV tower, and at the Hotellcentralen accommodations bureau at the central train station.

Maps and timetables for all city transportation networks are available from the Stockholm Transit Authority (SL) information desks at Sergels Torg, the central train station, and at Slussen in Gamla Stan. You can also obtain information by phone (tel. 08/600–1000).

The subway system, known as T-banan, is the easiest and fastest way of getting around the city. Fares are based on zones, starting at SKr 14, good for travel within one zone, such as downtown, for one hour. You pay more if you travel in more than one zone. Single tickets are available at station ticket counters, but it is cheaper to buy the SL Tourist Card, which is valid on buses and the subway and also gives free admission to a number of sights and museums. It can be purchased at Pressbyrån newsstands and SL information desks and costs SKr 60 for 24 hours.

A 10-km (6-mi) taxi ride will cost SKr 97 between 9 AM and 4 PM on weekdays, SKr 107 on weekday nights, and SKr 114 on weekends. It can be difficult to hail a taxi on the street, so call ahead if possible. Major taxi companies are Taxi Stockholm (tel. 08/150000), Taxikurir (tel. 08/300000), and Taxi 020 (tel. 020/939393).

Exploring Stockholm
Numbers in the margin correspond to points of interest on the Stockholm map.

Anyone in Stockholm with limited time should give priority to a tour of **Gamla Stan** (the Old Town), a labyrinth of narrow, medieval streets, alleys, and quiet squares on the island just south of the city center. Ideally, you should devote an entire day to this district. Be sure to spend at least a day visiting the large island of Djurgården. Although it's only a short walk from the city center, the most pleasant way to approach it is by ferry from Skeppsbron, in Gamla Stan.

❶ The **Stadshuset** (city hall) was constructed in 1923; architect Ragnar Östberg's ornate facade has become a Stockholm landmark. Lavish mosaics adorn the walls of the Golden Hall, and the Prince's Gallery features a collection of large murals by Prince Eugen, brother of King Gustav V. Take the elevator halfway up, then climb the rest of the way to the top of the 348-ft tower for a magnificent view of the city. *Hantverkargatan 1, tel. 08/508–29000. Admission: SKr 40. Tours daily at 10 and noon; also at 11 and 2 in summer. Tower admission: SKr 15. Tower open May–Sept., daily 10–4:30.*

❷ You should get to the **Kungliga Slottet** (Royal Palace), preferably by noon, when you can see the colorful changing-of-the-guard ceremony. The smartly dressed guards seem superfluous, as tourists wander at will into the palace courtyard and around the grounds. Several separate attractions are open to the public. Be sure to visit the Royal Armory, with its outstanding collection of weaponry and royal regalia. The Treasury houses the Swedish crown jewels, including the regalia used for the coronation of King Erik XIV in 1561. You can also visit the State Apartments, where the king swears in each successive government. *Gamla Stan, tel. 08/666–4466. Admission: SKr 35 daytime, SKr 40 evening, not including coupons or passes for rides. Late Apr.–early Sept. Prices and hrs subject to change; call ahead.*

The *Vasa,* a restored 17th-century warship, is one of the oldest preserved war vessels in the world and has become Sweden's most popular tourist sight. It sank ignominiously in Stockholm Harbor on its maiden voyage in 1628 because it was not carrying sufficient ballast. Recovered in 1961, the ship has been restored to its original appearance and ❸ is housed in a spectacular museum, the **Vasamuseet.** Film presentations and exhibits are also on site. *Gälarvarvet, tel. 08/666–4800. Admission: SKr 60. Open daily 10–5, Wed. 10–8.*

❹ **Gröna Lund Tivoli,** Stockholm's major amusement park, is a family favorite, with traditional rides and new attractions on the waterfront each season. *Djurgårdesvägen, tel. 08/ 670–7600. Open late Apr.–early Sept. Prices and hours are subject to change; call ahead.*

❺ The **Nordiska Museet** (Nordic Museum) provides insight into the way Swedish people have lived over the past 500 years. The collection includes displays of peasant costumes, folk art, and Sami (Lapp) culture. Families with children should visit the delightful "village life" play area on the ground floor. *Djurgårdsvägen 6–16, tel. 08/666–4600. Admission: SKr 60. Open Tues.–Sun. 11–5; July daily 10–5.*

More than 150 reconstructed traditional buildings from all ❻ over Sweden have been gathered at **Skansen,** an open-air folk museum with a variety of handicraft displays and demonstrations. There is a zoo, with native Scandinavian lynxes, wolves, and elks, as well as an aquarium and an old-style *tivoli* (amusement park). *Djurgårdsslätten 49–51, tel.*

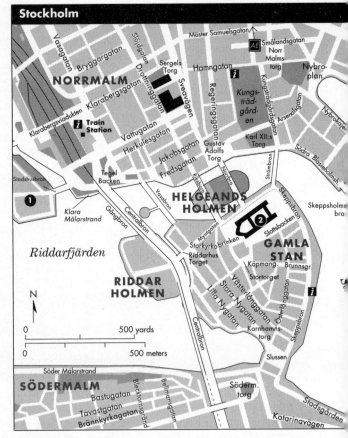

Stockholm

Gröna Lund
Tivoli, **4**

Kungliga
Slottet, **2**

Nordiska
Museet, **5**

Skansen, **6**

Stadshuset, **1**

Vasamuseet, **3**

Riddargatan

Syrmangatan

Storgatan

Linnégatan

Strandvägen

Strandvägen

Djurgårdsbron

Djurgårdsbrunnsviken

5

Rosendalsvägen

3

DJURGÅRDEN

Alkärret

Djurgårdsvägen

6

SKEPPSHOLMEN

Svensksundsvägen

Falkenbergsg.

4

Djurgårds
Slatten

Allmänna Gränd

Saltsjön

KASTELL-
HOLMEN

BECKHOLMEN

Strömmen

KEY

AE American Express Office

— Rail Lines

i Tourist Information

08/442–8000. Admission: Sept.–Apr., SKr 30 weekdays, SKr 40 weekends; May–Aug., SKr 50. Open Sept.–Apr., daily 9–5; May–Aug., daily 9 AM–10 PM. Prices and hours subject to change; call ahead.

Shopping

Shop till you drop means hitting the street **Hamngatan** with a vengeance. The **Gamla Stan** area is best for antiques shops, book shops, and art galleries. **Sturegallerian** (Stureg.) is an elegant covered shopping gallery built on the site of the former public baths at Stureplan. **Västerlånggatan,** one of the main streets in the Old Town, is a popular shopping area brimming with boutiques and antiques shops.

Turkish Coast and Kuşadası/Ephesus

Some of the finest reconstructed Greek and Roman cities, including the fabled Pergamum, Ephesus, Aphrodisias, and Troy, are found along the Aegean. Bright yellow road signs pointing to historical sites or to those currently undergoing excavation are everywhere here. There are so many Greek and Roman ruins, in fact, that some haven't yet been excavated and others are going to seed. Grand or small, all the sites are steeped in atmosphere and are best explored early in the morning or late in the afternoon, when there are fewer crowds. You can escape the heat of the day on one of the sandy beaches that line the coast.

Currency

The monetary unit is the Turkish lira (TL), which comes in bank notes of 50,000, 100,000, 250,000, 500,000, 1,000,000 and 5,000,000. Coins come in denominations of 5,000, 10,000, 25,000, 50,000, and 100,000. At press time, the exchange rate was 428,115 TL to the U.S. dollar, 282,817 TL to the Canadian dollar, and 681,048 TL to the pound sterling. These rates are subject to wide fluctuation, so check close to your departure date. Be certain to retain your original exchange slips when you convert money into Turkish lira—you will need them to reconvert the money. Because the value of Turkish currency can sometimes fall significantly over a very short period, it is advisable to change enough money for only a few days at a time.

Telephones

The country code for Turkey is 90. When dialing a number from outside the country, drop the initial zero from the local area code. All telephone numbers in Turkey have seven local digits plus three-digit city codes. Intercity calls are preceded by 0. Pay phones are blue, push-button models. Many take *jetons* (tokens), although increasingly, particularly in large cities, they are being replaced with phones that take phone cards or, to a lesser extent, credit cards. Tokens can be purchased for 7¢ at post offices and, for a couple of cents more, at street booths. Telephone cards are available at post offices. Multilingual directions are posted in phone booths. For all international calls dial 00, then dial the country code, area or city code, and the number. You can reach an international operator by dialing 132. To reach an **AT&T** long-distance operator, dial 00800-12277; **MCI,** 00800- 1177; **Sprint,** 00800–14477.

Shore Excursions

The following are good choices along the Turkish coast. They may not be offered by all cruise lines. Times and prices are approximate.

IN İZMIR

City Tour. Visit the fairly well-preserved Velvet Fortress and Archeological Museum followed by a belly-dancing performance and a folkloric show. *3¾ hrs. Cost: $30.*

Ephesus. Drive 1 hour and 15 minutes to reach Ephesus, once the Roman capital of Asia Minor, where you'll tour the spellbinding ruins of Ephesus. Major sights include the Great Theater, the Library of Celsus, the Temple of Hadrian, and Curetes Street. *4½ hrs. Cost: $45.*

IN KUŞADASI

Ancient Ephesus. This is the tour to take—it explores one of the best-preserved ancient cities of the world. Be prepared to do a lot of walking. *3 hrs. Cost: $41.*

IN BODRUM

The Castle of Bodrum is easily explored on your own, and is within walking distance of the tender drop-off point.

Wooden Boat Ride. Sail one of the wooden boats that line Bodrum's harbor to small coves and bays for swimming and snorkeling. *4 hrs. Cost: $64.*

Coming Ashore

Whether your ship docks or drops anchor along the Turkish Coast, landing sites are conveniently located for independent exploration.

IN İZMIR

Ships calling at İzmir's harbor dock along the waterfront boulevard called Kordon. Depending on what you want to see, you can walk, take a bus, or hire a taxi to explore the sights.

IN KUŞADASI

Ships either dock or tender passengers ashore at Kuşadası. Shops and restaurants are within walking distance of the port.

IN BODRUM

Ships calling at Bodrum tender passengers ashore in the main harbor. Walking Bodrum's streets is truly the best and most pleasurable way to explore local sights.

Exploring the Turkish Coast

İZMIR

İzmir, Turkey's third-largest city, is also its most Mediterranean in feel. Called Smyrna by the Greeks, it was a vital trading port that was often ravaged by wars and earthquakes. The city was almost completely destroyed by a fire in 1922 during the final stages of Turkey's war of independence against Greece. The center of the city is **Kültürpark,** which is a large green park that is the site of İzmir's industrial fair from late August until late September.

On top of İzmir's highest hill is the **Kadifekale** (Velvet Fortress), built in the 3rd century BC by Lysimachos. It is easily reached by dolmuş and is one of the few ancient ruins that was not destroyed in the fire of 1922.

At the foot of the hill is the restored **Agora,** the market of ancient Smyrna. The modern-day marketplace is in **Konak Square,** a maze of tiny streets filled with shops and covered stalls. *Open Mon.–Sat. 8–8.*

KUŞADASI

The major attraction near Kuşadası is **Ephesus,** a city created by the Ionians in the 11th century BC and now one of the grandest reconstructed ancient sites in the world. It is the showpiece of Aegean archaeology. Ephesus was a powerful trading port and the center for the cult of Artemis, Greek goddess of chastity, the moon, and hunting. The Ionians built a temple in her honor, one of the Seven Wonders of the Ancient World. During the Roman period, it became a shrine for the Roman goddess Diana. Some of the splendors here are the two-story Library of Celsus; noblemen's houses, with their terraces and courtyards; a 25,000-seat amphitheater, still used today during the Selçuk Ephesus Festival of Culture and Art; remains of the municipal baths; and a brothel. The city is especially appealing out of season, when it can seem like a ghost town with its shimmering, long, white marble road grooved by chariot wheels. Allow yourself the full day for Ephesus. *4 km (2½ mi) west of Selçuk on Selçuk–Ephesus Rd., tel. 232/892–6402. Admission: $5. Open daily 8:30–6 (summer), 8:30–5 (winter).*

BODRUM

Sitting between two crescent-shape bays, Bodrum has for years been the favorite haunt of the Turkish upper classes. One of the outstanding sights in Bodrum is **Bodrum Kalesi** (Bodrum Castle), known as the Castle of St. Peter. Between the two bays, the castle was built by crusaders in the 15th century. It has beautiful gardens and the Museum of Underwater Archaeology. *Kale Cad., tel. 252/316–2516. Castle and museum admission: $3. Open Tues.- -Sun. 8:30–noon and 1–5.*

The peninsula is downright littered with ancient Greek and Roman ruins, although getting to some of them involves driving over rough dirt roads. Five kilometers (3 miles) from Bodrum is **Halikarnas,** a well-preserved 10,000-seat Greek amphitheater built in the 1st century BC and still used for town festivals. *Admission free. Open daily 8:30– sunset.*

Varna, Bulgaria

Bulgaria, a land of mountains and seascapes, of austerity and rustic beauty, lies in the eastern half of the Balkan peninsula. From the end of World War II until recently, it was the closest ally of the former Soviet Union and presented a rather mysterious image to the Western world. This era ended in 1989 with the overthrow of Communist Party head Todor Zhivkov. Since then, Bulgaria has gradually opened itself to the West as it strives to become a member of the European Union and struggles along the path toward democracy and a free-market economy.

Founded in 681 by the Bulgars, a Turkic tribe from central Asia, Bulgaria was a crossroads of civilization even before that date. Archaeological finds in Varna, on the Black Sea coast, give proof of civilization from as early as 4600 BC. Bulgaria was part of the Byzantine Empire from AD 1018 to 1185 and was occupied by the Turks from 1396 until 1878. The combined influences are reflected in Bulgarian architecture, which has a truly Eastern feel. Five hundred years of Muslim occupation and nearly half a century of communist rule did not wipe out Christianity, and there are many lovely, icon-filled churches to see.

Currency

The unit of currency in Bulgaria is the lev (plural leva). There are bills of 100, 200, 500, 1,000, 2,000, 5,000, 10,000, 20,000, and 50,000 leva. Although prices are sometimes quoted in dollars, all goods and services must be paid for in leva. The value of the lev continues to fluctuate, and the exchange rate and price information quoted here may be outdated very quickly. At press time, the rate quoted by the Bulgarian State Bank was 1.83 leva to the U.S. dollar, 1.21 to the Canadian dollar, and 2.91 leva to the pound sterling.

Telephones

The country code for Bulgaria is 359. When dialing from outside the country, drop the initial zero from the regional area code. Local calls cost 2 leva and can be made from your hotel or from pay phones. Phone cards can be purchased at post offices, hotels, and street kiosks. Calls to the United States can be made from Bulfon or Betkom phones by using a local calling card to reach the international operator and then a long-distance calling card to reach the States. To place a call using an **AT&T USADirect** international operator, dial tel. 00–800–0010.

Shore Excursions

The following is a good choice in Varna. It may not be offered by all cruise lines. Time and price are approximate.

Varna Tour. You'll see the city's major sites before visiting one of the area's renowned Black Sea spas. *Half day. Cost: $45.*

Coming Ashore

Ships calling at Varna dock at the city harbor. Varna's main sights can be reached on foot. Buses are inexpensive; make sure to buy your ticket in advance from the kiosks near the bus stops.

Exploring Varna

Begin with the **Archeologicheski Musei** (Archaeological Museum), one of the great—if lesser-known—museums of Europe. The splendid collection includes the world's oldest gold treasures from the Varna necropolis of the 4th millennium BC, as well as Thracian, Greek, and Roman treasures, and richly painted icons. *41 bul. Maria Luiza, in park, tel. 052/23–70–57. Open Tues.–Sat. 10–5.*

In Mitropolit Simeon Square, the monumental **Tsurkva Yspenie Bogorodichno** (Cathedral of the Assumption), 1880–86, is worth a look for its lavish murals. Opposite the cathedral, in the city gardens, is the **Starata Chasovnikuh Kula** (Old Clock Tower), built in 1880 by the Varna Guild Association. *pl. Nezavisimost*

The 1602 **Tsurkva Sveta Bogoroditsa** (Church of the Holy Virgin) is worth a look for its beautifully carved iconostasis. *ul. Han Krum at ul. Knyaz Alexander Batenberg.*

Wander through the remains of the **Rimski Termi** (Roman Baths), dating from the 2nd to the 3rd century. Signs in English detail the various steps of the bath ritual. *ul. Han Krum just south of Tsurkva Sveta Bogoroditsa.*

The **Morski Muzei** (Marine Museum) has exhibits on the early days of navigation on the Black Sea and the Danube. *2 bul. Primorski, tel. 052/22–26–55. Open weekdays 8–4.*

In the extensive and luxuriant **Primorski Park** (Seaside Park) are restaurants, an open-air theater, and the fascinating Copernicus Astronomy Complex, near the main entrance.

Southern end of bul. Primorski. Astronomy Complex: tel. 052/22–28–90. Open weekdays 8–noon and 2–5.

Venice, Italy

For hundreds of years Venice—La Serenissima, the Most Serene—was the unrivaled mistress of trade between Europe and the Orient, and the staunch bulwark of Christendom against the tide of Turkish expansion. Though the power and glory of its days as a wealthy city-republic are gone, the art and exotic aura remain. Many of its magnificent palazzi are slowly crumbling, but somehow in Venice the shabby, derelict effect is magically transformed into one of supreme beauty and charm. Hot and sultry in the summer, Venice is much more welcoming in early spring and late fall.

Currency

The unit of currency in Italy is the lira (plural, lire). There are bills of 1,000, 2,000, 5,000, 10,000, 50,000, 100,000, and 500,000 lire (this largest bill being almost impossible to change, except in banks); coins are worth 50, 100, 200, 500, and 1,000 lire. In 1999 the euro began to be used as a banking currency, but the lira will still be the currency in use on a day-to-day basis. At press time, the exchange rate was about 1,822 lire to the U.S. dollar, 1,203 lire to the Canadian dollar, and 2,900 lire to the pound sterling. When your purchases run into hundreds of thousands of lire, beware of being shortchanged, a dodge that is practiced at ticket windows and cashiers' desks, as well as in shops and even banks. Always count your change before you leave the counter.

Telephones

The country code for Italy is 39. Do not drop the zero in the regional code when calling Italy. For all local calls, you must dial the regional area codes, even in cities. Most local calls cost 200 lire for two minutes. Pay phones take either 100-, 200-, or 500-lire coins or *schede telefoniche* (phone cards), purchased in bars, tobacconists, post offices, and TELECOM offices in either 5,000-, 10,000-, or 15,000-lire denominations. To place international calls, many travelers go to the Telefoni telephone exchange (usually marked

TELECOM), where the operator assigns you a booth, can help place your call, and will collect payment when you have finished. To dial an international call, insert a phone card, dial 00, then the country code, area code, and phone number. For **AT&T USADirect,** dial access number tel. 172–1011; for **MCI Call USA,** access number tel. 172–1022; for **Sprint Express,** access number tel. 172–1877. You will be connected directly with an operator in the United States.

Shore Excursions

The following are good choices in Venice. They may not be offered by all cruise lines. Times and prices are approximate.

Canals of Venice. See Venice from the water on this boat tour that glides down the bustling Grand Canal as well as some of the city's more intimate, narrow canals. Take time out for a visit to a glass factory. *3½ hrs. Cost: $60–$118.*

Venice Tour. Visit St. Mark's Square and Cathedral, Doge's Palace, and the Bridge of Sighs. *3 hrs. Cost: $50.*

Coming Ashore

Ships typically dock in Venice at the main port terminal, an unappealing building whose saving grace is its relative nearness to St. Mark's Square.

Cruise passengers may find that getting around Venice presents some unusual problems: the complexity of its layout (the city is made up of more than 100 islands, all linked by bridges); the bewildering unfamiliarity of waterborne transportation; the apparently illogical house numbering system and duplication of street names in its six districts; and the necessity of walking whether you enjoy it or not. It's essential to have a good map showing all street names and water-bus routes; buy one at any newsstand, and count on getting lost more than once.

Walking is the only way to reach many parts of Venice, so wear comfortable shoes. ACTV water buses run the length of the Grand Canal and circle the city. There are several lines, some of which connect Venice with the major and minor islands in the lagoon. **Line 1** is the Grand Canal local, calling at every stop, and continuing via San Marco to the Lido. (It takes about 45 minutes from the Santa Lucia train station to San Marco.) **Line 41** and **Line 42** follow long loop routes in opposite directions: take Line 41 from San Zaccaria to Murano, but Line 42 from Murano to San Zaccaria; Line 42 from San Zaccaria to the Redentore, but Line 41 from the Redentore back to San Zaccaria. **Line 51** runs from the railway station to San Zaccaria via Piazzale Roma and Zattere and continues to the Lido. **Line 52** goes along the same route but in the opposite direction, so from the Lido it makes stops at the Giardini, San Zaccaria, Zattere, Piazzale Roma, the train station, Fondamente Nuove (where boats leave for the islands of the northern lagoon), San Pietro, and back to the Lido. **Line 82** runs in a loop from San Zaccaria to Giudecca, Zattere, Piazzale Roma, the train station, Rialto (with fewer stops along the Grand Canal than Line 1), and back to San Zaccaria (and out to the Lido in the afternoon). The fare is 6,000 lire on all lines. A 24-hour tourist ticket costs 18,000 lire. Timetables are posted at every landing stage, but there is not always a ticket booth operating. You may get on a boat without a ticket, but you will have to pay a higher fare on the boat. For this reason, it may be useful to buy a *blochetto* (book of tickets) in advance. Landing stages are clearly marked with name and line number, but check before boarding, particularly with the 52 and 82, to make sure the boat is going in your direction.

If you mustn't leave Venice without treating yourself to a gondola ride, take it in the evening when the churning traffic on the canals has died down and the palace windows are illuminated and the only sounds are the muted splashes of the gondolier's oar. Make sure he understands that you want to see the *rii,* or smaller canals, as well as the Grand Canal. There's supposed to be a fixed minimum rate of about 120,000 lire for 50 minutes, and a nighttime supplement of 30,000. Come to terms with your gondolier *before* stepping into his boat.

Motoscafis, or water "taxis," are excessively expensive, and the fare system is as complex as Venice's layout. A minimum fare of about 50,000 lire gets you nowhere, and you'll pay three times as much to get from one end of the Grand Canal to the other. Always agree on the fare before starting out. Contact the **Cooperativa San Marco** (tel. 041/ 522–2303).

Few tourists know about the two-man gondolas that ferry people across the Grand Canal at various fixed points. It's the cheapest and shortest gondola ride in Venice, and it can save a lot of walking. The fare is 700 lire, which you hand to one of the gondoliers when you get on. Look for TRAGHETTO signs.

Exploring Venice

Numbers in the margin correspond to points of interest on the Venice map.

1 Even the pigeons have to fight for space on **Piazza San Marco,** the most famous piazza in Venice, and pedestrian traffic jams clog the surrounding byways. Despite the crowds, San Marco is the logical starting place for exploring Venice. Napoléon called this "the most beautiful drawing room in all of Europe."

2 The **Basilica di San Marco** (St. Mark's Basilica) was begun in the 11th century to hold the relics of St. Mark the Evangelist, the city's patron saint. Its richly decorated facade is surmounted by copies of the four famous gilded bronze horses (the originals are in the basilica's upstairs museum) taken from Constantinople by the Venitians in 1204. Inside, golden mosaics sheath walls and domes, lending an extraordinarily exotic aura: half Christian church, half Middle Eastern mosque. Be sure to see the Pala d'Oro, an eye-filling 10th-century altarpiece in gold and silver, studded with precious gems and enamels. From the narthex, climb the steep stairway to the museum: the bronze horses alone are worth the effort. *Piazza San Marco, tel. 041/ 5225205. Admission free for Basilica. Open Mon.–Sat. 9:45–4:30, Sun. 1–4:30;'last entry 30 mins before closing.*

3 During Venice's heyday, the **Palazzo Ducale** (Doge's Palace) was the epicenter of the Serene Republic's great empire. More than just a palace, it was a combination White House, Senate, Supreme Court, torture chamber, and prison. The building's exterior is striking; the lower stories consist of two rows of fragile-seeming arches, and above rests a massive pink-and-white marble wall, whose solidity is barely interrupted by its six great Gothic windows. The interior is a maze of vast halls, monumental staircases, secret corridors, and the sinister prison cells and torture chamber. The

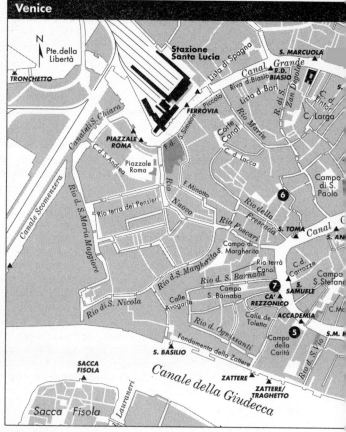

Venice

Basilica di San
Marco, **2**

Ca' Rezzonico, **7**

Campanile di
San Marco, **4**

Gallerie dell'
Accademia, **5**

Palazzo
Ducale, **3**

Piazza San
Marco, **1**

Santa Maria
Gloriosa dei
Frari, **6**

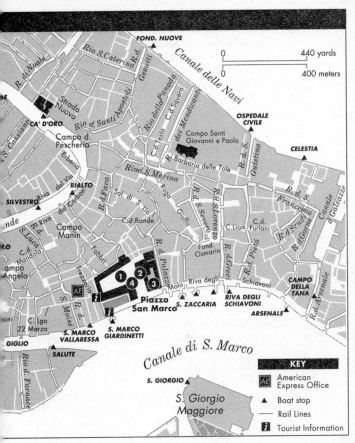

FOND. NUOVE

Canale delle Navi

| 0 | | 440 yards |
| 0 | | 400 meters |

R. di Noale

Rio S.Caterina R. d.

Gesuiti

Strada Nuova

CA' D'ORO

Rio d. Santi Apostoli

C. S. Cassiano

Campo d. Pescheria

Erberia

Riva del Vin

RIALTO

SILVESTRO

Rio d. S. Marina

R.d.Fava

Sal. di S. Lio

C.s.d.Bande

OSPEDALE CIVILE

Campo Santi Giovanni e Paolo

R: Barbaria delle Tole

CELESTIA

R. d. S. Giustina

R. d. S. Francesco

Canale d.Galeazze

Ruga Giuffa

R. d. S. Lorenzo

R. d. S. Severo

C. Lion

C. d. Furlani

R. d. S. Francesco

R. d. Scudi

R. d. Corte

Campo Manin

C. d. Mandola

S. Luca

Riva Carbon

Grande

Campo S. Angelo

C. Frezzaria

Fabbri

AE

i

R. d. Moisè

S. MARCO VALLARESSA

S. MARCO GIARDINETTI

Piazza San Marco

Molo

Riva degli

Schiavoni

Fond. Osmarin

R. d. Greci

R. d. Pietà

Fond. della Pietà

S. ZACCARIA

RIVA DEGLI SCHIAVONI

ARSENALE

R. d. Arsenale

CAMPO DELLA TANA

GIGLIO

C. lga 22 Marzo

SALUTE

Rio d. Fornace

Canale di S. Marco

S. GIORGIO

S. Giorgio Maggiore

KEY

AE American Express Office

▲ Boat stop

— Rail Lines

i Tourist Information

palace is filled with frescoes, paintings, and a few examples of statuary by some of the Renaissance's greatest artists. Don't miss the famous view from the balcony, overlooking the piazza, St. Mark's Basin, and the church of San Giorgio Maggiore across the lagoon. *Piazzetta San Marco, tel. 041/522–4951. Admission: 17,000 lire. Open Apr.–Oct., daily 9–7; Nov.–Mar., daily 9–5. Last entry 1 1/2 hrs before closing.*

For a pigeon's-eye view of Venice take the elevator up to the top of the **Campanile di San Marco** (St. Mark's bell tower) in Piazza San Marco, a reconstruction of the 1,000-year-old tower that collapsed one morning in 1912, practically without warning. Fifteenth-century clerics found guilty of immoral acts were suspended in wooden cages from the tower, sometimes to live on bread and water for as long as a year, sometimes to die of starvation and exposure. Look for them in Carpaccio's paintings of the square, which hang in the Accademia (*see below*). *Piazza San Marco, tel. 041/522–4064. Admission: 8,000 lire. Open June–Sept., daily 9:30–10; Oct.–May, daily 9:30–4:15; last entry 30 mins before closing. Closed two wks in Jan.*

The **Gallerie dell'Accademia** (Accademia Gallery) is Venice's most important picture gallery and a must for art lovers. Try to spend at least an hour viewing this remarkable collection of Venetian art, which is attractively displayed and well lighted. Works range from 14th-century Gothic to the Golden Age of the 15th and 16th centuries, including oils by Giovanni Bellini, Giorgione, Titian, and Tintoretto, and superb later works by Veronese and Tiepolo. *Campo della Carità, tel. 041/5222247. Admission: 12,000 lire. Open Tues.–Sat. 9–7, Sun. and Mon. 9–2; longer hrs June–Sept.*

The church of **Santa Maria Gloriosa dei Frari**—known simply as the I Frari—is one of Venice's most important churches, a vast, soaring Gothic building of brick. Since it is the principal church of the Franciscans, its design is suitably austere to reflect that order's vows of poverty, though paradoxically it contains a number of the most sumptuous pictures in any Venetian church. Chief among them are the magnificent Titian altarpiece, the immense *Assumption of the Virgin,* over the main altar. Titian was buried here at the ripe old age of 88, the only one of 70,000 plague victims to be given a personal church burial. *Campo dei Frari, San Polo, tel. 041/5222637. Admission: 3,000 lire. Open Mon.–Sat. 9–6, Sun. 1–6.*

Just off Piazzetta di San Marco (the square in front of the Doge's Palace) you can catch Vaporetto 1 at either the San Marco or San Zaccaria landing stages (on Riva degli Schiavoni) to set off on a boat tour along the **Grand Canal.** Serving as Venice's main thoroughfare, the canal winds in the shape of a backward S for more than 3½ km (2 mi) through the heart of the city, past some 200 Gothic-Renaissance palaces. Your vaporetto tour will give you an idea of the opulent beauty of the palaces and a peek into the side streets and tiny canals where the Venetians go about their daily business.

❼ The **Ca' Rezzonico**—the most spectacular palace in all of Venice—was built between the mid-17th and 18th centuries and is now a museum of sumptuous 18th-century Venetian paintings and furniture. The Ca' Rezzonico is the best chance to glimpse Venetian splendor and is a must-see; its magnificent ballroom hosted the grandest Venetian costume balls, the last given for Elizabeth Taylor and Richard Burton in the 1960s. The museum will be closed for restoration until 2001. *Fondamenta Pedrocco, 3136 Dorsoduro, tel. 041/2410100.*

Shopping

Venetian glass is as famous as the city's gondolas, and almost every shop window displays it. There's a lot of cheap glass for sale; if you want something better, try Carlo Moretti's chic, contemporary designs at **L'Isola** (San Marco 2084). On the island of Murano, **Domus** (Fondamenta dei Vetrai) has a good selection.

For Venetian fabrics, **Norelene** (Calle della Chiesa 727, in Dorsoduro) has stunning hand-painted material that makes wonderful wall hangings or elegantly styled jackets and chic scarves. **Venetia Studuim** (Calle Larga XXII, Marzo 2430) is famous for Fortuny-inspired lamps and elegant accessories.

Try to visit the famous **Rialto market** when it's in full swing (start from the Salizzada S. Giovanni side of the bridge on Tuesday to Saturday mornings; Monday is quiet because the fish market is closed), with fruit and vegetable vendors hawking their wares in a colorful and noisy jumble of sights and sounds. Not far beyond is the fish market, where you'll probably find sea creatures you've never seen before (and possibly won't want to see again). A left turn into Ruga San Giovanni and Ruga del Ravano will bring you face to face with scores of shops: At **La Scialuppa** (Calle delle Saoneri, 2695 San Polo) you'll find hand-carved wooden models of gondolas and their graceful oarlocks known as *forcole*.

Ports of Embarkation and Disembarkation

Athens/Piraeus

Athens is the gateway for cruises to the Greek Islands and to the eastern Mediterranean, including cruises of the Black Sea.

FROM THE AIRPORT

Piraeus lies 10 km (6 mi) from Athens. You can take a taxi for about 1,100 dr. or buy a transfer from the cruise line in advance.

Istanbul

Istanbul is a major jumping-off point for cruises of the eastern Mediterranean.

FROM THE AIRPORT

Atatürk Airport lies very close to the pier, but traffic in Istanbul is notoriously bad, so plan on half an hour for the transfer. You can take a cab from the airport to the ship, but buying a cruise-line transfer in advance is a good idea.

Rome/Civitavecchia

For reasons as much geographical as historical, Rome is a very popular starting or ending port for cruises of the eastern or western Mediterranean.

FROM THE AIRPORT

Civitavecchia, the port city for Rome, is an hour and 15 minutes from the city. Cruise-line transfers are your best bet for getting to the ship.

Southampton

Southampton is where the *Queen Elizabeth 2* arrives and departs on transatlantic crossings. There's not much in the

immediate vicinity except a coffee shop and berths for ferries going to the Isle of Wight. The train station is about ¼
mi from the pier.

FROM THE AIRPORT

Southampton is 90 km (56 mi) southwest of London. The
trip by BritRail takes an hour and 40 minutes from central
London's Waterloo Station. Driving from London to
Southampton takes less than two hours.

INDEX

NOTES

NOTES